DISCARD

**BLOOMFIELD
COLLEGE LIBRARY**
≈≈≈≈≈≈≈≈≈≈≈≈≈
Presented by
Larry Qualls

WITHDRAWN

LARRY QUALLS
141 Wooster Street
New York, NY 10012

Stage and Screen: Studies in Scandinavian Drama and Film

Essays in honor of Birgitta Steene

Edited by
Ann-Charlotte Gavel Adams
and Terje I. Leiren

DreamPlay Press Northwest
Seattle

All rights reserved. No part of this publication may be reproduced, stored in a retrieval system or transmitted in any form, except for brief excerpts quoted in reviews, without the prior permission of DreamPlay Press.

Copyright © 2000 by DreamPlay Press Northwest.

Cover design: Lena Eliasson
                Grafiska Språnget
                Stockholm, Sweden

ISBN 1-930721-00-5

DreamPlay Press Northwest
University of Washington
Department of Scandinavian Studies
Box 353420
Seattle, Washington 98195-3420
http://depts.washington.edu/scand/

Table of Contents

Tabula Gratulatoria vii

Preface xiii

Birgitta Steene: Teacher and Scholar 1
Terje I. Leiren

DRAMA 7

Inga-Stina Ewbank 9
"Where do I find my *home*land?"
Ibsen, Strindberg, and Exile

Harry G. Carlson 31
Ibsen's Mythic Ornithology: Poetic
Images as Clues to Character

Ann-Charlotte Gavel Adams 45
Delacroix's murals in Église Saint-Sulpice
and Strindberg's *Jacob wrestles* and
To Damascus I

Anne-Charlotte Hanes Harvey 63
The Theatrical Compulsion of Strindberg's
Charles XII

Otto Reinert 91
Meaning Compounded: Strindberg's
Charles XII and the Question of Genre

Matthew M. Roy 105
History Revisited and Rewritten: August
Strindberg, Magnus Smek, and Heliga Birgitta

FILM 119

Astrid Söderbergh Widding 121
   Deep Staging and Light: Notes on
   Hasselblads and Georg af Klercker

Mark Sandberg 131
   Maternal Gesture and Photography in
   Victor Sjöström's *Ingeborg Holm*

Tytti Soila 159
   Desire Disavowed in Victor Sjöström's
   The Phantom Carriage

Rochelle Wright 177
   Realism Refined and Retouched: Alf
   Sjöberg's *Bara en mor*

Marilyn Johns Blackwell 193
   Cross-Dressing and Subjectivity in the
   Films of Ingmar Bergman

Maaret Koskinen 209
   Ingmar Bergman and The Mise en
   Scene of the Confessional

Egil Törnqvist 229
   "This is my hand." Hand Gestures in
   the Films of Ingmar Bergman

Bibliography 245
A. Gerald Anderson

The Contributors 261

The Editors 265

TABULA GRATULATORIA

Asbjørn Aarseth
University of Bergen
Bergen, Norway

A. Gerald Anderson
University of Washington Seattle,
Washington

Randie Aulie
Seattle, Washington

John Austin
Illinois College
Jacksonville, Illinois

Coni Baker
Kent, Washington

Steven and Kelly Barker
Redmond, Washington

Theodore Beck
Seattle, Washington

Diana Behler
University of Washington
Seattle, Washington

Dennis and Betty Behrens
Bothell, Washington

Aina Bellis
Stockholm, Sweden

Ulf Beijbom
Emigrantinstitutet
Växjö, Sweden

Marilyn Blackwell
The Ohio State University
Columbus, Ohio

Irene Blekys
Seattle, Washington

Bernt and Elisabeth Bodal
Lynnwood, Washington

Trond and Debbie Bodal
Lynnwood, Washington

Susan Brantley
University of Wisconsin
Madison, Wisconsin

Margareta Brundin
Royal Library
Stockholm, Sweden

Harry Carlson
Queens College
Flushing, New York

Lars Göran Carlson
Enskede Gård, Sweden

Patricia L. Conroy
University of Washington
Seattle, Washington

Kerstin and Lars Dahlbäck
Stockholm University
Stockholm, Sweden

Lena Daun
Swedish Institute
Stockholm, Sweden

Elizabeth de Noma
University of Wisconsin
Madison, Wisconsin

Paul and Marie Louise Dietrichson
University of Washington
Seattle, Washington

Ia Dübois
University of Washington
Seattle, Washington

Tom DuBois
University of Washington
Seattle, Washington

Gunnar Edander
Stockholm, Sweden

viii *Stage and Screen*

Eric Einhorn
  University of Mass.
  Amherst, Massachusetts

Hans-Göran Ekman
  Uppsala University
  Uppsala, Sweden

Ingrid and Rune Eliasson
  Hässelby, Sweden

Leslie Eliason
  The Monterey Institute
  Monterey, California

Lena Eliasson
  Grafiska Språnget
  Stockholm, Sweden

Gunnel Engwall
  Stockholm University
  Stockholm, Sweden

Lone Erritzoe
  Copenhagen, Denmark

Inga-Stina Ewbank
  University of Leeds
  Leeds, U.K.

Margaretha Fahlgren
  Uppsala University
  Uppsala, Sweden

Marna Feldt
  Red Bank, New Jersey

Bill Fischer
  University of Washington
  Seattle, Washington

Penny and Kjetil Flatin
  Oslo, Norway

Marianne Forssblad
  Nordic Heritage Museum
  Seattle, Washington

Syrene and Don Forsman
  Seattle, Washington

Helena Forsås-Scott
  University College
  London, U.K.

Anni Fuller
  University of Washington
  Seattle, Washington

Lars Furuland
  Uppsala University
  Uppsala, Sweden

Gunilla Gavel and
Göran Johansson
  Stockholm, Sweden

Lotta Gavel and Birney Adams
  University of Washington
  Seattle, Washington

Ulf and Agneta Gavel
  Linköping, Sweden

Sverker Göransson
  Gothenburg University
  Gothenburg, Sweden

Sophie Grimal
  Université Marc Bloch-Stras.
  Strasbourg, France

Anne-Charlotte Hanes Harvey
  San Diego State University
  San Diego, California

Katherine Hanson and Michael Schick
  University of Washington
  Seattle, Washington

Stina Hansson
  Gothenburg University
  Gothenburg, Sweden

Nils Hasselmo
  Association of American Universities
  Washington, D.C.

Hon. Consul Jahn R. Hedberg
  Seattle, Washington

Margareta Hedberg
  Seattle, Washington

Tabula Gratulatoria ix

Erik Hedling
*Lund University
Lund, Sweden*

Eva Heggestad
*Uppsala University
Uppsala, Sweden*

Vreni Hockenjos
*Stockholm University
Stockholm, Sweden*

Birgitta Holm
*Uppsala University
Uppsala, Sweden*

Roger Holmström
*Åbo Academy
Åbo, Finland*

Christine Ingebritsen
*University of Washington
Seattle, Washington*

Niels and Faith Ingwersen
*University of Wisconsin
Madison, Wisconsin*

Gunnar Iversen
*Trondheim University
Trondheim, Norway*

Barry Douglas Jacobs
*Montclair State University
Upper Montclair, New Jersey*

Claes Jernaeus
*S.I.S.
New York, New York*

Carl Jarvie
Seattle, Washington

Carl Olof Johansson
*Strindberg Society
Stockholm, Sweden*

Majella Johnson
Seattle, Washington

Hon. Consul Jon Marvin Jonsson
Seattle, Washington

Maria Karlsson
*Uppsala University
Uppsala, Sweden*

Hon. Consul Mart Kask
Seattle, Washington

Alf Knudsen
Seattle, Washington

Maaret Koskinen
*Stockholm University
Stockholm, Sweden*

Glenn Kranking
*University of Washington
Seattle, Washington*

Olaf Kvamme
Seattle, Washington

Agneta Lalander
*Strindberg Museum
Stockholm, Sweden*

Philip E. Larson
Seattle, Washington

Dr. Willard Larson
Everett, Washington

Sirkku Latomaa
*University of Tampere
Tampere, Finland*

Terje and Ingunn Leiren
*University of Washington
Seattle, Washington*

O. Hall and Carol Leiren
Vancouver, British Columbia

Barbara Lide
*Michigan Tech. University
Houghton, Michigan*

Lars Lönnroth
*Gothenburg University
Gothenburg, Sweden*

Arne Lunde
*University of California
Berkeley, California*

Lars Malmström
    Stockholm, Sweden

Merete Mazzarella
    University of Helsinki
    Helsinki, Finland

Lars Mathiesen
    Seattle, Washington

Björn Meidal
    Uppsala University
    Uppsala, Sweden

Martin Metzon
    Seattle, Washington

Laina Molbak
    Seattle, Washington

Mark Mussari
    Villanova University
    Villanova, Pennsylvania

Stanley Nelson, Jr.
    Seattle, Washington

Hon. Vice Consul Kim Nesselquist and Krystn Nesselquist
    Seattle, Washington

Per Nilsson
    Stockholm, Sweden

Ingeborg Nordin Hennel
    Uppsala University
    Uppsala, Sweden

Anna Nordlund
    Uppsala University
    Uppsala, Sweden

Margareta Nordström
    Stockholm University
    Stockholm, Sweden

Linda Norkool
    University of Washington
    Seattle, Washington

Paul Norlén and Ari Santander
    University of Washington
    Seattle, Washington

Mary Kay Norseng
    UCLA
    Los Angeles, California

Daniel Nye
    Seattle, Washington

Peter Ohlin
    McGill University
    Montreal, Canada

Elvi M. Olsson
    Seattle, Washington

Rose-Marie Oster
    University of Maryland
    College Park, Maryland

Anita and Peter Oxburgh
    Migma Film AB
    Stockholm, Sweden

Anita Persson
    Stockholm, Sweden

P. O. Qvist
    Uppsala, Sweden

Otto Reinert
    University of Washington
    Seattle Washington

Michael Robinson
    University of East Anglia
    Norwich, U.K.

Helge Rønning
    University of Oslo
    Oslo, Norway

Tiina Rosenberg
    Stockholm University
    Stockholm, Sweden

Sven Rossell
    University of Vienna
    Vienna, Austria

Matthew Roy
    University of Washington
    Seattle, Washington

Tabula Gratulatoria

Mark Sandberg
*University of California
Berkeley, California*

Per Sandsmark
Seattle, Washington

Kathy Saranpa
*University of Oregon
Eugene, Oregon*

Willmar Sauter
*Stockholm University
Stockholm, Sweden*

Ebba Segerberg
*University of California
Berkeley, California*

Henning Sehmsdorf
*University of Washington
Seattle, Washington*

Uldis Seja
Portland, Oregon

Kerstin Sirkiä
Västra Frölunda, Sweden

Jan Sjåvik
*University of Washington
Seattle, Washington*

Guntis Smidchens
*University of Washington
Seattle, Washington*

Astrid Söderbergh Widding
*Stockholm University
Stockholm, Sweden*

Inga Söderblom
*Linköping University
Linköping, Sweden*

Tytti Soila
*Stockholm University
Stockholm, Sweden*

Steven Sondrup
*Brigham Young University
Provo, Utah*

Eva-Britta Ståhl and
Björn Sundberg
*Uppsala University
Uppsala, Sweden*

Barbro Ståhle Sjönell
*Stockholm University
Stockholm, Sweden*

Hon. Consul Thomas A. Stang
Seattle, Washington

Anita Steene
Ljungskile, Sweden

Mikael and Åse Uhrdin Steene
Stockholm, Sweden

Thure Stenström
*Uppsala University
Uppsala, Sweden*

Bengt Sundelius
Stockholm, Sweden

Alan Swanson
*University of Groningen
Groningen, The Netherlands*

Robyn Tarbet
Seattle, Washington

Joan Templeton
*Long Island University
Brooklyn, New York*

Birgitta and Karl-Axel Thorstenson
Växjö, Sweden

Mariann Tiblin
*University of Minnesota
Minneapolis, Minnesota*

Roland Thorstensson
*Gustavus Adolphus College
St. Peter, Minnesota*

Egil Törnqvist
*University of Amsterdam
Amsterdam, The Netherlands*

Henk van der Liet
University of Amsterdam
Amsterdam, The Netherlands

Jim and Joan Vatn
Seattle, Washington

Rune Waldenkranz
Stockholm, Sweden

Lars Warme
University of Washington
Seattle, Washington

Ingrid and Kingsley Weatherhead
Eugene, Oregon

Margit Weingarten
Seattle, Washington

Arnold Weinstein
Brown University
Providence, Rhode Island

Hon. Consul E.N. Westerberg
Seattle, Washington

Boel Westin
Stockholm University
Stockholm, Sweden

Lynn Wilkinson
University of Texas
Austin, Texas

Margareta Wirmark
Lund University
Lund, Sweden

Gurli Woods
Carleton University
Ottawa, Ontario

Monica Wranne
Stockholm, Sweden

Rochelle Wright
University of Illinois
Urbana-Champaign

Clas Zilliacus
Åbo Academy
Åbo, Finland

Virpi Zuck
University of Oregon
Eugene, Oregon

Institutions

Center for Ibsen Studies
University of Oslo
Oslo, Norway

Dept. of Cinema Studies
Stockholm University
Stockholm, Sweden

Dept. of Scandinavian Studies
University of Washington
Seattle, Washington

Folke Bernadotte Memorial Library
Gustavus Adolphus College
St. Peter, Minnesota

Litteraturvetenskapliga Inst.
Gothenburg University
Gothenburg, Sweden

Litteraturvetenskapliga Inst.
Åbo Academy
Åbo, Finland

Lund University Library
Lund University
Lund, Sweden

Scandinavian Department
University of Amsterdam
Amsterdam, The Netherlands

The Strindberg Society
Stockholm, Sweden

The Strindberg Museum
Stockholm, Sweden

Swedish Institute
Stockholm, Sweden

University of Minnesota Libraries
Minneapolis, Minnesota

University of Washington Libraries
Seattle, Washington

Preface

The publication of *Stage and Screen* introduces a new publishing venture, DreamPlay Press Northwest, affiliated with the Department of Scandinavian Studies at the University of Washington, Seattle. For its initial publication, DreamPlay Press Northwest is pleased to honor Professor Birgitta Steene with a collection of essays by some of the most important scholars of Scandinavian drama and film. Dr. Steene has not only been a groundbreaking researcher and a dedicated teacher herself, but she has also served as a supportive colleague, and a faithful friend to several generations of scholars and students of Scandinavian studies.

The cover for *Stage and Screen*, elegantly designed for this publication by the Swedish artist Lena Eliasson of *Grafiska Språnget* in Stockholm, is intended to reflect the interplay and opposition between drama and film as represented in the chess match between Victor Sjöström and August Strindberg. The motif, of course, is inspired by the well-known scene in Ingmar Bergman's film, *The Seventh Seal*. It had been the editors' original intention to place Bergman himself as Strindberg's opponent, but the illustrious director declined our invitation saying he considered himself Strindberg's interpreter, not his opponent. During a subsequent conversation with one of the editors, Linn Ullmann, the Norwegian journalist, author, and daughter of Bergman, said: "He's actually been playing chess with Strindberg all his life."

The publication of *Stage and Screen* could not have been accomplished without the generous support of several people and organizations. The editors wish to express their sincere thanks to the *Holger och Thyra Lauritzens stiftelse* and to the *Swedish Institute* in Stockholm for their financial support toward this project. In addition, the *Department of Scandinavian Studies* and the *Center for Advanced Research Technology in the Arts and Humanities (CARTAH)* at the University of Washington and the *Sverre Arestad Research Fund* generously contributed to the publication of this book. We also thank Matthew Roy and Glenn Kranking for their work in preparing the manuscript, and Linda Norkool for her assistance with DreamPlay Press. For this book, the editors chose to invite scholarly contributions from friends, colleagues, and several generations of students of Birgitta Steene and, thereby, demonstrate not only her wide influence on the study of Scandinavian drama and film, but also to present to a broader public examples of the rich intellectual environment that is represented by the fields of Scandinavian drama and film.

Terje I. Leiren and
Ann-Charlotte Gavel Adams
Seattle, Washington

Birgitta Steene

Brigitta Steene – Teacher and Scholar

Terje I. Leiren

Following her initial university studies at Uppsala University in Sweden, Kerstin Birgitta Steene came to the United States as one of the first recipients of a stipend from the *Sverige-Amerika stiftelsen* in 1955. The decision to study in the United States as an exchange student at the University of Kansas proved to be the decisive initial step in the creation of a career that would see her develop as one of America's foremost interpreters of Scandinavian literature, drama, and film. Eventually, Birgitta would assume positions of leadership in the national and international communities of scholars of Scandinavian studies and, combined with her teaching and dedicated scholarship, she would come to influence several generations of students and scholars of Scandinavian studies.

Proudly reflecting on his young instructor of Swedish and German in November, 1957, Dr. J. A. Burzle, the chairman of the Department of Germanic and Slavic Languages and Literature at the University of Kansas, told of Birgitta's success at her first stop on the North American continent. Writing to the College of Arts and Sciences at the University of Washington, Burzle noted that Birgitta's classes at Kansas have seen the largest enrollment in the Swedish language since the end of World War II. In addition, he wrote that her course on Scandinavian literature taught in English "had a larger than normal enrollment." He praised her for her "ingenuity" and "originality" in the classroom.

In the autumn of 1956, Birgitta began her doctoral studies at the University of Washington in the Department of Comparative Literature and was offered a teaching assistantship as a pre-doctoral associate for freshman English. A year later, in December, 1957, she was invited by Sverre Arestad, Chair of the Scandinavian Department, to replace Walter Johnson during his sabbatical leave. It was the beginning of her association with the Department that would eventually see her assume the leadership as Chair in 1973.

During her doctoral studies, in order to make financial ends meet, Birgitta took an evening job with Skyway Luggage Company in Seattle. At Skyway, she would later recall an incident in which a fellow woman employee was fired when the company discovered she had become pregnant. Subsequently, when reflecting on the impact of this incident on her, Birgitta noted that she sensed this to be "an early warning of the discriminatory treatment of working women in postwar America."

Birgitta completed her Ph.D. in 1960 with a critically acclaimed dissertation "The American Drama and The Swedish Theater, 1920-1958." In her dissertation, Steene pointed to the Swedish theater tradition as that of a programmatic and realistic theater with strong nationalistic overtones and a lyrical and visionary theater that reached its fullest expression with interpretations of Strindberg's dream plays in the 1930s. She pointed out that both of these trends were reflected in the production of American plays between 1920 and 1958. A subsequent article published in the journal *Modern Drama*, on the "Critical Reception of American Drama in Sweden," helped to bring her to the attention of other scholars and potential employers.

Despite booming enrollment in American universities in the early 1960s, it was not common for women to receive offers of employment from the country's leading academic institutions. Consequently, with her Ph.D. in hand, Birgitta accepted her initial teaching job at the newly established New Orleans branch campus of Louisiana State University. Teaching took place in barracks constructed during the Korean War and under the watchful eye of United States marshals who were there to enforce federal mandates on increased admission for African-Americans. While in the South, Birgitta became actively involved in the Civil Rights movement joining in sit-in protests against segregated restaurants and bussing.

As was the pattern for an ambitious academic in the decade of the 60s, Birgitta moved from New Orleans to the University of Calgary in Alberta, Canada, then to the University of Pennsylvania where she also reworked her dissertation for publication in Sweden while teaching all three Scandinavian languages. This unique ability made her particularly attractive to universities because it meant greater return on their investment. As she prepared to teach advanced Norwegian in 1964, she wrote to Sverre Arestad asking for advice on text books and dictionaries which might be available for Norwegian instruction, while also noting, tongue in cheek, that he should nominate her for "'Storkorset' for spreading Norwegian culture in the wilderness!!!"

Having paid her dues by moving to all corners of the North American continent, the retirement of Walter Johnson in 1973, saw Birgitta Steene invited to join the faculty of the University of Washington as the Chair of the Scandinavian Department. The circle had been completed when Birgitta Steene returned as a Full Professor to the campus where she had first arrived as a promising graduate student seventeen years earlier. Now, too, she had become an established scholar of Scandinavian drama and film. She had published books on Strindberg and Bergman, and she was asked to assume the directorship of the new Film Studies Program at the University of Washington.

Throughout her career, Birgitta Steene has been a frequent guest lecturer at several American and European universities. She served as visiting professor at Humboldt (Freie) University in Berlin in 1976, Göteborg University in 1984 and 1988, Åbo University in 1990, Stockholm University in 1990-94, and two summers at the University of California, Berkeley, in 1970 and 1973. In 1982, Birgitta's Swedish alma mater,

Uppsala University, surprised her by awarding her an honorary doctorate for her outstanding contributions to the scholarship of Scandinavian drama and film. In addition, she was further honored by being awarded commemorative medals by the King of Sweden and the Governor of the State of Washington. Twice, Birgitta hosted visits by King Carl Gustav to the University of Washington.

Both major professional organizations in the field of Scandinavian Studies elected Birgitta Steene as their President. The International Association of Scandinavian Studies (IASS) chose her to lead them in 1984-86, and the Society for the Advancement of Scandinavian Study (SASS) elected her president in 1987-1989. She has also been instrumental in organizing several international symposia such as the IASS meeting at the University of Washington in 1984, the Strindberg Conference in 1988, also in Seattle, and the Strindberg-Bergman-Sjöberg symposium in Stockholm in 1998. She has served on the boards of several journals, including the *Journal of Cinema Studies* and *Scandinavica*. For the past five years, Birgitta Steene has served as the capable editor of the major scholarly publication in Strindberg studies, *Strindbergiana*

Although a major university's academic department does not develop because of the work of any single individual, the scholarship, teaching, and service of Birgitta Steene to the University of Washington Department of Scandinavian Studies has been an invaluable source of strength for the Department. She has contributed to its overall growth through her dual roles of scholar and teacher. Her colleagues, students, and friends present this volume of essays to her as a gesture of thanks for her long and faithful service to Scandinavian studies in North America and Scandinavia.

Note: The information presented in this essay has been based on material gathered through interviews with Professor

Birgitta Steene and many of her friends and colleagues, as well as from her student and faculty files at the University of Washington.

Drama

"Where do I find my *home*land?" Ibsen, Strindberg, and Exile

Inga-Stina Ewbank

My dear Brandes, you don't live for 27 years in great, free, and liberating cultural conditions without it affecting you. In here, or rather up here, among the fjords is my *native* land. But—but—but: where do I find my *home*land?[1]

HUNTER
... all languages can be called foreign,
And foreigners we remain, in relation to each other. Incognito we all travel,
GIRL
and incognito to ourselves![2]

In the English language, the word *exile* signifies either a condition or a person. In any language, there are exiles and exiles, just as there are crimes and crimes. *The Oxford English Dictionary*, defining the condition of exile, foregrounds the "enforced" aspect of "removal from one's native land" but also admits that the "prolonged absence" from that land may be "voluntarily undergone for any purpose" (sb.1 and b. *gen.*). Both kinds of exile have been—for centuries, and in due course on both sides of the Atlantic—a source of strength to the academic world. The creative possibilities inherent in voluntary academic exile are happily exemplified in the career of Birgitta Steene: equally at home, it seems, in her native land of Sweden and her self-chosen homeland of the United States, in her writings she has shown a rare ability to move between the two cultures, and to make the two dramatic and cinematic traditions cross-illuminate each other. As a small tribute to her achievement, this paper sets out to explore the significance of exile in some of the works of the two great Scandinavian dramatists on whom she has herself written so illuminatingly.

From Sappho to Salman Rushdie, exile has been the enforced or freely chosen lot of innumerable writers. It has been the subject, or subtext, or even more intangible impulsion and source, of innumerable works and, according to Harry Levin, "writers in exile have been among the most impressive witnesses to human experience."[3] Neither Ibsen nor Strindberg belongs as obviously in a list of European writers in exile as do such writers as Heine, Conrad, Joyce, Beckett, or Nabokov. But both of them lived and wrote for long periods far from their native lands: Ibsen from 1864 to 1891 and Strindberg between 1883 and 1889 and again between 1892 and 1898. Strindberg liked to refer to his departure from Sweden in 1883 as an exile like Heine's (*SV* 15:372); and in the *Kristiania* poem in his Heine-inspired cycle entitled *Exile* (*Landsflykt*) he obviously has Ibsen (as well as Bjørnson) in mind when he refers to "your great men/ Who have had to go into exile" (*SV* 15:108). To both Ibsen and Strindberg the notion of exile seems over the years to have stretched across a range of sometimes contradictory meanings and associations: exile as release into freedom and as a vantage site for cultural criticism; exile as deprivation and feelings of nostalgia; exile as an existential condition. All these can be read in, under, and between the lines from Ibsen's letter to Georg Brandes in June 1897, quoted at the head of this paper;[4] and Strindberg's last play, *The Great Highway* (1909), from which the second quotation derives, encompasses them all. The range I referred to is not simply a matter of chronological development or evolution: with both writers, various notions co-exist in time, often inextricably interwoven. Although in both the sense of existence itself as exile belongs more to late works, even then the specific—feelings for and against the "native land"—feeds into the general. The conditions which the Hunter in *The Great Highway* sees into are those of Swedish theater[5] as well as of all humanity; and when Rubek and Maja in the opening scene of *When We Dead Awaken* talk of the journey that took them back to their native country,[6] the train stopping for no reason at each isolated and silent station, then the image is rooted in Norway but grows to reflect a whole world of individuals wrapped up in silence—travelling "incognito" to others and to themselves. In my exploration, however, I will proceed from the localized to the existential.

Home and Abroad and Home Again

The binary opposition which Ibsen constructs in his 1897 letter, between, on the one hand, "the great, free, and liberating cultural conditions" abroad and, on the other, "up here" where "all the channels of understanding are blocked," had informed his thinking for thirty years and more. It was spelled out in his letters from Italy in the 1860s, was implicit in his great verse plays of that decade, and came to the fore in "contemporary" plays of the late 1870s and early 1880s. Osvald Alving, in *Ghosts* (1881), speaks to an uncomprehending Pastor Manders of "the beautiful, glorious life out there," and of its "joy of life," which brings to mind Scandinavian artists' colonies on the Continent, like the one at Grèz where Strindberg was to spend the early weeks of his first exile. It was not only painters and writers who thus found "freedom." In *Pillars of Society* (1879) Lona Hessel remembers how she had hoped—in vain, as it proved—that the young Karsten Bernick's time in Paris would have inspired him to defy the narrow prejudices of his home culture, since he had "lived out there in a large/great and liberated world which gave you the courage to think freely and largely/greatly." There is a translation problem here, as in the quoted Ibsen letter, in that in both Swedish and Norwegian the adjective *stor* means "big" or "large" when it refers to physical size and "great" when it refers to matters of mind and spirit. The resulting ambivalence enables a sliding between the largeness of other countries—more populous than the (in this sense) small Scandinavian nations—and their greatness. Ibsen avails himself of this in *Pillars of Society*, where the text insistently dichotomizes "at home" (her hjemme) and "the large countries" (de store samfund) which are an abomination to home-pillars like Rørlund but "great" to the enlightened—who are also the exiles. *Hjemme* becomes a metaphor for self-satisfied and pernicious parochialism, resisted by Dina who thinks she would be good if only she was "far away," and who defines "a beautiful thing" as "something which is great (*stort*)—and far away." As the curtain falls, there is more hope in Dina's and Johan's escape across the sea to America than in Lona's belief that Bernick's half-hearted confession has established "the spirit of truth and of freedom" at home.

"Isn't it disastrous to be buried alive as we now are with three dead languages and two and a half royal houses?" Strindberg wrote to Edvard Brandes, from Paris, in June 1885.[7] Allowing for the characteristically over-stated in his rhetorical question (so rhetorical that, in the original, he has not even bothered to end it with a question mark), it still gives an idea of what it felt like to be an ambitious and radical writer in nineteenth-century Scandinavia—that is in a marginalized culture. From Dresden Ibsen projects a more specific version of the same image when he tells his readers, in the preface to the second edition of *Catilina* (1875; first ed. 1850), of the experience of writing that play in the aftermath of the European revolutions of 1848, "at loggerheads with the small community in which I lived, cramped as I was by private circumstances and by conditions in general." (*HU* I:120)[8] In such contexts, exile meant release from being "cramped" and "buried alive"; and it meant a movement from the margin to the center. Strindberg is explicit about wanting to be "a European" (*Brev* IV:158); Ibsen, typically, is more explicit about what he does not want to be: he won't come back to Norway, he writes to his mother-in-law in December 1865, because he doesn't want his little boy to "belong to a people whose aim is to become Englishmen rather than human beings" (*HU* 16:119). England may be *large* but, seen as epitomizing an ideology of compromise, it is not *great*.

Of course, Strindberg's reference to "dead" languages belies the intimacy with which both he and Ibsen were bound to the native culture by the native language—and continued to be so in exile. Neither was forced to experience that which Nabokov called his private tragedy: having to abandon one's mother tongue. Ibsen remained resolutely monoglot as a writer. Strindberg, keenly aware of a minority (not "dead") language as a barrier between his works and a European audience, wrote a number of essays and articles in French, and some shorter pieces in German. Misgivings about a Swedish reception, combined with the desire for a wider readership, led him to compose *A Madman's Defense*, *Inferno* and part of *Legends* in French. But he never truly changed languages—unlike Nabokov, who could see Lolita as his "love affair with the English language," or Joseph Conrad and Karen Blixen who, each for his or her own reasons, chose to write in English. Beckett composed in both English and French and translated himself, producing in effect separate originals. Strindberg, who translated three of his own plays[9] into French, was, as Gunnel Engwall has shown, not necessarily the best translator of his own Swedish.[10] He was ambivalent about working in another language, finding French at times a straitjacket but at other times a creative stimulus. "My brain crackles when it has to give birth to the right word in the foreign language," he wrote when in the midst of *Le Plaidoyer d'un Fou*, "but this exertion produces a full vision of what I have experienced" (*Brev* VI:389). The attention given to verbal details in Ibsen's draft manuscripts suggests that, if his brain crackles, it is when he searches for the exactly right word in his own language; and the real Strindbergian crackle was surely when he bent the Swedish language to his own ends.

Though each left his own country feeling misunderstood, unappreciated, indeed rejected, neither Ibsen nor Strindberg was strictly in political exile—although Strindberg came to feel like it over the blasphemy trial which took him back to Stockholm in October–November 1884. Celebrated for those few short weeks as a fighter for freedom of thought and expression, by June 1885 he could look homeward and construct his native nation as "four and a half million enemies" (*Letters* I:145).[11] And Ibsen's criticism of his country initially focussed on the political betrayal by Norway and Sweden of Denmark when attacked by Prussia. Both writers record the not unusual experience of feeling that distance gives a clearer vision of conditions at home.[12] *Brand*, Ibsen insists, is the direct result of such insight compounded by comparison with "what I have seen is possible out here" (*HU* 16:123). He was still making the same point nearly ten years later, in his poem *Far Away* (*Langt borte*) where he rejects the pan-Scandinavianist celebrations he has nearly been drawn into, and contrasts the active politics, the genuine struggles towards national identity, in Italy and Germany with the ineffectual posturing and "mist-banks of phrases" in the North. It was the combination of fierce political-moral anger and aesthetic culture shock—meeting in Rome the art of High Renaissance and Baroque—that released the creative powers needed for the drama of *Brand*. In a well-known letter to Bjørnson he describes the epiphany in St. Peter's which gave him "a strong and clear form" for what he wanted to say (*HU* 16:110). With *Brand* and *Peer Gynt*, exile gave Ibsen his identity as a dramatist confident in his own power.

In contrast, Strindberg saw his first period of exile less dramatically, in more than one sense. For one thing, unlike Ibsen, he continued to have so many outlets other than drama

—polemical essays and articles, narrative fiction and non-fictive prose—for his cultural criticism. The exile years led up to the writing of his great naturalistic plays, but altogether they held far more continuity as well as multiplicity of literary activity than was the case with Ibsen. During the early years Strindberg was a very deliberate traveller, writing—or planning to write—accounts of "abroad" for Swedish newspapers and journals, and of Sweden for the French press. This was partly a matter of economic necessity—unlike Ibsen, Strindberg did not have a state stipend to support him and his family—but also because he was in the midst of a crisis of doubt in the value of fictive literature, relishing what he saw as his right as a journalist: "to be allowed to set down my thoughts on the questions of the day without having to package them in the chocolate boxes of fiction" (*SS* XVI:143). But his imagination was far too restive to be confined to discursive prose, and in the four long poems which make up his *Sleepwalking Nights* (*Sömngångarnätter*, 1884) travel-letters and fiction meet and merge. Each of these poems follows a pattern where the poet's mind detaches itself from his sleeping body in a faraway place (though not before the place has been thoroughly and often critically described) and sweeps back to re-visit, and to pass more or less scathing verdicts on, a Swedish institution—church, art, library, and science. Bjørnson is said to have stated that in Norway "one wouldn't put up with such lectures in verse" (*SV* 15:398), which may be taken as a measure of how much more thoroughly the "lectures" by Ibsen—as Brand lashes out against moral half-heartedness—had been transmuted into art and into a general, rather than Norway-specific, moral and intellectual challenge. The young Strindberg had heard in *Brand* "the voice of a Savonarola," all the more empowered to "arouse all thinking young people" because it sounded from far away (*SS* 17:208).

The Norwegian language provides Ibsen with a pair of rhyme words—*hjemmet* (home) and *fremmed* (strange, or foreign)—to ram home the idea of being *other*, a foreigner in and to one's home. He uses it in *Brand* (*SV* I:438), and twice in the poem *Far Away*. In the lyric, the stance—"alone, far away"—gets uncomfortably close to the kind of easy romanticizing of exile that Terry Eagleton envisages when he warns against "vulgariz[ing] the notions of exile and expatriation to some simple model of the 'outsider', with its banal image of a fixed ontological gap between isolated artist and inauthentic society."[13] *Brand* escapes such banality, both through the fierceness with which the gap between the hero and his society is realized and through the fact that the gap is not "fixed." Brand's stance is questioned, not only by the final "ontological" assertion that "He is *deus caritatis*" but by the inhuman sacrifices it demands.

Strindberg can infuriate by his would-be heroic insistence that he stands alone—whether it is against the four and a half million Swedes or all the world—and the beginning of the end of his friendship-in-exile with Bjørnson was his letter in which the sentence stating that "Now I stand as alone in my fight as neither you nor Ibsen have ever done" (*Brev* IV:355) was perhaps the least outrageous. But he is also remarkably capable of seeing the outsider's position as potentially absurd —never more so than in the novel *By the Open Sea* (*I Havsbandet*) which he began writing soon after returning from his first exile, in the summer of 1889, but—uncharacteristically—was not able to complete until the following summer. As Axel Borg, the scientist turned Inspector of Fisheries who is the novel's main, not to say only, character, becomes increasingly alienated from everyone because of his superior intellect, his *Übermensch* ego does not grow, but "swells out," making everything else, even the sea, seem "cramped." The swelling takes the form of a megalomania which in turn becomes a kind of parody on cultural criticism: his schemes swell from a restructuring of the geography of Sweden to a redrawing of the political, cultural, and religious map of Europe.[14] Borg's megalomania reaches its climax in a fantastic scene where he anticipates modern science and plays at being God by attempting, and only just failing, to create a human embryo in a test tube. Defeated, he disintegrates into grotesque pathos, rescuing a pile of dolls from a stranded ship and—in a haunting pre-echo of Ibsen's Aline Solness—nursing them as if they were his children. In the last few lines of the novel he resorts to the ultimate exile, sailing to his death on a sea which is "life's source and life's enemy."[15] The story of Borg is a compound of Strindberg's own interests and obsessions, translated into a work of magic realism long before this term had been invented; but at the heart of it is a complex—and far from "banal"—insight into the "tragedy" of the irreconcilable conflict between rootedness and otherness—or between Ibsen's *hjemmet* and *fremmed*.

That conflict underlies the nostalgia which is an inalienable attribute of exile; but nostalgia finds very different forms of expression in the two writers. Strindberg's expansive *Sleepwalking Nights* have a typically laconic—almost lapidary—equivalent in the poem *Burnt Ships* (*Brente skibe*) which Ibsen insisted on placing last in his 1871 volume of collected verse (*Digte*). In the first two stanzas a latter-day Viking leaves the snowy North for the sunny South and its "brighter" gods; in the third stanza the smoke of his burnt ship streaks northwards; but the fourth and last brings a *peripeteia*:

> To snow-hutted Norse-land,
> from thickets of light,
> gallops a horseman
> through each, single night.[17]

Strindberg writes far more often and fully of what he calls, in a play of words difficult to translate, "hemlig hemsjuka" (secret homesickness) and describes as "gnawing, wasting" (*SV* 21:162, 169).[18] In a letter to Albert Bonnier, and with a logic applicable only to himself, he argued that *Sleepwalking Nights* had to be published while he was still abroad, or else "the undertone, my homesickness, will be lost" (*SV* 15:389). Like many of his letters from abroad, the poems longingly evoke the kind of essentially "Swedish" images which later media, not least the cinema, have turned into clichés of a lost paradise:

> White birches in groves with lilies-of-the valley,
> Places where the wild strawberries grow . . .
> (*SV* 15:262)

To Strindberg these are not clichés. His rootedness in Swedish soil is part of his equipment as a writer; it conditions the concrete physicality of nearly everything he writes, at home or abroad. He can proudly proclaim himself, to Bonnier, "Sweden's most verbally-abused author," but the same letter has a parenthesis: "(My homesickness is purely physical, my body yearns for the landscape, 'the environment', the root for the soil)" (*Brev* V:121); and in the last part of *Son of a Servant*, written in 1886, he comments on exile, his own and others', that "the body has its own homesickness. The finest roots are damaged in replanting, a different soil gives alien nourishment" (*SV* 21:151). Ibsen could allow one of his dramatic characters the same image: in *Emperor and Galilean* (1873) Julian, about to become an apostate, defines the plight of Roman Christians as "vines replanted in a strange and unfamiliar soil" (*SV* II:190). But of himself he would use a more measured discourse. Honored in June 1885 by a workers' procession in Trondheim, on only his second visit to Norway since leaving in 1864 (the first was in 1874), he told them:

> It is after an absence of 11 years that I came home again to Norway 8 days ago.
> In these 8 days at home I have experienced more

joy of life [livsglæde] than in all the 11 years abroad. (*HU* XV:407)

It is not only the public occasion but also the typically Ibsenite reticence—so opposed to Strindbergian confessional concreteness—that puts feelings here into a sort of mathematical straitjacket. Nor need it be just the desire to find the appropriate discourse for a formal thank-you that makes Ibsen revalue words like "home" and "abroad" and their relation to "joy of life." In 1892, soon after his return to Norway, he added a stanza to *Burnt Ships* in which the returning horseman "found open each door"; so, he asks, "could the rider have ended / his long exile before?"[19] But by the time he writes his letter to Georg Brandes in 1897, he is no longer sure where his "*home*land" is. The returning horseman both is and is not the same man who defiantly burnt his ship. Strindberg develops this idea hauntingly in a poem which he wrote in the autumn of 1889, soon after his return from exile, and added as a *Fifth Night* to the second edition of *Sleepwalking Nights* (1890). In his manuscript he had given it the title *The Awakening*.

Returning in reality to where in the four earlier "Nights" he went in his dreams, the "he" of the *Fifth Night* finds everything changed—the city has grown and become modern, people have died or altered beyond recognition—and he ends up "erring around homeless," realizing in the end that he cannot be homesick for "what does not exist." But before then he has had an eerie confrontation with his own double. It is a scene which may well reflect Strindberg's excited "discovery" of Edgar Allan Poe at about the same time[20] and which also anticipates the experience of the hero of Henry James's story *The Jolly Corner* (1908) who returns to his house after 33 years abroad to find his *alter ego*, "un 'vrai' fantôme,"[21] still there. But most of all, as solidly observed reality dissolves into a serio-comic nightmare of nothingness, this scene anticipates some of Strindberg's own post-Inferno drama—*Advent*, or even *A Dream Play*. Through a window of his own old house "he" sees a man sitting at his own old desk, eagerly dipping his pen in the inkwell and writing away on long, white sheets of paper—without leaving a trace on them. And then this man, who only "believes he is writing," turns his face towards "him":

> Deadman's eyes as huge as teacups
> Stare darkly, through distended pupils,
> And he nods familiarly to his namesake,
> Points significantly to his work;
> And out of the depths of his throat he hiccups:
> "Look, I'm beginning to write in white!"
> (*SV* 15:232)[22]

This homecoming, then, holds an insight into the most extreme exile, the very deepest rootlessness—not only the discovery that home is not home but the fear, as expressed in Ibsen's last play, that "when we dead awaken, we see that we have never lived" (*SV* III:542).

Existential Exile

Intimations of exile as an existential condition are there in earlier Ibsen drama. Peer Gynt may boast of global citizenship,[23] but towards the end, though returned to his native country, he finds himself alone in a universe so unresponsive that his question stops being a question:

> Is there no one, no one to hear me even—
> No one in darkness, no one in heaven—![24]

At the very end Peer finds his home in Solveig's lap, and in her "faith, . . . hope and . . . love" (*SV* I:714); but at the end of *Ghosts* there is no such closure. As if in a negative of *Peer Gynt*'s ending, Mrs. Alving is left with her broken-down son in her lap, "in speechless horror." Osvald's exile may be from Paris, but hers is from what she took to be herself and into an indifferent universe.[25] If, however, *When We Dead Awaken* is Ibsen's most pronounced exile play, it is because its central action is a homecoming of individuals—Rubek and Irene— who have no home except in a lost paradise of the past when she was the model and inspiration of his art as a sculptor. When they try to recover it, they die, leaving the audience to wonder whether these characters were ever anything other than strangers to themselves and each other, and Rubek's art ever anything but "writing in white." And the geography of travel in this three-act movement from valley to high mountain, while rooted in the Norwegian landscape, has become, as in Strindberg's "wander-plays," an internalized, spiritual process.

When We Dead Awaken (1899) is the play that Ibsen wrote instead of the autobiography he had promised,[26] and also— very likely—after reading the first two parts of Strindberg's *To Damascus* (1898),[27] the drama that marked the end of Strindberg's second exile. An eventful period, containing his second marriage (including a macabre and abortive honeymoon visit to England) and divorce, it had led up to and through his Inferno-crisis; it had produced scientific or pseudo-scientific writings, but nothing that we would think of as exile-literature until the crisis itself was recorded in *Inferno* (1897). The concept of exile is now profoundly internalized. Paris or Dornach or Klam, however vividly realized, are important only as the settings for spiritual crises; they are places in the mind rather than on the map, and travelling back to Sweden is a "pilgrimage," undertaken "in order to endure enemy fire at yet another station on the road to atonement" (*SV* 37:273). The eye is not, as in *Sleepwalking Nights*, on the land he returns to but on his own spiritual state, observed with an extraordinary mixture of fervor and self-reflective humor: his smart new "flea-brown" coat looks like a Capuchin's cloak, "So it is in penitential garb that I make my re-entry into Sweden after six years of exile" (*SV* 37:279). In *To Damascus I*, deliberately structured as the stations of a turn-and-return pilgrimage, the hero is called "Den Okände"—The Stranger, or literally The Unknown One—and his sense of exile is absolute. He doesn't know, he says in the opening scene, "why I exist, why I'm standing here, where I am going, what I am to do" (*SV* 39:16). In Part II the Stranger's attempt to articulate such a sense of exile gives occasion for remarkable, surrealist prose-poetry—

> Where am I? Where have I been? Is it spring, winter or summer? In which century am I living and in which universe? . . . Are these my own inner organs that I see around me, are they stars or nerve ends in my eye, is this water or my own tears? . . . I must have slept a couple of thousand years, and I dreamt that I exploded and was turned into ether, could no more feel anything, suffer anything, rejoice at anything, but had entered a state of rest and equilibrium! But now! O, now! I am suffering as if I were the whole of humanity—
> (*SV* 39:265)

which anticipates the voice of that other great Strindberg exile, Indra's Daughter in *A Dream Play*, as she descends among, and finally ascends from, pitiable mankind.

Themes of exile weave in and out of Strindberg's immensely rich and varied post-Inferno production. His theater geography has larger dimensions than Ibsen's; it can quite literally take in heaven, earth and hell, as in *Advent* (1898) which ends with the Nativity, while the Magistrate and his wife are exiled to Hell, where "there are only entrances, no exits" and where "time has stopped, and a minute can be an eternity"

(*SV* 40:113, 117). It can also be firmly grounded in the Swedish landscape, as in *Easter* (1900) where Elis, exiled in a "stifling" southern town, yearns for the willow trees and row boats of "our own country, . . . Lake Mälaren."[28] But perhaps what is most characteristic of the post-Inferno plays is the combination of concrete, "rooted" localization with figures who are strangers in existence. As the Hunter in *The Great Highway* puts it, "A traveller in other people's countries / Is always a stranger, alone / . . . / Until his journey has reached its end— then he is at home" (*SV* 62:209). Yet, "at home" is more of a question mark than a lasting abode. The Chamber Plays (1907, 1909) do not dissolve time and space as radically as does *A Dream Play* or *To Damascus*, but they place rootless, alienated individuals in a detailed Stockholm environment; and only the first, *Storm* (Oväder), allows for a resolution that is a kind of homecoming, to "the serenity of old age" (*SV* 58:82). The Stranger who returns to the burned-out remains of his childhood home in *After the Fire* conjures his past out of the ruins. Its sights and sounds and smells are nearly as fully realized as are those of Gerda's and the Son's childhood Christmases and summer holidays in the holocaust of the final scene of *The Pelican*. Yet, the Stranger is not a sentimentally returning exile; he has been through other countries, including death, and knows he belongs nowhere. "And now, wanderer: out into the wide world again," are his closing words. He will continue to travel, "incognito," as *The Great Highway* tells us we all do.

The essential modernity of both Strindberg and Ibsen has much to do with their anticipation of what Julia Kristeva has called the "Copernican revolution" of the discovery of the Freudian unconscious—the discovery that "we are our own foreigners, we are divided."[29] In Ibsen's *The Lady from the Sea* (1888) Ellida's, the protagonist's, exile is that of a deeply divided psyche. At the level of physical geography it is expressed as a longing ("homesickness," she calls it) for the open sea, away from the brackish water of the fjord town where she is enclosed in what she perceives as a marriage of convenience. She is torn between her husband and the mysterious Stranger, the sailor who, like the sea, signifies to her all that is *unheimlich*.[30] For once Ibsen appears to offer an acclimatizing solution,[31] as Ellida chooses, "in freedom" and "on [her] own responsibility," to stay with Wangel. In the four last plays, all written after his return to Norway, there are no such easy homecomings. Here people remain strangers to themselves and others. *Fremmed*—which means both "strange" and "foreign"—becomes the keyword for defining relationships: John Gabriel Borkman and Vilhelm Foldal dissolve their friendship by declaring each other "fremmed"; after Little Eyolf's death his mother describes him as a "fremmed" little boy; and to Mrs. Solness "everything" has become "fremmed" (*SV* III:465, 414, 362). People in these plays are exiles in existence; they have a vision of a moment or state of perfection in the past and when, like Solness or Borkman or Rubek, they try to re-create, or return to it, they die. It is difficult not to believe in a similar doom for Rita and Alfred Allmers's plan to atone for the death of Little Eyolf by transforming their own home into a home for poor neglected children. Alfred's real homesickness, we have learned, is for a lost paradise, his pre-marital life together with Asta, the first Eyolf, and, alternatively, for the mountains where he and death walked together, "like two good travelling companions" (*SV* III:430).

By 1894 Ibsen could publicly define, in a proud distich, what he saw as his country:

As far as my works set the minds of people on fire
So far stretches my fatherland (fedreland).[32]

But if your works bring international fame—as they did to Ibsen and, more fitfully, to Strindberg—and if this, in defiance of your minority-culture origin, makes you a world citizen, the works themselves tell a different story of homelands. So do private communications, like Ibsen's letter to Brandes, and even public ones, as when Ibsen told the guests at his seventieth-birthday banquet that "he who has won for himself a home in many countries feels, in the innermost depths of his being, quite at home nowhere,—scarcely even in his own native country."[33] If this is a paradox, perhaps as such it also holds a key to these writers' modernity and continued appeal. For all the differences between them, the two Scandinavian playwrights both share in a paradigm articulated by Todorov, though not in its simple curve from rawness to strength to perfection:

> The man who finds his country sweet is only a raw beginner, the man for whom each country is his own is already strong, but only the man for whom the whole world is a foreign country is perfect.[34]

NOTES

[1] "Å, kære Brandes, man lever ikke virkningsløst 27 år ude i de store fri og frigørende kulturforhold. Her inde eller, rettere sagt, her oppe ved fjordene har jeg jo mit *føde*land. Men-men-men: hvor finder jeg mit *hjem*land?" Henrik Ibsen, letter to Georg Brandes, 3 June 1897, in *Samlede Verker*, ed. Francis Bull, Halvdan Koht, and Didrik Arup Seip, 22 vols. (Oslo: Gyldendal, 1928–57), XVIII:397. In this paper, Ibsen's letters and speeches are cited from this edition (*Hundreårsutgave*), with references to (*HU*) in the text. Ibsen's plays and poems are cited from *Samlede Verker*, ed. Didrik Arup Seip, 3 vols. (Oslo: Gyldendal, 1960), with references to (*SV*) in the text. Unless otherwise indicated, translations from the Norwegian are my own.

[2] "**JÄGARN** . . . alla språk kan kallas främmande, / Och främlingar vi äro, bli inför varandra. / Inkognito vi resa alla, / **FLICKAN** och inkognito inför oss själva." August Strindberg, *Stora Landsvägen* (*The Great Highway*), in *August Strindbergs Samlade Verk* (*Nationalupplaga*), ed. Gunnar Ollén, vol. 62 (Stockholm: Norstedts, 1992), 130. Strindberg's works are cited, in this paper, from this edition, with references to (*SV*)

in the text. Where *SV* volumes have not yet appeared, (*SS*) references are to *August Strindbergs Samlade Skrifter*, ed. John Landquist, 55 vols. (Stockholm: Bonnier, 1912–21). Unless otherwise indicated, translations from the Swedish are my own.

[3] Harry Levin, "Literature and Exile," in *Refractions* (New York, 1966), 62.

[4] The lines quoted are framed by intertextual recall of his play *The Lady from the Sea* (1888): "Here all the straits are closed, in every sense of the word; and all the channels of understanding are blocked.... The sea, more than anything, is what draws me."

[5] See the speech where the Hunter explains that he has been an "architect": "I built a great many houses; they weren't all good, but when I built good ones, they were angry with me because they were good! So they gave the work to others, who did worse! It was in the city of Thofeth, where I built the theater" (*SV* 62:205). Presumably the theater to which he refers is the Intimate Theater.

[6] See *SV* III:505.

[7] *Strindberg's Letters*, selected, edited, and translated by Michael Robinson, 2 vols. (Chicago: University of Chicago Press, 1992), I:186. (Hereafter referred to as *Letters*). When letters are cited directly from the Swedish, reference is to *August Strindbergs Brev*, ed. Torsten Eklund and Björn Meidal (Stockholm: Bonnier, 1948–), with references to (*Brev*) in the text.

[8] "[P]å krigsfod med det lille samfund, hvor jeg sad indeklemt af livsvilkår og omstændigheder." Quoted in James Walter McFarlane's translation, in *The Oxford Ibsen*, vol. I (London: Oxford University Press, 1970), 110.

[9] *The Father*, *Creditors* and *A Dream Play*.

[10] See her contribution to Nobel Symposium 110, in Sture Allén, ed., *Translation of Poetry and Poetic Prose* (Singapore: World Scientific, 1999), 151-59. For an insight into Strindberg's command of French, see Gunnel Engwall's fascinating study of the original manuscript of *Le Plaidoyer d'un fou*, of the published version (which was the result of Georges Loiseau's extensive corrections and revisions), and of John

Landquist's translation of this text into Swedish: "En dåres försvarstal i Samlade Skrifter", in Gunnel Engwall and Regina af Geijerstam, ed., *Från språk till språk* (Lund: Studentlitteratur, 1983), 168–96.

[11] Cf. Ibsen's letter to Clemens Petersen, 4 Dec. 1865, which concludes: "I have an insufferably oppressive feeling of standing alone" (*HU* 16: 122).

[12] For Strindberg, see e.g. *Brev* III:310, where he tells Bonnier that, since he does not expect to extend his "exile" beyond a year [sic], he has decided that the best way to use this year is "to scrutinize from a distance the state of things in Sweden." For Ibsen, see particularly his letter to Magdalene Thoresen, 3 Dec. 1865: "What has been decisive and significant for me is to have put sufficient distance between myself and home to see the hollowness behind all the self-made lies in our so-called public life and the wretchedness of all that private phrasemongering which always has words enough when it comes to speaking of 'A Great Cause,' but which never has either the will, the power or the sense of duty needed for a great deed" (*HU* 16:118).

[13] Terry Eagleton, *Exiles and Emigrés* (London, 1970), 219.

[14] "Europe must be one again. The way of the people was via Rome, that of the intelligentsia via Paris!": *By The Open Sea*, translated by Mary Sandbach (London: Secker & Warburg, 1984), 171.

[15] Ibid., 185.

[16] See Ibid., 170: "He could not journey away from it all, for he was rooted in this soil, in his small impressions, in his diet, and he could not be dug up by the roots. This was the tragedy of the northener which finds expression in his longing for the south."

[17] *Ibsen's Poems*, translated by John Northam (Oslo: Norwegian University Press, 1986), 121. For the original—"Mot snelandets hytter, / fra solstrandens kratt, / rider en rytter / hver eneste natt."—see *SV* III:646–47.

[18] Long before Freud used the German adjectives *heimlich* and *unheimlich* (*Das Unheimliche*, 1919) to explore the dynamic of the unconscious, Strindberg was able to take advantage of the uncanny relationship between Swedish *hem* (home) and *hemlig* (secret).

[19] Northam trans., 121. The original—"Nys steg han af hesten / fandt åpen hver dør—/ kunde hjemløse gæsten / kanske kommet lidt før?"—was published in *Dagbladet*, no. 21, 1892 (*HU* XIV:462).

[20] See his letter to Ola Hansson, 3 January 1889: "If you only knew what I've experienced since I read E.P.—experienced—because I've become aware of it!" (*Letters* I:301).

[21] The phrase is Tzvetan Todorov's, in *L'homme dépaysé* (Paris: Éditions du Seuil, 1996), 19. Todorov sees in *The Jolly Corner* a parallel to his own experience of returning to Sofia after 18 years in Paris and finding that "[j]e suis un fantôme, mieux: un revenant."

[22] The poem is in four-beat trochaic verse, rhyming abab cdcd, etc. (which contributes to the deadpan effect), but I have simply translated the words as literally as possible.

[23] *SV* I:637. (To Monsieur Ballon's question, "You are Norwegian, aren't you?", Peer replies: "By birth, yes! / But a world citizen by temperament.")

[24] *Peer Gynt*, trans. Rolf Fjelde (New York: Signet Classic, 1964), 235. For the original—"Er der ingen, ingen i hele vrimlen—, / ingen i avgrunnen, ingen i himlen—!" see *SV* I:711.

[25] I take the final scene's sunrise on the distant mountaintops to be a sign of this indifference.

[26] See his speech at the banquet in honor of his seventieth birthday, in Christiania on 23 March 1898 (*HU* XV:412): " . . . a book that will link my life and my authorship together into an illuminating whole."

[27] A copy of the first edition of *Till Damaskus. Del I och II* (Stockholm: Gernandt, 1898) was in Ibsen's library.

[28] The otherness of summer in the southern town is expressed through Elis's grotesque vision: "The middle of the day, and you see the long grey street winding its way like a trench—not a human being, and not a horse, not a dog.— But out of the mouths of the sewers come the rats, since the cats are on holiday. — . . . And out of the poor quarters crawl cripples who have been hiding, creatures without noses and ears, wicked

creatures and unhappy ones. — And they sit on the promenade sunning themselves, as if they had occupied the town" (*SV* 43:285).

[29] Julia Kristeva, *Strangers to Ourselves*, translated by Leon S. Rondiez (New York and London: Harvester, 1991), 169, 181.

[30] Cf. *SV* III:217: "Det grufulle, . . . som skremmer og drager."

[31] The tone of the ending is mixed: apart from the fact that another marriage of convenience (Arnholm and Bolette's) has been agreed on, the steamer which is the town's last outside contact for the year moves away down the fjord, and Ballested comments, in the phrase which Ibsen was to use in his 1897 letter to Brandes, that "soon all the straits will be closed" (*SV* III:234).

[32] *HU* XIV:463: "Sålangt min digtning tænder sind i brand / sålangt går grensen for mitt fædreland." This was published in *Morgenbladet*, 20 November 1894, with a note: "A couple of years ago Dr. Ibsen wrote for a Swedish literary album a very characteristic couplet, which the poet has recently also sent to a Dutch lady who had requested a few words from his hand" (*HU* XIV:529).

[33] "For det er sagen: at den, som har vundet sig et hjem ude i de mange lande,—han føler sig i sine inderste dybder ingensteds helt hjemme,—neppe nok i selve fødelandet" (*HU* XV:414).

[34] Tzvetan Todorov, *La conquête de l'Amerique*, quoted from Richard Howard's translation, *The Conquest of America* (New York, 1985), 250. Todorov claims a twelfth-century origin for the saying, and adds: "I myself, a Bulgarian living in France, borrow this quotation from Edward Said, a Palestinian living in the United States, who himself found it in Erich Auerbach, a German exiled in Turkey."

Ibsen's Mythic Ornithology:
Poetic Image as Clue to Character

Harry G. Carlson

Ibsen practiced many kinds of poetry. There is the brisk, sturdy verse of *Brand* and *Peer Gynt* and there is the poetry of psychological nuance of *The Wild Duck* and *Ghosts*, where a single word or gesture can vibrate in context with more poetic and dramatic intensity than entire texts of the verse dramas of lesser talents. There is the poetry of social interaction in plays like *Rosmersholm* and *Hedda Gabler*, where within the restricted confines of drawing rooms whole worlds are evoked in which the problems of the individual and of society interpenetrate in microcosmic/macrocosmic tension. And there is another poetry in Ibsen, one vibrating with the power and eloquence of myth. Like Sophocles, Shakespeare, and Racine before him, he was a major mythopoetic artist, a fact obscured when he is only narrowly identified with naturalism or the drama of social problems.

Modern literary uses of ancient mythic images are reminders of a continuity in Western poetic tradition that reaches back to the Greeks, but for actors in the theater they can serve another important purpose as well. A play's realistic surface may conceal or obscure mythic images of which an actor or an audience may be only dimly aware, but which can reveal meaning in interesting and important ways.

Sometimes these images appear only singly, as discrete elements, and sometimes, especially in Ibsen's case, they are grouped together in clusters of allusions that are associated with each other. A cluster of avian images is the subject of this essay, and the associative bonds within it are so strong that an image rarely appears singly. More often than not two or more images appear, almost as if the use of one image automatically called up others. The avian cluster appears again and again in Ibsen's work, as if he had been compelled to return to it as to an itch that continued to demand scratching. My central concern here is how it can supply clues to character relationships.

Certainly, no problem for the actor is more basic than the one he faces each time his character confronts another. Constantly, he must ask himself the questions: "What is the nature of our relationship? On how many levels does it exist? What am I trying to do to him/her and what is he/she trying to do to me?" An Ibsen scene that illustrates the difficulties such questions pose is Peer Gynt's confrontation with the statue of Memnon in the sands of Egypt. The actual statue is a massive black stone sculpture 68 feet high that still stands on the Theban Plain, and is known as the "singing colossus." Every day at sunrise it is said to utter a sound like the breaking of a lyre-string, probably because a flow of air, passing through an interior fissure in the stone, expands noisily as it is warmed by the sun.

In the play Peer has just abandoned the role of prophet after being tricked and humiliated by the seductive Anitra. He is now assaying a new role as a scientific researcher, and he wanders the sands of the desert, notebook in hand, jotting down his impressions in as scholarly a fashion as he knows how.

It is dawn and time for the statue to begin to sing. Ibsen provided a short song for the occasion and William and Charles Archer were among the first to translate it:

> From the demigods's ashes there soar, youth renewing,
>   birds ever singing
>   Zeus the Omniscient
>   shaped them contending.

> Owls of wisdom,
> my birds, where do they slumber?
> Thou must die if thou rede not
> the song's enigma!
> (Archer 180; *Billigutgave* II:196)

Not surprisingly, the song has puzzled scholars, translators, actors, and directors alike. To make sense of it we need to turn to the original myth. When Memnon was killed in the Trojan War, his grieving mother, Eos or Aurora, goddess of dawn, begged Zeus to honor her son. In response to her plea a flock of birds arose from the embers of Memnon's funeral pyre and flew around it three times. On the fourth circuit they divided into two flocks, fought with claws and beaks, and fell down upon the ashes as funeral sacrifice.

Some scholars speculate that the owl reference in the poem—which the Archers rendered as the plural "owls" for the singular "ugle" in Norwegian—was Ibsen's way of criticizing reactionary provincial professors at the University of Norway, the badge of which is the Owl of Wisdom (Bull 73–74; Fjelde 222). However interesting this explanation may be as a curiosity for scholars, it does little to help an actor looking for clues in the images to character relationships.

When we examine the song more closely, we find the references to birds related to other images in the cluster that may help us to understand not only this scene, but related scenes in many of Ibsen's works. The elements of the cluster include: dawn, birds, a mother grieving over a child in a pietà scene, and the promise of resurrection. A clue to Ibsen's possible intention with it can be found in a poem written a decade before *Peer Gynt* for Norwegian Independence Day: "Prologue Recited on the 17th of May, 1855, at the Norwegian Theatre." In the poem a reference to the Memnon statue is used by the author to provoke his countrymen into thinking about the true significance of their national holiday. Asking the question, "What is freedom?" the poem responds with another question:

> Is it only the right
> To send men to Parliament every three years —
> To sit there dully, wings of thought clipped . . . ?
> . . . .
> No, if it is in form *alone* that we have provided freedom,
> Then we have only in general understood what God intended!
>
> *
>
> Only he is free who boldly aspires forward,
> Whose deepest craving is the deed, whose goal is an heroic act of the spirit,
> . . . .
>
> *
>
> Have you ever heard tell of the Memnon statue,
> A granite sculpture in the East?
> When the rosy dawn colored the desert sands,
> A stream of sound issued mightily from Memnon,
> While the statue itself, cold as a wintry mountain,
> Stared with soulless glance toward the eastern horizon.
> And so it stood year after year in lethargic dreams, —
> For only from its lips would the sound stream forth.
>
> *
>
> And is it anything more than words and sound,
> If we hail the rosy dawn of freedom,
> And not understand that its finest fruit
> Can ripen only in the *light of the spirit*? . . . .
> (*Hundraårsutgave* 14:174–76)

New elements are apparent in the cluster: the challenge of freedom and the demands of the spirit. In the dawn of freedom "only he is free . . . whose goal is an heroic of the spirit," and slave is he who sits like the Memnon statue—inert in the sands, paying only lip service to life's challenges and demands. Memnon's birds no longer rise to do life's battles; they only slumber. The spiritual resurrection is aborted.

Returning to the Memnon scene in the play we can see another reading of the statue's cryptic song, one that suggests that the singer may be yet another of the strange voices from Peer's unconscious that sound throughout the play, like the Boyg, prodding him to work actively toward the goal of self-realization:

> From the ashes of the demigod there rise,
> life-bringing,
> birds singing.
> Zeus, in his knowing might,
> Shaped them born to fight.
> Owl of Wisdom, do you keep
> the secret of where my birds sleep?
> Do not from this riddle fly
> Solve it, or die!

(*Billigutgave* II:196)

Memnon's riddle, like the riddle posed to Oedipus by the Sphinx, is the ancient challenge to accept the call to freedom. Peer's spirit has yet to answer the call; his birds are asleep. Unfortunately, like a true pedant, he has only recorded the experience with the statue in his notebook, adding that it has no significance. He has heard everything but understood nothing.

When elements in the earlier poem are joined with those in the song, a larger pattern of meaning emerges, and it has three components. First, freedom is not a license to travel through life unhindered or unencumbered. Peer thinks it is a license for him "to swim in the river of history, / ... as in a dream." Though he says he wants to experience the dream, he means to do so as "only a spectator" (*Billigutgave* II:194).

Second, freedom is not just an outward journey to adventure. It is a profoundly intense inward search—"Within! Within! That's the word!" says Brand, "that's where the road leads" (*Billigutgave* II:33). But though he preaches this, he is unable to put it into practice in his own life. And third, freedom is not a privilege but an opportunity, a call to the spirit to take flight and soar toward self-fulfillment and realization. The two flocks of birds represent the duty to confront one's inner self, to accept the necessity of inner struggle, spiritual conflict. "To live," Ibsen said in an 1880 letter, "is to battle trolls in the vaults of the heart and mind" (McFarlane 91).

Bird, spirit, dawn, battle for self-realization, pietà—let us see how the cluster operates in the final scenes of *Peer Gynt* when Peer returns to find Solveig. It is not only dawn, but the dawn of Pentecost, the moment after the Crucifixion when God's bond with man was renewed, the moment when His grace descended through the Holy Spirit—traditionally depicted as a dove in flight—upon the Apostles. Peer is afraid. He has so long resisted the call to be himself truly and completely, he fears it may now be impossible. It may be too late for his spirit to lift its wings and soar. To make matters worse, he hears a predatory owl searching for prey—the owl again—and he is pursued by a Thin Person carrying a fowling net, the ancient way of capturing birds.

But then Peer finally locates his first love, Solveig, whose name in Norwegian means "way of the sun." As she cradles him in her arms and calls him her little boy, she becomes Eos hovering over the fallen Memnon as well as Mary over the crucified Christ. The mythic echoes give the scene another dimension, transforming profane time into sacred time. A mother has reclaimed her son. The journey ends where it began; the circle is complete; and the authority presiding over all is the ageless Magna mater, at once as virginal as spring and as ancient as the earth. But, as in countless other pietàs, an ambiguous note is struck, giving the moment a sadness that is as profound as life itself. Mother hovering over dead son is the reverse image of Madonna hovering over sleeping baby, and so, the fulfillment of promise is aborted.

There are other avian images in *Peer Gynt*, as there are in *Brand* and Ibsen's poetry. To explore their meaning further, however, would be to depart from our purpose. We must ask what happens to the avian cluster when Ibsen abandons verse drama, with its undisguised, undisplaced references to myth, and turns instead to writing realistic/naturalistic plays.

Toy and game images are plentiful in *A Doll House*, but the play might also be called *The Bird Cage*. Throughout, Torvald calls Nora, among other things, his lark and songbird—appropriate names for a woman whose role it is to be her husband's pet, to be cheerful and to entertain. In the end she realizes that her spirit has been trapped and suffocated and she must leave in order to see if it can still take flight.

There are no bird images in Ibsen's next play *Ghosts*, but echoes of the Memnon myth resound powerfully. Osvald comes home from abroad, apparently dying of a strange disease. Scholars tend to diagnose the malady as syphilis, but psychiatrist Derek Russell Davis has described how the young man might well be suffering instead from mental illness brought on by being deprived of his mother's love (Davis 369–83). Mrs. Alving, in order to protect her son from what she saw as her husband's evil influence, had the boy sent to live away from home at the age of seven. When Osvald now returns as the prodigal and says he feels "åndeligt nedbrutt," which some translators have rendered as "suffering from a mental breakdown," and others as "spiritually broken," Mrs. Alving must bear at least part of the blame for the fact that his spirit is crippled and earthbound.

Allusions to the Memnon myth are especially apparent in the final act. First, there is the reference to a funeral pyre in the burning of the orphanage, where Oswald remained too long after the fire was extinguished and caught a chill. Later, back home with his mother, they watch the sunrise, with its implicit promise of resurrection. But it is too late; he sinks down in his mother's lap in a delirium. We are left with another pietà, as Mrs. Alving hovers over her son while he mumbles pathetically, "the sun, the sun" (*Billigutgave* III:156).

In *The Wild Duck*, as in the earlier plays, bird in flight is a metaphor for the spirit's thrust toward self-realization. There is marvelous irony in the species of fowl that live in the artificial forest of the loft area in the Ekdal home: like Nora, most of them serve tamely decorative or domestic purposes—Tumbler and Pouter pigeons and chickens. Only one of the loft's avian residents has known freedom apart from man: the wild duck. But that freedom, for this particular bird, is a thing of the past. Wounded by a hunter (Gregers's father) and no longer able to fly, its spirit is crippled, like everyone else in the Ekdal home, animal or human. The association of duck and spirit is clearer in Norwegian, where the sounds of the words resemble each other: *and* for duck and *ånd* for spirit.

As in the other plays, characters find it natural to speak in avian metaphors and similes. Gregers Werle resents that his father expected him to hurry home "on the wings of filial piety," for the father's second marriage (*Billigutgave* III:228). And Hjalmar Ekdal, when describing how his daughter Hedvig is going blind, says: "chirping like a happy and carefree little bird, she flutters into life's eternal night" (*Billigutgave* III:236).

In the later play, *The Lady From the Sea*, the central themes are freedom and the emancipation of the spirit. At the opening, Ellida Wangel senses uneasily that her marriage has withered. She feels trapped, like Nora Helmer, with a man to whom she sold herself in exchange for security. A crisis is precipitated by the return of her first love, the Stranger, who comes to reclaim her and liberate her from her marriage. For Ellida, long-buried feelings are aroused, feelings she describes as "grufulle" (*Billigutgave* III:356), which in English only partially translates as a sense of dread. When her husband presses her for a closer definition, she describes it as a feeling of attraction and repulsion, a combination of fear and fascination (*Billigutgave* III:370). The freedom the Stranger promises is thus clouded. In Ibsen's emotional language, when freedom is chosen only as an outward movement it often means simply escape—escape from responsibility and love.

Nevertheless, the Stranger's claim has validity. Calling to her from a part of herself that was never completely developed, he is like a creditor figure in a fairy tale, returning to collect an unfulfilled pledge. And Ellida expresses her awareness of the claim in a marvelous image that suggests in the Stranger's arrival the approach of a dark, predatory bird: Ellida says that she senses it "like silent black wings" hovering over her (*Billigutgave* III:380). An 1889 Ibsen letter makes reference to an actor he admired as the Stranger, an actor with a "hawk face" (Macfarlane 119).

Just before Ellida must face the Stranger, Wangel gives her the emancipation she has been hungering for. He releases her from her marital responsibilities, leaving her free to choose to leave or to stay, and, most importantly, he expresses the love for her that he was so long unable to articulate. The Stranger's spell is suddenly broken, and Ellida elects to remain with Wangel. Peer Gynt was similarly threatened by ominous birds in the Boyg scene. But the redemptive power of the love Aase and Solveig had for Peer caused church bells to ring, and so the birds withdrew, admitting defeating in simple but powerful words: "He was too strong. There were women behind him" (*Billigutgave* II:159). One might say that Ellida is saved because there was a man behind her.

Among Ibsen's so-called realistic/naturalistic plays, *The Master Builder* marks the high point of his experimentation with the avian image cluster. Solness is a builder whose own creative spirit is dead, and who keeps his successful business going by exploiting the talents and energies of his colleagues and workers through denying them independence of action.

Like the sick old king of legend, he clings tenaciously to an authority he is no longer morally entitled to wield.

The most serious threat to this authority, ironically, comes not from within but from without—from a young woman, Hilde Wangel, whose unwitting mission is to serve, like Gregers Werle in *The Wild Duck* and the Stranger in *Lady From the Sea*, as a messenger or angel of death. Her given name is close not only to *Hildr*, one of the Valkyries, whose duty it was to guide dead warriors to Valhalla, but to the folkloric *huldra*, which Einar Haugen defined as both a "wicked, alluring siren inhabiting hills and mountains" and "any beautiful, alluring woman, femme fatale."

Hilde is akin to the Lady in Green in *Peer Gynt*, whose child Peer Gynt fathered, and to the Stranger in *Lady from the Sea*—all figures from the past who come to collect on long-unpaid debts or promises. Hilde remembers that it is ten years since Solness's visit to her town for the dedication of one of his building projects. It was memorable for her because the visit coincided with her awakening as a woman. The importance of the moment was heightened by an incident that may have been just a figment of her imagination, for Solness cannot recall it. She says he kissed her passionately and promised her a kingdom with the magic name of Orangia. Now, she has come to claim this kingdom.

The idea of the promise of resurrection that is inherent in the Memnon myth appears also in *Master Builder*, but it is tragically blunted. Long ago, a fire destroyed the Solness home, and afterward, as an indirect result, Solness's twin sons perished. Aline, their mother, caught a fever—like Osvald, who lingered too long near the orphanage fire—and as a result, couldn't nurse her infant boys properly and they died. Since then, she has been in perpetual mourning, dressed entirely in black—yet another evocation of a pietà.

What died long ago, or perhaps what never came to life, was Solness's spirit. He is unfulfilled professionally and in his family life. Rather than becoming an architect, he remained a builder, constructing other men's visions. And he allowed the capacity to love to die within him after the fire and the loss of his sons. He and Aline are permanently alienated from each other, both of them bitter and filled with guilt.

For further evidence of the connection established between Solness and the Memnon myth we need to go back to a stanza in Ibsen's 1855 poem about the statue where he describes that "When the rosy dawn colored the desert sands, / A stream of sound issued mightily from Memnon." As we noted earlier, the sound issuing from the "singing colossus" was like that of the breaking of a lyre-string. When the adolescent Hilde first saw Solness, she excitedly watched him climb to place a wreath high on the scaffolding of his building. She found it "so marvelously thrilling," to see him stand on the very top, apparently without a touch of trepidation. He starts to protest that her recollection made him sound more romantically courageous than he actually was. She waves aside his protest with the assertion that he must have been brave, for

> How else could you stand up there singing?
> SOLNESS (stares astonished at her)
> Sang? *I* sang?
> HILDE
> Yes, of course you did.
> SOLNESS (shaking his head)
> I never sang a note in my life.
> HILDE
> But at that moment you sang. It sounded like harps in the air.
> (*Billigutgave* III:450)

Solness has unfortunately remained ever since like the statue, inert, his spirit refusing to respond to the call of his destiny. He is unable to reconcile the polarity between youth versus age. He not only needs Ragnar, his young assistant, he regards him as a potential threat. He has lost faith that he too can be become young again, at least metaphorically, by renewing himself, by returning to his early promise. One part of Hilde's mission was to awaken this possibility within him. The scene between them when he realizes, part consciously, part unconsciously, her meaning in his life is one of the most evocative in the play and is saturated with Memnon associations.

Like Peer before the statue, another hero stands on the brink of a profound confrontation with everything he has hidden from himself, everything he could have become. And once again, there is the message of the birds and the challenge of the sunrise:

> SOLNESS (staring intently at her)
> Hilde—you're like some wild forest bird.
> HILDE
> Oh, no I'm not. I don't hide away under bushes.
> SOLNESS
> No. No, you're more like a bird of prey.
> HILDE
> That's closer—perhaps. (impulsively) And why not a bird of prey? . . . .
> SOLNESS
> Hilde—you know what you are?
> HILDE
> Yes, I'm some strange kind of bird.
> SOLNESS
> No. You're like a dawning day. When I look at you—it's as if I looked into the sunrise.
> HILDE
> Tell me, Mr. Solness—are you quite sure that you've never called for me? Within yourself, I mean?
> SOLNESS (slowly and quietly)

I almost think I must have.
HILDE
What did you want with me?
SOLNESS
You, Hilde, are youth.
HILDE (smiling)
The youth that you're so afraid of?
SOLNESS (nodding slowly)
And that I so deeply long for.
(*Billigutgave* III:467)

But Solness's potential has slumbered for too long. He is not, perhaps never was, equal to the call that Hilde's arrival implies. When she now provokes him to climb the heights that he has avoided for a decade, he is ill-equipped for the challenge, and his subsequent fall is as inevitable and fateful as that of Icarus.

The Memnon statue must have aroused for Ibsen some of the same bitter, almost mocking sadness and sense of waste and loss that Shelley felt and expressed about another sculptural ruin in the desert: Shelley's *Ozymandias*. In each case, we have an image of both the potential and the vanity of human aspiration, of the call to responsibility and the inevitability of broken promises. Perhaps this helps to explain the ambivalence evoked by the ending of *The Master Builder*, a mixture of triumph in defeat and defeat in triumph. As others stare in horror at Solness's broken body, Hilde exults: "But he reached the top. And I heard harps in the air" (*Billigutgave* III:482).

Even as the "lonely and level sands stretch far away," there is always the dawn and the sound of the song.

Works Cited

Bull, Francis. *Henrik Ibsens Peer Gynt: Diktningens tilblivelse og grunntanker.* Oslo: Gyldendal, 1947.

Davis, Derek Russell. "A Reappraisal of Ibsen's Ghosts," in *Family Process*, vol. 2, no. 1, 1963. Rpt. in *Henrik Ibsen: Penguin Critical Anthology.* Ed. James McFarlane. Baltimore, Maryland: Penguin Books, 1970. 369–83.

Haugen, Einar. *Norwegian English Dictionary.* Oslo: Universitetsforlaget and Madison: University of Wisconsin, 1974.

Ibsen, Henrik. *Samlede verker, hundreårsutgave.* (The Centenary Edition). Ed. Halvdan Koht, Francis Bull, and Didrik Arup Seip. 21 vols. Oslo: Gyldendal, 1928–58.

—————. *Ibsens samlede verker i billigutgave.* Oslo: Gyldendal Norsk forlag. II. *Fra Brand til Keiser og Galilær: 1865–73*; 13. utgave; 2. opplag, 1972. III. *Nutidsdramaer: 1877–99*; 13. utgave, 1962.

—————. *Peer Gynt.* Trans. Rolf Fjelde. 2nd ed. Minneapolis: University of Minnesota Press, 1980.

—————. *Peer Gynt.* Trans. William and Charles Archer. London, The Walter Scott pub. co., ltd.; New York, C. Schribner's sons, 1904.

McFarlane, James, ed. *Henrik Ibsen: Penguin Critical Anthology.* Baltimore, Maryland: Penguin Books, 1970.

Delacroix's murals in Église Saint-Sulpice and Strindberg's *Jacob wrestles* and *To Damascus I*

Ann-Charlotte Gavel Adams

DEN OKÄNDE
Jo, jag märker allting sedan en tid tillbaka; ej som förr dock då jag endast såg ting och händelser, former och färger, utan nu ser jag tankar och betydelser. Livet som förr var ett stort nonsens har fått mening, och jag märker en avsikt där jag förr endast såg slumpen.

[THE STRANGER:
Yes. I have started to notice all kinds of things lately; not like before when I only saw objects and events, forms and colors, but now I see ideas and significance(s). Life, which before was a big nonsense, has now acquired a meaning, and I see a purpose where I formerly saw only chance.] (*Till Damaskus I*, SV 39: 18)

During Strindberg's last stay in Paris from August 26, 1897 to April 3, 1898, he wrote the novel *Legends*, the fragment *Jacob wrestles*, and the drama *To Damascus I*. These works reflect a new artistic formula or vision, a successful attempt on Strindberg's part to create something new. In the epilogue to *Jacob wrestles*, Strindberg explains the fragment as a failed experiment to portray the author's religious struggles in figurative or metaphorical form. Critics and scholars do not agree with Strindberg's critical assessment of *Jacob wrestles*. Even Strindberg's contemporaries, who had disliked his novel *Inferno* a year earlier, praised *Jacob wrestles* unanimously as an artistic high point in his career. In this work they recognized the rebellious author from the 1880s, reborn and as powerful a stylist as ever.[1]

Strindberg's next attempt at "figurerad skildring" [figurative description], *To Damascus I*, is considered to be a milestone in the history of modern drama (Törnqvist 94). Here Strindberg succeeded in giving physical, theatrical form to man's spiritual struggles, to present his inner confrontations on stage. Scholars have attempted to identify the impulses behind the formation of Strindberg's new artistic vision. Göran Stockenström took Strindberg's mystical view of existence as the point of departure for his analysis and concluded that Strindberg's formal innovations are above all based in the subjective interpretations of his reading of Swedenborg (Stockenström 467). Evert Sprinchorn suggests that the Postimpressionists provide important clues to Strindberg's new literary and dramatic techniques: "Strindberg transferred to the stage the allegorical quality of Puvis [de Chavannes], the ironic allusiveness of Gauguin, and the subjectivism of Munch, along with the conventional and overt symbolism of the Pre-Raphaelite painters" (Sprinchorn 384–385). In addition to Strindberg's visual imagination, Harry Carlson has explored his broad range of interests from myths to Occultism, Orientalism and Medievalism as decisive influences behind Strindberg's post-Inferno reawakening as an artist.

This essay seeks to highlight another important, and immediate, source of inspiration: Delacroix's striking allegorical murals in Chapelle des Saints-Anges in Église Saint-Sulpice, which Strindberg often stopped to contemplate on his daily walks by the church while he was writing the drama, and which have left tangible imprints in both *Jacob wrestles* and *To Damascus I*. One finds both visual and allegorical traces from Delacroix's murals in these works.

Strindberg lived at Hôtel de Londres on rue Bonaparte, close by the river Seine during his entire last stay in Paris. He had brought his French manuscript to *Inferno* with him to Paris in the hope of getting it accepted by the publisher

Chamuel. Between September 22 and October 17, he worked on a sequel to *Inferno*, which he also wrote in French and eventually gave the title *Légendes*. Mornings and evenings he got his daily exercise by walking from his hotel to Place Saint-Sulpice and Jardin du Luxembourg. He would return to his hotel via boulevard Saint-Michel and quai des Augustins. These walks are so vividly described in *Jacob wrestles*, that visitors to Paris find the book a useful travel guide. Strindberg began to write *Jacob wrestles* some time in November 1897 and abandoned it as a fragment in January 1898.

One of the highlights of his walks was to stop by Église Saint-Sulpice where he admired Eugène Delacroix's famous murals in Chapelle des Saints-Anges. In particular, the painting of *Jacob wrestling with the Angel* made a great impression on him. The narrator in *Jacob wrestles* tells that he specifically enters the church to gain strength by looking at the painting:

> —j'entre souvent dans l'église pour me fortifier à la contemplations de la lutte de Jacob avec l'Ange d'Eugène Delacroix. C'est que cette scène me donne toujours à réfléchir, m'inspirant des pensées impies, malgré l'orthodoxie du sujet. Et en sortant au milieu des agenouillés je garde le souvenir du lutteur qui se tient debout en dépit de son hanche lesée.[2]

The image of the wrestler, who keeps himself upright in spite of his injured hip, stays in his mind after he has exited the church. Strindberg's ability to absorb visual images and transform them into literary metaphors and similes has been well documented by Karl-Åke Kärnell and Harry Carlson. Carlson mentions Delacroix's painting of *Jacob wrestling with the angel*, in passing, as a catalyst for the reference in the play to The Stranger being found unconscious after a mysterious wrestling match at the top of a mountain (Carlson 305).[3] However, the impact of all three of Delacroix's paintings in the chapel goes far beyond that single reference.

Delacroix's murals in Chapelle des Saints-Anges in Église Saint-Sulpice deserve a closer presentation in order to highlight aspects which seem to have left imprints in Strindberg's works. From their unveiling in 1861, Delacroix's murals have impressed artists of all genres. None of his other works met with such passionate public debate as these. Charles Baudelaire, among others, praised them for their imagination and artistic aspects, rather than their religious themes.[4]

The murals were painted between 1856 and 1861, less than four decades before Strindberg started making the chapel a frequent stopping point on his daily walks to Jardin du Luxembourg. For his first plans to the paintings, Delacroix was inspired by an unusual baptismal font he saw in the chapel. It was a giant shell of a *tridachna gigas* placed on top of a baroque marble stand.[5] Delacroix's first ideas for the paintings were inspired by this font: baptism, original sin, and expiation. The baptismal font was later moved to another location in the church, which deeply upset Delacroix who felt that he now had to change his entire conception of the murals in the chapel. Of his original plans only the idea for the painting in the ceiling remained: *The Archangel Michael defeating the Devil*, taken from Revelations 12: 7–9. This painting, portraying the struggle between good and evil, is generally regarded as the artistically least successful of the three paintings in the chapel. Strindberg however, seems to have been impressed with both theme and execution, because Delacroix's representation of *Michael defeating the Devil* reappear both in *Jacob wrestles* and in *To Damascus I*.

As new subjects for the two walls in the chapel, Delacroix chose *Heliodorus driven from the Temple*, from II Maccabees 3: 1–40, and *Jacob Wrestling with the Angel* from Genesis 32: 24–29. Both these paintings portray battles between men who have dared to defy the authority of God, and avenging

Baptismal font in Église Saint-Sulpice.

angels punishing the hubris of the offenders (Hannoosh 183). Delacroix placed the figures of the combatants in the very forefront of the paintings, almost as if they were performing on a stage. The paintings of Heliodorus and Jacob face each other on the chapel's west and east wall respectively, and they can be read and interpreted in sequence. The first one represents the crushing of the hubris of the Syrian officer Heliodorus, who committed the sacrilege of plundering the temple of

Jerusalem of its treasures. In the painting, Delacroix depicts him at the very moment when he is about to be crushed under the hoofs of an angel (with wings) on horseback. Two other heavenly avengers—without wings, but somehow suspended in mid-air—dive down on him, whipping him with bundles of switches. Heliodorus himself is lying on his back amid his stolen treasures at the bottom of the painting, trying to shield himself from his attackers. All movements in the painting are channeled from the top to the bottom of the painting, from the people on balcony who look down on the battle, to the staircase leading down to the man on the ground. The downward movement is emphasized by the rays of light from above, by the wind moving the draperies and by the angels swooping down on Heliodorus from each side. All downward moving lines in the painting reinforce the theme of the man who is being crushed because he has transgressed the law of God. A spectator standing in front of, or rather under this monumental 7.14 m by 4.88 m painting, with Heliodorus's horizontal body just above eye-level, cannot help but feel the power and weight of all heavenly forces coming crashing down.

The subject of the painting on the opposite wall of the chapel, *Jacob wrestling with the Angel* is taken from Genesis 32: 24–29. In this passage, Jacob is on his way home to make peace with his brother Esau, whom he had cheated out of their dying father's blessing. In doing so, he had defied divine law. Jacob encounters an angel who wrestles with him all night. By daybreak, the angel has not succeeded to lay him down. To end the struggle, the angel touches Jacob's thigh, making him lame. Jacob refuses to give up, not letting go of the angel unless he blesses him. Jacob is then given the name of Israel, the man who fought with God and prevailed. Although Delacroix's theme in this painting is similar to that of Heliodorus, man being punished for having defied divine authority, in the case of Jacob, man prevails because of his refusal to give up. Characteristically, Delacroix selected a mo-

Heliodorus driven from the Temple.

ment of intense combat between Jacob and the angel as his motif, rather than the resulting act of the blessing. Again the action, the struggle takes place in the forefront of the painting as if the combatants were on a stage. As a contrast to the Heliodorus painting with its geometric architectural background, the setting for *Jacob wrestles* is a landscape with intense greenery and a couple of giant oaks with rounded forms and upward curving branches in the center. All movements in this painting seem to predict the positive outcome of the struggle. They are all directed upwards diagonally, from the spear in the still life in the lower right corner which points to Jacob who is lunging at the taller and more powerful figure of the angel, to the giant oaks which stretch their limbs upwards towards the sky.

The two paintings can be read in sequence: the man who defies the laws of God will be punished, but the man who persists in his struggle will prevail. Delacroix's biblical juxtaposition and interpretations may not be considered traditional, but then Delacroix was not known to be conventional in terms of religion. He had received his commission to paint the murals from the state and did not feel any obligation to please the representatives of the Catholic Church (Spector 8). When the paintings were first unveiled, the Catholic community found them offensive in spite of their biblical motifs. Lacking in serenity and piety, the paintings seemed out of place in church dedicated to peace and contemplation. Art critics, on the other hand, immediately became enthusiastic about the murals. *Jacob wrestles with the Angel* was not interpreted as biblical, but rather as autobiographical, as the artist wrestling with the insurmountable difficulties of struggling with his art (Hannoosh 185).

Delacroix's paintings are highly dramatic, portraying the confrontations of Heliodorus and Jacob with divine authorities as physical battles. These battles are acted out on center stage in bold colors, Heliodorus in gold-gray and Jacob in intense green.

Delacroix does not seem to have forgotten the unusual shell-shaped baptismal font which give him the first ideas for the plans for the chapel. Although Delacroix made many sketches of the very large oak trees in the forest of Senart

Jacob wrestling with the Angel.

near Barbizon, which he used as models for the giant oaks in the painting of *Jacob wrestling with the angel*, none of the actual oak trees from the forest of Senart can be recognized in the painting. In his study of Delacroix, René Huyghe offers another source of inspiration for the oaks in the painting. Huyghe recognizes in the round curvy shapes of the branches of the oaks the shell-shaped baptismal font on its baroque stand, which he suggests has undergone "visual contagion" and been transformed. Huyghe even sees the baroque marble stand of the baptismal fount as the central knoll on which the oak trees grow in the painting (Huyghe 413).

Strindberg's many visits to Chapelle des Saints-Anges did not fail to make an imprint on the works he wrote during this same time period. It is not surprising that Strindberg would identify with Delacroix's representation of Jacob who wrestles with a divine power but refuses to give up. Strindberg clearly recognized it as a visual metaphor for his own spiritual struggles in recent years, and, like the narrator in *Jacob wrestles*, he must have felt "fortified" by the image of the man who stays upright in his confrontation with the angel. Delacroix's murals also seem to have demonstrated to Strindberg how a spiritual, interior struggle could be made visible, be communicated through a physical showdown. This is precisely Strindberg's technique in *Jacob wrestles* in the description of the encounter in Jardin du Luxembourg between the narrator and the Christ-like figure of "l'inconnu." Strindberg was, however, dissatisfied with his description of the narrator's pursuit of and confrontation with "l'inconnu," as an experiment to portray an inner struggle as a physical one in narrative form. Shortly after writing this passage Strindberg suddenly, in the middle of a page, switches from French to Swedish. The Swedish continuation of the story leads nowhere and he abandons it, leaving it a fragment. He may have found that the narrative format was unsuitable for such a dramatic confrontation. In the epilogue to *Jacob wrestles*, dated 23 April 1898, Strindberg addresses the readers and elaborates:

> Som läsaren troligen genomskådat, är denna andra avdelning kallad *Jakob brottas* ett försök att i figurerad skildring teckna författarens religösa kamp, och som sådan

misslyckad.

[As the reader has probably guessed, this second part, entitled *Jakob wrestles*, is an attempt to portray the religious struggles of the author in a figurative/metaphorical description, and as such a failure.]

Strindberg's visits to Chapelle des Saints-Anges also left traces of "visual contagion" from Delacroix's paintings in other passages of *Jacob wrestles*. On his daily walks to Jardin du Luxembourg and back, the narrator passes the Fontaine Saint-Michel where he finds Francisque Duret's 18 foot tall sculpture of the archangel Michael killing the devil. Interestingly, Strindberg's description of this sculpture in *Jacob wrestles* calls forth the image of Delacroix's version of Michael and the devil rather than the one by Duret: "le sublime Archange, tueur du serpent [. . .] qui ricane la lance au cœur" (*SV* 38: 99). The devil in Delacroix's version is grinning although the archangel is aiming the spear at his heart. In Duret's sculpture group in Fontaine Saint-Michel, the archangel does not aim his spear at devil's heart, he triumphantly swings a sword high over his head. The image of Delacroix's archangel, ready to thrust his spear into the heart of the devil, is superimposed on Duret's sculpture in Strindberg's memory at the time of the writing, illustrating another example of "visual contagion" from the paintings in Chapelle des Saints-Anges.

The unusual baptismal font with the basin made from the shell of a *tridachna gigas* in Saint-Sulpice, which inspired Delacroix, attracts the attention of all who enter the church. It is not surprising that it also caught the eye of Strindberg. The image of the shell-shaped font can also be found in *Jacob wrestles*, but here it reappears in another church, Saint-Germain l'Auxerrois near the Louvre. One Sunday morning, the narrator passes by the church and enters as it seems invitingly small and intimate. Feeling somewhat like an intruder, he stays

The Archangel Michael defeating the Devil.

by the door, watching the people dip their fingers in the basin with holy water before making the sign of the cross on their way out. After he is left alone in the church, he timidly approaches the basin described as "hugget i gul marmor i form av ett musselskal" [sculpted in yellow marble in the form of a mussel shell] (*SV* 38: 141). Since there is no font in that shape in Saint-Germain l'Auxerrois, we must assume that it is the image of the font from Saint-Sulpice that is being superimposed on the basin with holy water in Saint-Germain l'Auxerrois.

Soon after abandoning his attempt to portray his religious struggles "i figurerad skildring" [in figurative description] in prose form in *Jacob wrestles*, he embarks on a new project. On 19 January 1898, Strindberg noted in his *Occult Diary*: "Fick åter teatervurm och anlade Robert le Diable" [Was again struck by the theater bug and laid out the plans for Robert le

Diable]. In a note added later, Strindberg clarifies within brackets: "[Som blef Damaskus]" [Which became Damascus]. Already seven months earlier, Strindberg had played with an idea for a work in an unnamed genre about Robert le Diable (*Occult Dairy*, 10 July 1897). Now in January, he turns from allegorizing the legend of Robert le Diable to the biblical story of Saul /Paul who on his way to Damascus encounters God and is converted (The Acts 22: 5–11). Strindberg had already tried to portray his own "religiösa kamp" [religious struggles] in narrative form and had in his own estimation failed. Now he "is struck by the theater bug" and turns to the dramatic genre. It is not possible to assert that the visual impact of Delacroix's murals in Chapelle des Saints-Anges provided Strindberg with the ideas for the dramatic structure of *To Damascus I*. One can, however, note that both Delacroix and Strindberg in these works dramatize similar inner struggles of the soul, using biblical stories to allegorize them, allowing clear descending and ascending movements to reinforce and make visible the inner action of their protagonists. Strindberg had, of course, already in *Inferno* borrowed both title and structure of a descent into hell from Dante, but in *To Damascus I* the descent into the soul of man—which is portrayed visually on stage—suggests, as Sprinchorn noted above, a visual source of inspiration.

In the Asylum scene, the turning point of the drama, we also find what might be a visual remnant from Église Saint-Sulpice. From the refectory, there is a door in the back leading to a chapel. On the left wall of the chapel hangs a painting of the archangel Michael killing the devil. During the Stranger's interaction with the Confessor, he lifts his eyes and sees the image of Michael, which causes him to look down again (*SV* 39: 107). It would not be farfetched to suggest that the image Strindberg had in mind was that of Delacroix's painting of the archangel Michael in the ceiling of Chapelle des Saints-Anges, since that is the painting he both describes and alludes to in *Jacob wrestles*.

Peculiarly enough there seem to be no visual references to Delacroix's *Jacob wrestling with the angel* in *To Damascus I* other than the interior struggle made visible. In his first discussion with the Abbess, the Stranger wants to know how he ended up in the asylum. She explains that they had found him after he had fallen down a mountaintop. He was feverish and delirious but seemingly not physically hurt. He had broken off a cross from one of the calvaries with which he threatened someone up in the clouds. Although he complained about pain in his hip, they had not been able find anything wrong (*SV* 39: 104). The allusion to Genesis 32: 24–29 is clear, but there is no visual similarity to Delacroix's painting. The Stranger is said to have wrestled with a mysterious power, but he did not succeed in staying upright and he did not seem to receive any blessing.

Strindberg finished his manuscript to *To Damascus I* on 6 March 1898 and two days later he mailed it to Gustaf af Geijerstam, the literary editor at Gernandts Förlag in Stockholm with the words: "Härmed en pjes, om hvars värde jag icke har en aning" [Hereby a play, I have no idea if it has any value] (*Brev* 12: 272). Less than a month later, Strindberg returned to Sweden. *To Damascus I*—of questionable value to Strindberg at the time—has come to be considered one of the most innovative plays in the history of modern drama. It possesses visual, allegorical, and maybe structural elements from Delacroix's imaginative, irreverent, and bold murals in Chapelle des Saints-Anges.

NOTES

[1] Even Oscar Levertin, one of Strindberg's most ardent critics, was not blind to the visual fire works of Strindberg's style in *Jakob brottas*: "denna tjusande kornblixtglans, som ensamt Strindbergs stil besitter".

Although not in favor of Strindberg's new world view, Levertin finds that the fragment "genomsusas af en fläkt af den förtviflans sublimitet, inför hvilken hvarje inkast tystnar". The Strindberg who raises his fist and demands accountability from God is the one who impresses Levertin the most.

[2] I am quoting from Strindberg's original French, soon to be published in volume 38 of *August Strindberg's Samlade Verk* (*SV* 38).

[3] This wrestling match is however not described visually in the drama. The abbess tells the Stranger about it in a single line. It is therefore more accurately described as one of numerous references to Genesis 32: 24–32, which Strindberg liked to use both before and after he had the opportunity to view Delacroix's mural. In *Inferno*, for example, written in Lund in May and June of 1897, before he went to Paris, there are at least six references to the narrator as a Jacob wrestling with an unknown power (cf. *SV* 37: 13, 27, 137, 241, 245, 257).

[4] Baudelaire's laudatory article on Delacroix's murals in Chapelle des Saints-Anges first appeared in *Revue fantaisiste* on 15 September 1861, and later in expanded form in *Opinion nationale* on 2 September and 14 and 22 November 1863.

[5] The baptismal font was a gift to François I (1494–1547) from the republic of Venice.

Works Cited

Anderson Trapp, Frank. *The Attainment of Delacroix*. Baltimore, London: The Johns Hopkins Press, 1971.

Carlson, Harry G. *Out of Inferno: Strindberg's Reawakening as an Artist*. Seattle, London: University of Washington Press, 1996.

Hannoosh, Michele. *Painting and the Journal of Eugène Delacroix*. New Jersey: Princeton University Press, 1995.

Huyghe, René. *Delacroix*. Translated by Jonathan Griffin. New York: Harry N. Abrams, Inc., 1963.

Kärnell, Karl-Åke. *Strindberg's bildspråk*. Stockholm: Almqvist & Wiksell, 1969.

Spector, Jack J. *The Murals of Eugène Delacroix at Saint-Sulpice*. New York: The College Art Association of America, 1967.

Sprinchorn, Evert. Introduction to "To Damascus" in *Selected Plays II* by August Strindberg. Translated by Evert Sprinchorn. Minneapolis: University of Minnesota Press, 1986.

Stockenström, Göran. *Ismael i öknen: Strindberg som mystiker*. Uppsala: Acta Universitatis Upsaliensis, 1972.

Strindberg, August. *August Strindbergs Brev XII: december 1896–augusti 1898*. Edited by Torsten Eklund. Stockholm: Bonniers, 1970.

Strindberg, August. *Inferno.* Edited By Ann-Charlotte Gavel Adams. Volume 37 of *August Strindbergs Samlade Verk.* Edited by Lars Dahlbäck. Stockholm: Norstedts, 1994.

Strindberg, August. *Legender.* Edited by Ann-Charlotte Gavel Adams. To be published as Volume 38 of *August Strindbergs Samlade Verk.* Edited by Lars Dahlbäck. Stockholm: Norstedts, 2000.

Strindberg, August. *Till Damaskus.* Edited by Gunnar Ollén. Volume 39 of *August Strindbergs Samlade Verk.* Edited by Lars Dahlbäck. Stockholm: Norstedts, 1991.

Törnqvist, Egil. *Strindbergian Drama: Themes and Structure.* Stockholm, 1982.

The Theatrical Compulsion of Strindberg's *Carl XII*

Anne-Charlotte Hanes Harvey

"Bekänn, hjärta! Du leds vid den konservativa republiken och längtar efter Karl den tolfte, hjärta!"

[Confess, heart! You are weary of the conservative republic and long for Charles XII, heart!] (*SV* 15: 120)

"Interv.[iewaren]: Herrn har vågat angripa Ibsen; det är farligt det?
Författaren: Den som har angripit Carl XII, herre, den fruktar varken fan eller trollen!"

[Interviewer: Do I understand that you have dared to attack Ibsen, sir?
Author: He who has attacked Charles XII, sir, he fears neither trolls nor the devil!] (*SS* 14: 33)

Throughout his life, as reflected in his entire *oeuvre*, Strindberg's attitude to Charles XII is overwhelmingly negative and critical.[1] His criticism hits on three levels: first, against Sweden's nineteenth century worship of Charles XII, which to Strindberg was synonymous with a sick, provincial society's glorification of an unworthy subject, confirming the rottenness of both. What John Landquist calls "känsligheten för tryck" [the sensitivity to pressure] made Strindberg lash out against not only the oppression associated with by the absolute monarch Charles XII but also the pressure exerted by the late nineteenth century popular worship of Charles.[2]

Second, Strindberg attacks Charles XII as a ruler and military leader. Charles is described as a monarch without a conscience (*SS* 40: 51; *SS* 53: 40, 51) who displays lack of concern for Swedish prisoners of war on foreign soil (*SS* 4: 75; *SS* 8: 248; *SS* 53: 44–46); a king who is tyrannical (*SS* 50: 252; *SS* 53: 5, 37, 48, 53) and politically stupid.[3] Drawing on his own experiences as a vice corporal in the army, Strindberg scrutinizes Charles's particular lack of skill as a military strategist and roundly condemns the storming of Poltava, concluding that "detta tämligen idiotiska belägringssätt blev Sveriges ruin" [this rather idiotic form of siege turned out to be the ruin of Sweden].[4] Most often, Strindberg refers to the king not by name but by one of over forty colorful invectives: "Sveriges förstörare, mordbrännaren, storinkvisitorn, falskmyntaren" [Sweden's destroyer, the arsonist, the Grand Inquisitor, the counterfeiter] (*SS* 40: 53); "Sveriges bödel" [Sweden's henchman] (*SS* 53: 57); "ödeläggaren" [the annihilator] (*SS* 54: 138); "den store brottslingen" [the great criminal] (*SS* 50: 251) and "barbaren" [the barbarian] (*SS* 50: 251). In the drama *Carl XII* [*Charles XII*]—and only in the drama—he is also referred to, with a certain theatrical flair, as "boven" [the villain].[5]

Third, Strindberg attacks Charles, the man. Here Strindberg scours historical sources for unflattering tidbits and fills out the picture with unsympathetic traits of his own invention. Thus Charles is, according to Strindberg, variously beardless (i.e., effeminate) (*SS* 12: 387; *SS* 53: 37, 38), unimpressive (*SS* 12: 379), of bad stock (*SS* 12: 382), ill-bred (*SS* 12: 388; *SS* 53: 51) and coarse (*SS* 10: 57; *SS* 12: 383; *SS* 53: 51), cowardly (*SS* 8: 247; *SS* 10: 36–37; *SS* 25: 118, 158, 195; *SS* 50: 252; *SS* 53: 51) and afraid of the dark (*SS* 12: 383). He is slovenly (*SS* 12: 383; *SS* 53: 51) and a notorious glutton (*SS* 53: 51), vain (*SS* 53: 54) and selfish (*SS* 8: 247). He is dim-witted (*SS* 53: 51), deranged (*SS* 11:

53), and insane (*SS* 47: 543). In a letter to Carl Larson Strindberg even once refers to him as "en brödsvullen skitpys" [a bread-swollen shit].[6]

In Strindberg's summary treatment of Charles we see a hatred which, according to Lamm, had become an *idée fixe*.[7] Perhaps because of this fixation, Strindberg's references to Charles XII are, in spite of the creativity shown in the rich repertoire of invectives, almost formulaic—the more negative, the more formulaic. The same arguments are repeated over and over again, giving the impression of incantation or recitation of a lesson learned by rote.

There are, on the other hand, exceptions—instances when Strindberg shows what Ollén calls "en ganska stor portion motvillig beundran" [a sizeable portion of reluctant admiration] for Charles.[8] Here the language is more vibrant and varied, the portrait less one-sided and negative. Such less negative portraits, they are never wholly positive, are found in two of Strindberg's works: sketched 1891 in the short story *Vid likvakan i Tistedalen* [At the Wake in Tistedalen] and developed ten years later in the drama *Carl XII*.[9] Here Strindberg's attitude toward the king is ambivalent: Charles emerges as potentially sympathetic—especially in the drama, both on the page and—as born out in production—on stage. What may be the explanation for this ambivalence? And how is it achieved?

It is doubtful that Strindberg's attitude change is due to an outside influence. Why would he suddenly allow anyone to influence his opinion of Charles after years of negativity? Neither the ambivalence of one of his main sources, the historian Anders Fryxell, nor the renewed Carolinian fervor of the 1890s had improved his opinion—rather the opposite. Strindberg's two ambivalent portraits, in *Tistedalen* and *Carl XII*, are bracketed and separated by works in which he criticizes the king in his usual way. We must seek the answer elsewhere.

Several factors have a probable or potential bearing on

Strindberg's ambivalent, more sympathetic portrayal of Charles in *Tistedalen* and *Carl XII*. For one thing, both are fictional treatments of Charles—the only ones in Strindberg's entire *oeuvre*—and set in the king's own time. In both, the historical perspective, which otherwise dominates Strindberg's condemning portrayals of Charles, is almost entirely cut away and appears only as arguments voiced by Medicus and Horn, respectively. Completely absent is the to Strindberg so abhorrent nineteenth century worship of Charles. Second, being fictional, these treatments need not keep up an appearance of objectivity and historical "accuracy." This may allow for, even invite, idiosyncratic and contradictory perspectives. There is more space for character development, hence more depth of characterization is possible. And there is potentially more emotional involvement on the part of the author. Strindberg, quite understandably, is more involved with the character in the drama, in which Charles is alive, as opposed to the short story, in which he figures as a corpse.

Although both *Tistedalen* and *Carl XII* show a certain sympathy for Charles, there are notable differences between the short story and the drama. Not only is the drama more fully developed—*Tistedalen* is a kind of precursor, figuring in Strindberg's drafts of the drama as a sixth act that was never written—it reflects a different time in Strindberg's life.[10] One may, in fact, speak of a definite shift in Strindberg's outlook during the ten years that separate the creation of *Tistedalen* and *Carl XII*. This shift has generally been explained biographically—Martin Lamm and Gunnar Ollén see in the drama the aging poet's greater self-identification with Charles—or specifically ascribed, as by Göran Stockenström, to Strindberg's post-Inferno worldview and the overwhelming impact of his introduction to Swedenborgianism in the late 1890s.[11] In 1891, Strindberg, the Naturalist, sees Charles XII wholly as an agent, responsible for his own and Sweden's fall. In 1901, Strindberg, the Swedenborgian, sees Charles primarily as a victim, at the mercy of the Powers, and only partly as an agent chastised for setting himself up against Destiny and World History. As he puts it in *Öppna brev till Intima Teatern* [Open Letters to the Intimate Theater], Charles "går under i kampen mot makterna" [goes under in his struggle against the Powers] (*SS* 50: 251), which gives him a claim to tragic heroic stature. Strindberg identifies with Charles, or, as Stockenström puts it, "his process of change is projected onto Charles XII."[12]

The drama *Carl XII*, then, shows a more nuanced portrait of the king than the short story because the drama—by virtue of its greater length—allows, even demands, more scope, more depth, and more emotional involvement (empathy), but especially because its aging author identifies more with the king and interprets his fate according to his own new-found worldview.[13]

But there is another reason for the drama's potentially more sympathetic Charles. The difference in our perception of Charles in the short story and in the drama—on the page as well as on the stage—brings us to a consideration of what can be called the "theatrical compulsion" of *Carl XII*—the drama and its title character.

With the comprehensive term "theatrical compulsion" I understand the impact of a work of literary fiction resulting from it being written in dramatic form and intended for presentation/perception on stage, as well as the emotional and intellectual impact of that work resulting directly and specifically from it being seen in performance, or "in your mind's eye," in imagined performance. Some aspects of this "compulsion" affect primarily a reader, some affect both reader and viewer, and some only a viewer. [The compulsion could be called "dramatic/theatrical," though I prefer "theatrical," since ultimately the interaction between work and recipient that I am concerned with here derive from the performative, not the literary, aspects of the work.] For the purpose of this discussion I am dealing primarily with an imagined performance of the play, based on a close reading of the dramatic text and its *Nebentext*, but also with responses to the 1902 premiere performance which took place at the Royal Dramatic Theater in Stockholm on February 13, 1902.

One fundamental aspect of drama that affects a reader is its incompleteness, the fact that the text demands to be "fleshed out," whether in the mind's eye or on stage. Reading a play text is difficult, Strindberg warns, "nästan som att läsa partitur; det är en svår konst" [almost like reading a musical score; it is a difficult art].[14] The experienced theater practitioner reads a play as "commanding form"—Susanne Langer's term for "blueprint for performance"—and is continually challenged and stimulated by the text to "complete the picture."[15] This active involvement draws the reader into the text, and his/her response is two-fold: first, the imaginative creative response to the printed text and *Nebentext*; and second, the crucial response to his own creation, the "performance" in his mind's eye. Naturally, a playwright's response to his own play is of a similar yet uniquely intense kind. He did, after all, conceive the action, and the characters have lived in his imagination and mind—perhaps for a long time and very vividly—before being captured in print on the page. Over time, an author's response to his own creation may lose some of its original intensity, approaching the response of one of his readers.

That Strindberg at the turn of the century was a sensitive and skilled reader of drama we know. He "completed the picture" and responded to it. In *Memorandum* he writes: "Jag har aldrig sett uppföras . . . Schillers *Don Carlos*, aldrig Shakespeares *Stormen*, men jag har sett dem likafullt när jag har läst dem" [I have never seen a performance of . . . Schiller's *Don Carlos*, never Shakespeare's *Tempest*, but I have seen them nevertheless when I have read them] (*SS* 50: 14). He was a reader who—with Coleridge and other nineteenth century poets—not only celebrated the performance in "his mind's eye," but even at times preferred it to the tawdry and imperfectly realized *mises-en-scène* of contemporary commercial theater. It was more perfect and it was more involving. One may argue that Strindberg sought production for his own dramas not in order for his vision to be creatively completed or interpreted, but in order to be heard, recognized, and remunerated.

Strindberg was not alone in doubting the ability of the theater to realize any playwright's vision, a doubt which was reinforced by the practice of coordinating premieres of significant new plays with their appearance in print.[16] The public had the opportunity to read a play, see it, or both—and then compare. All the reviewers attending the premiere performance of *Carl XII* had already read the play. August Brunius, who thought the evening "a fiasco," concedes that "mångt och mycket gör en större verkan vid läsningen än vid den, på huvudpersonen när, klena sceniska framställning, som bestods skådespelet igår . . . " [many elements have a greater impact when you read it (the play) than they had in the weak production it was given yesterday—weak except for the leading character . . .][17]

One may think that the incompleteness of the dramatic form would affect only a reader, but anyone who has attended a theater performance can attest to the compulsion to "complete the picture," to interpret everything in the *mise-en-scène* and arrive at some kind of closure. Even the accidental, the unintended is interpreted, since—as Tadeusz Kowzan puts it—in the theater, whatever the intention, "all is sign."[18] And as performance answers questions, it asks new ones; as it fills in missing links, it creates new gaps. To the "compulsion" of the intriguingly open play text, performance adds a new dimension.

Another source of "theatrical compulsion" is genre expectations. I would suggest that although Charles is far from a classical tragic hero—his turning point (Altranstädt, 1706) is located in the distant pre-plot story, his *anagnorisis* fragmented and barely verbalized—he still exhibits certain traits of the tragic hero. He is a "great" man who falls, he defies fate with reasonable integrity, and he gains *some* measure of insight.[19] Just as Strindberg, when talking about *Carl XII* in *Öppna brev*, somewhat loosely invokes *Antigone* and the classical tragedies of fate and character, so the viewer (and the sensitive reader) who is swept up in the fall of the tragic protagonist feels the general compulsion of the tragic trajectory.[20] What goes up, must come down. The compulsion on stage is the stronger because Charles shares our waiting for its completion. We see Charles wait, and we wait.

Another component of "theatrical compulsion" is conflict. Drama uses dialogue—*deixis*—as its chief medium which, regardless of type of literature, invites, almost demands, multiplicity of perspectives, paradoxically without fragmenting the overall unity of the piece.[21] The author's voice is naturally fractured into a spectrum of diverse voices. In this sense, the dialogue form affects not only the reader/viewer but also the author. Even August Strindberg is invited by the nature of drama to voice a wider than usual range of opinions—good and bad—of Charles XII when he writes the play. This formal consideration may to some extent apply also to the short story *Tistedalen*, which approaches dramatic form by consisting largely of an extended dialogue between the accuser, Medicus, and the defender, the Lieutenant.[22]

Dialogue is a chief vehicle of conflict, and conflict is central to drama and to the theatrical compulsion of a play. Of the three basic types of conflict—internal (man vs. self), social (man vs. man), or metaphysical (man vs. some higher power)—only the last one, between Charles and the Powers, is fully developed in *Carl XII*, peaking in the Gethsemane-like moment when Charles prays, "Gånge denna kalken ifrån mig!" [Let this cup be taken from me!][23]

It is true that the play is structured largely as a series of social confrontations, most spectacularly between Charles and the three women Emerentia Polhem, his sister Ulrika Eleonora, and Queen Katarina Leszczynska of Poland. The 1902 reviewers praised the scenes with the three women as dramatic high points in the play. Regardless of whether they found Charles's stance more Strindbergian than historically defensible, the battle of the sexes still injected a vibrant and colorful note in the overall "grått i grått" [shades of grey].[24]

Yet each confrontation is brief, and several reviewers commented on the play's overall lack of conflict. The theater historian Herman A. Ring insists that "[n]ågon motspelare i egentlig mening mot Carl finnes icke. Man kan därför knappast tala om en konflikt i dramatisk mening" [strictly speaking Charles has no antagonist, so one can hardly speak of a true dramatic conflict], and goes as far as to suggest what events in Charles's life Strindberg *should* have written about and how.[25] If there is any overarching antagonist, Ring says, it is Charles himself, his own past actions and mistakes.

But there are types of conflict and tension other than that created through overt conflict between conscious wills. For both reader and viewer, there is the tension resulting from contradictory information and a playwright who gives no reliable "facts" to go on. For a reader, and even more so for a viewer, there is the tension created through contradictions and inconsistencies in a character who will say one thing and do another—just as in life. Especially for a viewer there is the tension between different theatrical sign systems created for simultaneous perception, e.g., the tension between action and setting, the tension between text and subtext, or the tension between verbal and gestural expression so well explored in Absurdist drama. Thus Charles can be *shown* on stage—in spite of the minimally sympathy-inducing dialogue—as ill, unhappy, broken, neurotic, sensitive, anxious, gentle, kind, tired, old, good-natured, etc. Which aspects of the character are underlined depends on the director and the actor. Attesting to the elasticity of the role and the latitude of characterizations possible are the different aspects stressed by some of this century's great Swedish actors: August Palme (1902) emphasized "storhetens, originalitetens, olyckans ensamhet" [the loneliness of greatness, originality, and misfortune], Lars Hansson (1940) stressed the character's simplicity and dignity, and Anders Ek (1967) played up his illness and exhaustion.[26]

There is also the potential for considerable tension between what an audience expects and what it is given. Paradoxically, the "ensidighet" [one-sidedness] of which Ring accuses Strindberg's Charles does not lessen but increases this tension, since every aspect of Strindberg's creation is instantly set against the Charles everybody "knows," Tegnér's blue-and-yellow "unge hjälte" [young hero]. To paraphrase Ring, Charles's antagonist is more than his own past self, it is his centuries-old heroic public persona. The tension between the two Charles, the one everyone "knows" and the one Strindberg presents, permeates the play.

There is, in other words, plenty in the drama *Carl XII* to stimulate the imagination of reader and audience and draw them in: urge to "complete the picture" and resolve ambiguity, the tragic form, and the tension of contradiction and conflict. Of these, Strindberg used especially contradiction—contrast and conflict between clearly stated and irreconcilable data—and ambiguity—deliberate lack of clarity—to communicate his ambivalence about Charles.

Of Strindberg's historical characters, Charles XII is particularly rich in ambiguity and contradictions. Strindberg was certainly not alone in his ambivalence toward the king—cf. Voltaire, Fryxell, Heidenstam—but his research method contributes to the complexity and contradictoriness of the portrait. Voracious reading of a wide range of sources and indiscriminate assembling of "facts" from all directions resulted in lists of features, traits, incidents, and situations, all jotted down over an extended period of time and saved in the famous carpetbag *"gröna säcken."* From *Miss Julie* on, Strindberg often uses a patchwork technique to create complex dramatic characters. Time and again Strindberg clearly recognizes drama's ability to create lifelike images of human beings through contradiction:

> Enkla sinnen tala alltid om motsägelser och inkonsekvenser, men allt levande är sammansatt av element som icke äro homogena, utan måste vara sammansatta för att hålla ihop...
>
> [Simple minds are always speaking of contradictions and inconsistencies, but all living things are composed of elements which are not homogenous, but rather have to be opposites in order to hold together...] (*SS* 50: 80–81)

But Strindberg does not balance the picture of Charles simply by giving *boven* (the villain) a few human traits or good qualities. Instead, the same trait is interpreted differently by different people, adding to the fluidity and ambiguity of the whole play. Or the same person—the Man, Malcontent, Luxemburg, the Sailor—shows what Walter Johnson calls "a strange blend of respect and disrespect, liking and dislike, reliance and suspicion, blind admiration and fear."[27] The Man concedes: "Tänk att jag kunde inte bli riktigt ond på den där karln! En helvetes karl var det i alla fall!" [Strange, but I couldn't get really angry with that man! A helluva man he was, when all's said and done!] (*SV* 47: 149)

The powerful attraction of ambiguity is attested to in reviews of the play, in which "mystikens stämning" [the mood of mysticism] (*NDA*) is seen as a positive aspect, as is the vagueness of the king's portrait:

> ... att gestalten blott är antydd, aldrig fullt utförd, finner

jag icke vara något konstnärligt fel, snarare tvärtom. Åskådarens fantasi har dock på förhand ett så rikt stoff att röra sig med, att den blott behöfver ledas i rätta riktningen, för att utfylla de fasta om också tunna konturerna, gestalten har i sig själv en sådan tragisk storhet och ett sådant mänskligt djup, att man är tacksam, då författaren endast med försynthet rör vid den.

[. . . that the character is merely suggested, never fully executed, I do not consider an artistic flaw, on the contrary. Since the imagination of the viewer has such rich material to work with in advance that it only needs to be pointed in the right direction to fill out the firm albeit thin contours (of the portrait); the character possesses in itself such tragic greatness and such human depth that one is grateful when the author only delicately touches it.] (*SVD*)

In other words, the reviewer assumes that the audience will fill out the vague portrait on stage along the lines of the Charles everyone "knows," and that the more they do so, the better.

Ambiguity and contradiction are found throughout the play. The script is a masterful "commanding form" for various scenic means of portraying the many-faceted character and inner journey of the elusive king. Ambiguity is created, alternately, by a paucity of signs, unclear or non-committal signs, or contradictory or complex signs. Strindberg often creates ambiguity visually, while contradiction is created through what we are told. For example, according to contemporary sources the historic Charles was inscrutable and non-committal.[28] Strindberg's Charles looks equally inscrutable, but the contradictions in his personality are pointed out by what people say about him.

Charles is taciturn, non-communicative, enigmatic—more noticeably so on stage than on the page. He speaks inaudibly in Act I; Act II's stichomythic dialogue is carried on in a hoarse whisper; in Act III he is not present; and in Act V he again speaks little. Yet in Act IV there *is* verbal "flow" in Charles's three-partite confrontation with Woman, showing him as human, witty, communicative. Speaking about the play, Strindberg may protest all he likes that he portrays "den halvgalne despoten som icke värdigas säga ett ord" [the half-crazed despot who does not deign to speak a word] (*SS* 50: 252), but an actor communicates beyond words, and Strindberg himself laid the foundation for a more "eloquent" Charles by his use of contradictions.

Is Charles commanding, regal? In Act I, he is frozen, exhausted, and can barely speak, yet there is something about him which demands attention and absolute obedience. Strindberg shows this mysterious power through the impact it has on others, as in Act I when it forces the representatives of the Four Estates to their knees against their will. The Peasant muses: " . . . jag kan inte förstå—(borstar av sina knän)—men det var som om någon slagit undan benen på en—det vill säga, det var inte jag, som föll på knä..." [. . . I can't understand it—(brushes off his knees)—but it was as if someone had kicked my legs out from under me—that is, it wasn't me who went down on my knees . . .] (*SV* 47: 27).

Is he impressive? In the scenes where he might look most imposing—together with his Dwarf Luxemburg—he is also least dignified and most human. He is called a giant, yet seen lying down for nearly half the time he is on stage (for much of two acts out of four), and his bed—an army cot or camp bed—is prominently present in three acts. Strindberg often uses the prone position of a character to express defeat or imminent death—compare the king's bed with, e.g., the emasculating sofa in *The Father* and the *chaise-longue* in *Dance of Death*. Strindberg hints at the significance of Charles's lying down as a sign of inactivity—"I andra akten 'ligger' han i Lund och gör ingenting" [In the second act he 'lies' in Lund doing nothing][29]—and specifically mentions three times in Act V that

Charles is prostrate.

Charles is chameleon-like. Even the king's height is open to speculation. When Gyllenborg asks Horn in Act II about the king's appearance, Horn finds it difficult to describe him conclusively:

> Gyllenborg:... Är han högväxt?
> Horn: Svårt att säga! ty han går inte efter vanliga ögonmått—Jag har sett honom stor som en Theseus och liten som en page! Och hans ansikte?
> Gyllenborg: Vad är det med det?
> Horn: Ja, jag har sett tjugo olika! Han är icke en människa, ty han är legio!
>
> [Gyllenborg:... Is he tall?
> Horn: Hard to tell! Because he can't be measured by normal standards—I have seen him great as a Theseus and small as a page! And his face?
> Gyllenborg: What about his face?
> Horn: Well, I have seen twenty different (faces)! He is not a single human being, he is a multitude!] (*SV* 47: 40–41)

We hear that he deserted prisoners of war in Siberia, but we see him being kind to Luxemburg. We hear about *boven*, (the villain), but what we see is a man suffering from indecision, isolation, defeat. Similarly, he wears the same plain blue woolen uniform as his men, but his camp bed is draped with blue silk and his chair with ermine. Strindberg scenically underscores the contrast between "the king's two bodies,"[30] the anointed monarch and the man. The silk, ermine, and ceremony belong to the body politic, the woolen uniform, hoarseness, and exhaustion to his temporal body. Yet Strindberg's point is not to uphold the sanctity of the king's politic body: the death of absolute monarchy and Charles's weary body both are imminent. The most significant turning point in Act III—in the entire play, according to Strindberg—is the lowering of the flag outside Görtz's house at the news of Louis XIV's death, signifying "Enväldets fall—och Carl XII:s stundande slut" [the fall of Absolute Monarchy—and the imminent end of Charles XII] (*SS* 50: 252). No wonder Strindberg was unhappy that Act III was cut in the premiere production.[31] The stage picture in Act III, the facade of Görtz's house, is an image of the public persona of the monarch, while the garden of the same house in Act IV shows an image of his private self. The garden is a private space: a refuge, an arena for personal encounters, a Gethsemane. The garden is not open to the public, closed off both with iron gates downstage left and a wall with plank doors upstage center.[32] An allée of trees leads up to the plank doors, whose barring function is further stressed by *spanska ryttare*,[33] spikes and barbs to keep the rabble from climbing over the wall.

But more compelling than either of the above-mentioned factors is something which is experienced by the viewer of a live performance, namely the power of live action in a shared time and space. The act of watching an actual person (the actor) create a virtual person (the character) has a strong and unique power to involve and compel. This unique power, attested to by Plato's condemnation and Aristotle's defense equally, manifests in empathy—often leading to sympathy—and a kinesthetic response to the action on stage. This power derives from—but is not synonymous with—a mental and physical involvement with the action, as well as an awareness and appreciation of the tension between the virtual and the actual, i.e., aesthetic distance.

In performance, Charles—though silent—is physically present on stage most of the time, which means a potentially much more forceful cumulative emotional involvement on the part of the audience. *Carl XII* is the only work in which Strindberg gives the king a chance to "speak" directly to us—

ironically, often by being silent—and defend himself against the standard Strindberg accusations, here voiced by the Man and Luxemburg. We see the king's isolation and empathically share his mental and physical states, e.g., his embarrassment in Act II when Horn unwittingly criticizes him, his exhaustion, and his utter despair in the "Gethsemane‧scene" in Act IV.

The power of live presence is known by all theater practitioners, yet surprisingly little is written about it. In one of the few attempts to analyze the nature of this power, psychologist Charles Neuringer teamed with theater director Ronald A. Willis to identify eight factors contributing to the empathy (identification) fundamental to the power of live presence in the theater.[34] Of these eight, four—narrowed focus, emotion without obligation, creation of community, and belief affirmation—require a group of audience members, while the other four—enhanced feedback loops, physical proximity, stimulus richness, and unpredictability (risk)—affect all audience members, singly or in a group, but have a potential impact also on a single sensitive reader.

And Strindberg was a sensitive reader, especially of his own works. He clearly "saw" his dramas vividly as he was working on them. Anyone writing a drama envisions the action, records it, shapes it in a feedback loop, and finally responds to it as it plays itself out in his "mind's eye." But Strindberg, in addition to being a master of dialogue, had an unusually highly developed visual sense and skillfully utilized visual elements in his theatrical "text." His earliest sketches for a given play were often a floor plan and list of "Scenerier" [settings].[35] His carefully worked out "stage pictures" in the five acts in *Carl XII*—later significantly called *tableaux*[36]—are both strikingly visualized compositions and a text to be interpreted.

Strindberg does show a good deal of empathy for Charles. No doubt, as Lamm, Ollén, and Stockenström point out, this is partly due to identification of his own situation with Charles's—or the reverse—but it is also, I maintain, due to "theatrical compulsion," a compulsion that is especially strong in live performance. But how can the power of live performance have had anything to do with any empathy (or sympathy) Strindberg may have developed for Charles in the writing of *Carl XII*, even allowing for the fact that Strindberg was a sensitive reader?

A partial answer may lie in certain unusual circumstances surrounding the writing of *Carl XII*. Strindberg labored over *Carl XII* and the play was written in at least four stages over a long time (August 1899 to June 1901). Strindberg was baffled by Charles's contradictory nature and by his own inability to reconcile historical fact with his personal scheme for the play as "karaktärs- och katastrofdrama" [a drama of character and catastrophe (fate)].[37]

Two influences seem to have helped Strindberg resume his work and complete it. The first one was the Swedish eighteenth century mystic Emanuel Swedenborg, in whose works Strindberg claims to have found "god ledning vid förklaringen af det svåra problemet Karl XII:s personlighet" [a good key to the explanation of the big problem of Charles's personality].[38] The young Swedenborg had actually been a member of Charles XII's engineer corps in Lund, and could therefore be written in as a character in the play, where he serves as an "explainer" of the king's personality.[39]

Second, during one of the critical stages in the writing, in the beginning of 1901, Strindberg had the help of August Palme, a leading actor at the Royal Dramatic Theater. They discussed the play, especially the character of Charles, at meetings in Palme's rented villa at Oakhill. It is at this stage that Strindberg would have begun to respond to the "compulsion" of Charles's live presence, affected by the four empathy-producing factors that do not require a group response, namely enhanced feedback loops, physical proximity, stimulus richness, and unpredictability (risk). If Palme, even for a moment, assumed the character of Charles, these four would begin to operate instantly. Palme's interest was professional but apparently unselfish, since Strindberg to begin with had the actor Brór Olsson at The Swedish Theater in mind for the role. (Strindberg may have been persuaded by his work with Palme, who usually played romantic leads, that Olsson would better fit Strindberg's image of "den instängde, manlige, lugne Karl" [the introvert, manly, calm Karl].)[40] As it turned out, The Swedish Theater refused the play in early August 1901, while the Royal Dramatic Theater accepted it a month later for the current season, so Palme happily ended up playing the part he had helped Strindberg bring to life. The premiere, first set for Charles's birthday November 30, took place on February 13, 1902.

The exact number and dates of the meetings between Strindberg and Palme is not known, but their significance and nature can be gleaned in a letter from Strindberg to Palme the day after the opening, congratulating him on his performance of Carl XII:

> Jag lyckönskar Dig till din framgång; och jag tackar Dig icke blott för rollen, ty Du var med och uppehöll mitt intresse, när den gåtfulle karakteren började taga lif hos författaren. De oroliga, icke alltför ljusa stunderna på Oakhill—det är ett år sedan—skola derför alltid hos mig i minnet kvarstå vid sidan af Carl XII.

> [I congratulate you on your success; and I thank you not only for (creating) the part, for you were there and kept my interest up, when the enigmatic character began to come alive in the (mind of the) author. The anxious/uneasy, not too light moments at Oakhill—it's now one year ago—will therefore in my memory always remain associated with Carl XII.] (*Brev* 14: 170)

The Theatrical Compulsion 81

Palme fills in the picture: "När Strindberg höll på med 'Carl XII' voro vi dagligen tillsammans och talade då nästan oupphörligt om stycket eller rättare sagt om Carl XII." [When Strindberg was working on 'Charles XII' we were together daily and talked almost incessantly about the piece or rather about (the character of) Charles.][41] Furthermore, the play itself and Palme's portrayal attest indirectly to the unique collaboration that "delivered" Charles. The title character in *Carl XII* is the most carefully developed of all Strindberg's protagonists, judging from the numerous and detailed stage directions and the amount of space Strindberg devoted already in his drafts to the description of the king's character.[42] The play is filled with the kind of fine-tuning stage directions often associated with Ibsen—Hedda Gabler "suppresses an almost imperceptible smile"—such as: the king "fixerar nu Horn såsom om han ville läsa hans innersta tankar och se efter om där finnes några baktankar. Munnen står öppen och överläppen rycker" [now fixes Horn with his glance as if he wanted to read his innermost thoughts and see if he has any ulterior motives. His mouth is open and his upper lip twitches] (*SV* 47: 46). He "tyckes söka ord som han ej finner" [appears to be looking for words but in vain] (131) and "darrar på rösten utan att höja den" [his voice is trembling without being raised] (51). Charles "far med handen över ögonen såsom om han samlade minnen och tankar" [passes his hand over his eyes as if collecting memories and his thoughts] (50), shortly thereafter he "far med handen över ögonen som om han ville befria sig från ett nät" [passes his hand over his eyes as if wanting to free himself from a net] (53)—a fine distinction, and difficult, if not impossible, to convey.

What do these stage directions tell us? Do they merely reflect the "shift of emphasis from a public historical world to the private inner world of his protagonist"?[43] Do they tell us that Strindberg did not trust the actor Olsson—or any actor, for that matter—to sufficiently "understand" Charles? That he tried to compensate for the paucity of spoken lines with expanded stage directions to chart Charles's subtext? That he had an unusually keen psychological insight into the character, derived from his personal identification with the king and/or his readings with Palme? Did he, for whatever reason, "see" the character more clearly, more fully, more compellingly, than usual?[44]

One other play with a great amount of specific directions for the actor is *Kristina* [Queen Christina] (1901). But the detail in *Kristina* was probably intended to help his young wife Harriet Bosse in creating the role.[45] (Strindberg had previously written several roles for his first wife Siri von Essen, but without the careful coaching found in *Kristina*.) *Carl XII* is unique in that Strindberg was directly assisted in the creation by a professional actor. The wives were neophytes, not professionals; recipients of advice, not dispensers, and their roles were written to promote their careers by an author in full command of his pen. Working with Palme, Strindberg was the recipient of suggestions: he had no reason to develop the character for Palme's sake, since neither of them knew that Palme would end up playing the role. Palme helped Strindberg get "unstuck" and flesh out the character. The king's hoarseness and tiredness, for example, were added during the writing, probably after working with Palme.

Palme's unusually strong involvement with the character of Charles can be gleaned from the reviews of the 1902 premiere. All agree that the role's physical aspects, realized through makeup and costume, are gratifyingly "lifelike," i.e., correspond to the popular image of Charles "known" to everybody through Per Krafft's portraits. Though some of the reviewers deplore that the author has added disconcerting psychological traits and left out Tegnér's beloved "unge hjälte," Palme is universally praised for the unusual subtlety and rich

The Theatrical Compulsion 83

detail of his portrayal:

> Han tolkade... med förstånd och god uppfattning af hvad författaren menat grundtonen hos karakteren samt med icke obetydlig nyanseringsförmåga de skiftningar som finnas...
>
> [He... interpreted the basic tone of the character with intelligence and a clear understanding of the author's intention, and also rendered the character's finer nuances with a not inconsiderable ability...] (*NDA*)
>
> Som Karl XII hade hr Palme sin bäst och samvetsgrannast lösta uppgift under de senare åren.... Det var tydligen ett mycket allvarligt och ärligt studium nedlagdt på uppgiften...
>
> [In (the character of) Charles XII Mr. Palme had his best and most conscientiously solved acting challenge of the past few years.... Obviously very serious and honest study had been devoted to the task...] (*SVD*)
>
> Herr Palme, som ibland spelar sina roller i största allmänhet, har här med framgång lagt sig vinn om att studera, karaktärisera, och individualisera.... väl detaljerad i öfverensstämmelse med diktarens intentioner.
>
> [Mr. Palme, who sometimes makes his characters very general, has here successfully made an effort to study, characterize, and individualize.... (the character is) carefully detailed in agreement with the poet's intentions.] (*DN*)
>
> Herr Palme följde i sin tolkning af denne originelle Carl XII noga författarens intentioner och gjorde detta med en erkännansvärd konsekvens.

[In his interpretation of this original Charles XII Mr. Palme carefully followed the author's intentions and did so with commendable consistency.] (*ST*)

Alfred Lindkvist (*ST*) praises Palme's strong identification with the role: "Carl XII eller August Palme—de tu äro här ett—tala" [Charles XII or August Palme—here those two are one—are speaking]. The praise is unusual for its time: this kind of identification of actor with role is rarely attempted, achieved, or critically recognized before the introduction of Stanislavsky's "method" in the 1920s. Strindberg is an exception: in his *Memorandum* he twice addresses the actor's complete identification with the role (*SS* 50: 16, 22).

I suggest that Palme acted as midwife to *Carl XII* by reading draft passages and discussing the subtext with Strindberg, perhaps suggesting or trying on the specific behavior of Charles reflected in the stage directions. By doing so he both laid the foundation for his own eventual detailed work with the role and began to create a fleshed out, "compelling" character that Strindberg could—and did—respond to. Like the character of the Stepdaughter in *Six Characters in Search of an Author* visits her creator Pirandello at dusk and seduces him, so Charles/Palme may have "seduced" Strindberg at Oakhill or Karlavägen by his presence. One reviewer thoughtfully remarks after reading the play:

> Det är en tragisk storhet öfver denna gestalt, sådan den af författaren är tänkt—*sedd* skulle man snarare vilja säga—och gifven i några korta, antydande drag.
>
> [There is a tragic grandeur in this character, as it is thought/conceived—or rather *seen/envisioned*—by the author, and rendered in a few deft, suggestive strokes.] [italics mine](*SVD*)

No wonder, then, that Strindberg is ambivalent towards Charles in the drama. When formulaic negativity returns in Strindberg's references to Charles XII after the drama, it is aimed at the public political figure, but when he "sees" the inner man who finds release in the bullet from above, he is "compelled" to identify with him. This ambivalence finds powerful expression in the final verdict pronounced by The Man, the character who hates Charles the most:

Sjömannen: Sveriges aldra största konung är död! Gud bevare oss!
Mannen: Är boven död?
Missnöjd: Han är död! Och nu förlåter jag honom!
Mannen: Tänk att jag kunde inte bli riktigt ond på den där karln! En helvetes karl var det i alla fall!

[Sailor: Sweden's greatest king is dead! God preserve us!
Man: Is the villain dead?
Malcontent: He is dead! And now I forgive him!
Man: Strange, but I couldn't get really angry with that man! A helluva man he was, when all's said and done!]
(*SV* 47: 149)

NOTES

[1] There is some indication that the young Strindberg was caught up in the late nineteenth century Swedish mainstream idolization of Charles XII. At the age of 19, Strindberg participated in the inauguration of the J. P. Molin statue of Charles XII in Kungsträdgården, Stockholm. In the novel *Röda rummet* [The Red Room] (1879), Charles XII is referred to as Arvid's "gamla ideal" [old ideal]. *August Strindbergs Samlade Skrifter* (hereafter *SS*), ed. John Landquist, 55 vols. (Stockholm: Bonnier, 1912–21), 5: 80. When, almost forty years later, the Stranger in the drama *Brända tomten* [The Burned Lot] (1907) is voicing young Strindberg's distress at the celebration of "Sweden's worst king," the reference is probably projecting the mature Strindberg's feelings back onto the boy,

as Johan, Strindberg's alter ego in the autobiographical *Tjänstekvinnans son* [Son of a Servant] (1886), describes the event without criticizing either the king or his worshippers.

[2] "Kring Strindbergsstriden 1910," *Svensk litteraturtidskrift* 11, no. 2 (1948): 58.

[3] Charles's political stupidity is a frequently recurring theme in Strindberg's *oeuvre*: *SS* 8: 248; *SS* 12: 385; *SS* 16: 164–65; *SS* 42: 278–79; *SS* 53: 38, 50, 52, 56; *SS* 54: 318, 319–20, 375–76.

[4] "Sveriges förstörare," *Tal till svenska nationen*, *SS* 53: 55. All translations, unless otherwise indicated, are my own.

[5] Because of its strong associations to *teaterboven* [the stage villain], the epithet *boven* (*bov*: scoundrel, rogue, crook, villain) is here perhaps best rendered with "the villain." It is found only in the drama *Carl XII* and is used primarily by the Man, except for two references by the Peasant in Act I and one by Malcontent in Act III. *Teaterboven* is the mustache-twirling melodrama villain, thus *boven* has metatheatrical overtones of "the villain of the piece" and is a less critical, almost affectionate, epithet.

[6] Letter to Carl Larson, 2 March 1882, regarding suggestions for illustrations for the short story "Presten." *August Strindbergs Brev*, ed. Torsten Eklund, vols. 1–15 (Stockholm: Bonniers, 1948–76), ed. Björn Meidal, vols. 16–20 (Stockholm: Bonniers, 1989–96), 2: 376. Strindberg envisions the Crown Prince (later Charles XII) sitting with gaping mouth, "a bread-swollen shit," staring in the ceiling during a sermon. The short story was published in *Svenska folket* [The Swedish People] (1882) but the illustration was not executed according to Strindberg's suggestion, possibly because it would have deviated too much from an acceptable image of the king.

[7] Martin Lamm, *August Strindberg*, 2 vols. (Stockholm: Bonniers, 1942), 2: 89.

[8] Gunnar Ollén, *Strindbergs dramatik* (Stockholm: Prisma, 1966), 192.

[9] A third "positive" portrait is found in a brief essay in *Öppna brev till Intima teatern* [Open Letters to the Intimate Theater] (1909) (*SS* 50:

251–253). This essay is, however, merely a commentary on and explanation of the play *Carl XII*.

[10] "Drafts of Carl XII," SgNM 2: 6, 19 (Strindberg MSS, Royal Library, Stockholm).

[11] Lamm, *Strindbergs dramer*, vol. 2 (Stockholm: Bonniers, 1926), 280; Ollén, 195–96; Göran Stockenström, *Ismael i öknen*, Acta Universitatis Upsaliensis; Historia Literarum 5 (Uppsala: Almqvist & Wiksell, 1972).

[12] "*Charles XII* as Dream Play," *Strindberg's Dramaturgy*, ed. Göran Stockenström (Stockholm: Almqvist & Wiksell, 1988), 228.

[13] For a detailed discussion of Strindberg and Charles as scapegoats, see Stockenström "*Charles XII* as Historical Drama," *Strindberg's Dramaturgy*, 45.

[14] "Memorandum till medlemmarne av Intima teatern" [Memorandum to the Members of the Intimate Theater], *Öppna brev, SS* 50: 37.

[15] Susanne K. Langer, *Feeling and Form* (New York: Charles Scribner's Sons, 1953).

[16] In a letter to The Swedish Theater 14 July 1901 Strindberg states that if *Carl XII* is accepted for production by August 1, he will wait to have the play printed until the premiere, otherwise he will have it printed immediately (*Brev* 14: 102). The play was eventually published in time for the February 1902 premiere, though with a publication date of 1901.

[17] "Karl XII på Dramatiska teatern," *Vårt Land*, 14 February 1902. (This source hereafter abbreviated *VL*.)

[18] "The Sign in the Theater: An Introduction to the Semiology of the Art of the Spectacle," *Diogenes* 61 (Spring 1968): 57.

[19] Stockenström sees Charles's journey not as a fall but as a progression from suffering to religious awakening and transcendence ("*Charles XII* as Dream Play," 228).

[20] *SS* 50: 252. Ironically, from a careful reading of the passage it appears that Strindberg is really referring to *Oedipus Rex*.

[21] Throughout history the "compulsion" of dialogue has been used pedagogically by a wide variety of teachers and scholars, Plato, Leone di Somi, Galileo, Goethe, and Diderot among them.

[22] For example, after having Medicus sharply criticize Charles as a person, Strindberg immediately deflects the criticism in the words of the Lieutenant: "Fy för fan, vad ni är småaktig, medikus! Det hade jag aldrig trott om er . . . Dubbla tummar och skitiga strumpor, vad har det med mannen att göra?" [What the devil, how petty you are, medicus! I would never have believed that of you . . . Double thumbs and dirty stockings, what has that got to do with the man?] (*SS* 12: 383)

[23] *Karl XII*, in *August Strindbergs Samlade Verk* (hereafter *SV*), ed. Lars Dahlbäck, vol. 47 (Stockholm: Norstedts, 1993), 105.

[24] "Strindbergs *Carl XII*," *Stockholms-Tidningen*, 14 February 1902. (Hereafter abbreviated *ST*.)

[25] "Strindbergs *Carl XII*," *Nya Dagligt Allehanda*, 14 February 1902. (Hereafter abbreviated *NDA*.)

[26] "Karl XII på Dramatiska teatern," *Svenska Dagbladet*, 14 February 1902. (Hereafter abbreviated *SVD*.)

[27] Walter Johnson, *Strindberg and the Historical Drama* (Seattle: University of Washington Press, 1963), 170.

[28] Charles's own soldiers found him inscrutable: "[D]e säja alla, att de aldrig kunna röja och döma af hans ansichte och elljest åtbörder, hvad han menar och huru han är till mods, . . . [de] hafva ännu aldrig kunnat märkia . . . hvartill han mäst inclinerar." [They all say they have never yet been able to discover and judge from his face and gestures what he thinks and how he feels, . . . they have never yet been able to tell . . . what he prefers.] Letter from Anders Alstrin to J. Upmarck, Leipzig 18–28 May 1707, in *Historisk Tidskrift* 4 (1884): 180.

[29] *SS* 50: 252. Strindberg is here indulging in a pun: the expression *ligga i X* [X being the name of a university town] means "to attend the University of X." By putting quotation marks around "ligger" Strindberg indicates that Charles literally is lying down in Lund.

[30] Ernst Hartwig Kantorowicz, *The King's Two Bodies* (Princeton, NJ: Princeton University Press, 1957).

[31] Strindberg expresses his unhappiness several years later in *Öppna brev* (*SS* 50: 252). The reviewers generally applauded the cut of Act III since Charles does not appear in it, but mistakenly assumed that Strindberg had approved the deletion, i.e., that he would have had the power to keep the play intact if he had wanted to (*Dagens Nyheter*, 14 February 1902. This source hereafter abbreviated *DN*.)

[32] Stockenström even sees it as a "lost Garden of Eden," "*Charles XII* as Dream Play," 240.

[33] Literally "spanish horsemen," forged decorative iron spikes capping walls, gates, rooftops, to prevent public access. The first published translation of *Charles XII* (in Strindberg's *Queen Christina, Charles XII, Gustav III*, trans. Walter Johnson [Seattle: University of Washington Press, 1955]) is misleading. By translating Strindberg's description of the doors as "wooden gates decorated with the figures of Spanish knights" (p. 142), Johnson overlooks the closed-off character of the garden. Joe Martin, on the other hand, speaks of "doors made of planks, furnished on top with 'Spanish horsemen' spikes" in *Strindberg—Other Sides: Seven Plays* (New York: Peter Lang, 1997), 191.

[34] Charles Neuringer and Ronald A. Willis, "The Psychodynamics of Theatrical Spectatorship," *Journal of Dramatic Theory and Criticism* 11, no. 1 (Fall 1987): 96–109.

[35] For a fuller discussion of Strindberg's compositional schemes in his paintings and dramas, see my *Strindberg's Symbolic Room: Commanding Form for Set Design in Selected Strindberg Scripts from 1887 to 1907*, diss. University of Minnesota, 1984. Ann Arbor, Mich.: UMI, 1984.

[36] In the drafts the divisions are called "acts," but were later changed to "tableaux" (SgNM 2:16, 14).

[37] *SS* 50: 251, 253. Strindberg uses the word *katastrof* in its original Greek sense, denoting the entire unwinding of the tragic plot, not just a disastrous event.

[38] Interview, "August Strindberg hemma hos sig," *Svenska*

Dagbladet, 15 October 1900.

[39] For a full appreciation of Swedenborg's significance for Strindberg, see Stockenström *Ismael i öknen* and "*Charles XII* as Dream Play."

[40] Letter to Lars Nilsson, Secretary of The Swedish Theater, 3 July 1901. *Brev* 14: 97–98. It is also possible that Strindberg, who first offered the play to The Swedish Theater as the theater most likely to produce the play, is simply stating his preference of the actors available at that theater.

[41] Interview on the occasion of Strindberg's sixtieth birthday, *Dagens Nyheter*, 21 January 1909.

[42] Stockenström, "Kring tillkomsten av Carl XII," *Meddelanden från Strindbergssällskapet* 45 (May 1970): 22–25, and "*Charles XII* as Dream Play," 230.

[43] Stockenström, "*Charles XII* as Dream Play," 236.

[44] Or was Strindberg so unusually detailed in his portrait of Charles since he knew the reviewers would read the play before seeing it and thought they might find his unorthodox portrait more acceptable if they first encountered it on the page? Did he perhaps expect them to judge the performance according to how closely it followed the printed play? Several reviewers refer to the printed play, comparing the production with the text.

[45] Amy van Marken, "Strindbergs *Kristina*. En ny teknik," *Studi Nordici* 22 (1979): 165–76.

Meaning Compounded: Strindberg's *Charles XII* and the Question of Genre

Otto Reinert

> He left the name, at which the world grew pale,
> To point a moral, or adorn a tale.

Dr. Johnson's dismissive couplet in *The Vanity of Human Wishes* about Sweden's "hero king" is not Strindberg's text in *Charles XII*; the play points no moral and adorns no tale. What the play does do and is is harder to say. We are dealing with a question of genre.

Genre was never the monolithic, totalitarian "system" anti-genericists say it was. Johnson, a staunch neoclassicist who believed in generics, defended Shakespeare against the purists who objected to the mixture of tragedy and comedy in his plays. Genre is "an invitation to form" (Guillén 109), an open-ended repertory for exploration and exploitation. Genre study is not about filing away literary works but an inquiry into how works modulate the conventions of literary communication.[1] Its vocabulary is not limited to forms and modes but includes terms for ideology, for periods, for subjects and themes, authors' names denoting qualities ("Strindbergian"), and much else. Examining the genre of *Charles XII* doesn't help us tag a hard-to-classify play but to understand the whole by recognizing its parts and the way they work together. It's all right if we can't make any single genre label—or combination of labels—fit.

The main drama in *Charles XII* is in the ambivalence of the protagonist. Strindberg's opinion about the king seems like Voltaire's, "an odd blend of respectful admiration and fascinated revulsion" (Jenkins 9). In *Some Prefaces to the Historical Plays* (in Strindberg, *Open Letters* 259) Strindberg called Charles XII "Sweden's destroyer, the great criminal, the bully, the idol of thugs, the counterfeiter."[2] Dr. Neuman in the short story *Vid likvakan i Tistedalen* (1891) presumably speaks for Strindberg when he says that Charles XII was destined by his German heritage to become just another barbarian "viking" in his raids on the east (Printz-Påhlson, "Passions and Interests" 73). To Strindberg, Charles's most serious political misjudgment was his preference for alien Turkey over Russia under the Europeanizing Peter I as an ally for the West (*August Strindbergs Samlade Verk* [hereafter *SV*] 47:311). His bias sometimes shows in the play, but in no way is he simply dramatizing a polemic against Charles XII. There is no debunking. In the sentence following his calling the king names he says he wrote the play because "every criminal has the right to defend himself." But his play is no more a vindication (reluctant or not) of the king than a vituperation. The powerful tension in it comes from Strindberg's judgment on the king's elusive character—flawed yet innocent, admirable but pitiable, an enigma, a "bundle of contradictions" (Lide 86).

Strindberg makes the nation's resentment of Charles's rule and his wars understandable. The common people have suffered, multitudes have died in and out of battle, injustices have been committed, the land is desolate, the state bankrupt. The stage set of Tableau 1, with its symbolic realism of ruined village, a single rotten apple on a dying tree, wind carrying voices away, the king's delayed and mute entry, the distant and unexplained gunshot—points to the general devastation Charles XII has brought on Sweden, "the land of difficulties."[3] Every character and group of characters, high and low, voice discontent.

There may have been more to Strindberg's writing about the king than a wish to do him justice in the abstract. There are discernible affinities between author and subject. Both have a sense of reality as illusion, both see through the world's hypocrisies, both live with silences and with a loneliness anguished by the pressure of other people, both feel "sick," and both are residents, after long exile, in the town of Lund in the province of Scania (Ollén, *August Strindberg* 83). The veteran "Man," who has returned from captivity in Siberia, insists on calling the king "*boven*" (the villain, the scoundrel), but his epitaph on him at the end recognizes a kind of grandeur: "He was one hell of a guy, after all!"[4] The play is behind that sentiment.

Given all this, does *Charles XII* have intellectual integrity, or is Sven Delbanc right in considering the theme of royal hubris properly punished to be at odds with the Swedenborgian metaphysic in which the king is more an agent of the world will than a madman or a sinner (Delbanc 4:45)? Is there, as Göran Stockenström suggests (Stockenström, "*Carl XII* as Historical Drama" 55), a "metaphysical order" behind speeches and events? If there is, it is obscure, and the play's Swedenborg is no help.

But Birgitta Steene is right; the play is closer to being a tragedy than a history. It meets most of her criteria for a history play, but not the crucial one: a tragic hero has "a moral conscience"; the hero of a history play is more like an epic hero, acting rather than thinking and introspecting (Steene, "Shakespearean Elements" 210). Barry Jacobs sees a variant of a historical play in *Charles XII*, something one may call "'the nemesis play'" (Jacobs 169). Margareta Wirmark is right when she says it won't do to call plays as different as *Gustav Vasa* and *Charles XII* history plays; we need a new terminology. Of the two, *Charles XII* is by now the more modern and less "bizarre" because it has "much in common with the drama of the absurd" (Wirmark 206). It is not a psychological study, an "explanation" of an inaccessible man. Like Miss Julie, Charles is "characterless," remaining protean, opaque, till the end. Martin Lamm puts it admirably: "There is a misty shimmer about him, and he never yields the solution to his riddle. And it is precisely because he never comes out of obscurity that there is a dimension of greatness about him"[5] (Lamm 287). It is not a play about a king who is already dead but doesn't know it (Brantly passim); that reading creates more problems than it solves. To call him a "ghost," as Strindberg does, makes sense as metaphor but is not a fact of the drama. The king's real or virtual silences in the early scenes may be psychosomatic or simply a case of ordinary hoarseness, but they fit Strindberg's choice not to choose among interpretations of a character whom historical tradition has cast as inscrutable. The other characters are all even less psychologically transparent and complete. None of them is rendered in depth. Their dramatic function is confined to their relationship to the king.

The play begins at a point at which only the resolution of a ripe situation remains to be staged. Strindberg recognized that pattern of classical tragedy in his play (Strindberg, *Open Letters* 260). But the play does not, like *Oedipus Rex* and Ibsen's retrospective drama, rediscover and reassess the past in the process of showing its consequences in the present. Its dramatic structure is casual, not classically tight and taut. It has no plot (in the sense of an intrigue of cause-and-effect sequences) but does have an action. Gunnar Ollén's definition of it, "under great difficulties the king prepares a new campaign" (*SV* 47:303), puts undue weight on the Norwegian campaign, which is first mentioned in Tableau 2, ignored in Tableau 3, mentioned again, briefly, near the end of Tableau 4, and already implemented in Tableau 5. An alternative definition might be: the momentum of past events in a stasis in the present interacts with the king's perplexity to become deadly fate. The musical leitmotif—the Dwarf's Bach saraband from "the land of pain and sorrow"[6]—serves coherence but only as an image. In the succession of confrontations we see a radically isolated and thought-tormented man among shifting companies of resentful, ambitious, manipulative, and self-seeking people of both sexes and all social classes, some of them mute and sinister chorus figures, and most of them pygmies compared to him. As Horn says: "... every day new people."[7]

Strindberg did well when he changed the term of the divisions of his collage of semi-autonomous episodes filled with pauses from "acts" to "tableaux;" the latter properly suggests a succession of static scenic pictures rather than movement, action, and dialogue. Ollén quotes Pär Lagerkvist's comment in a theater review in 1918 on the "looseness, roughness, and improvised quality" that makes for the play's "special feel" (Ollén, *Strindbergs dramatik* 411). For plot dynamic, it substitutes a rhythm of its own: Tableaux 1, 3, and 5 are short and more talk than action; Tableaux 2 and 4 longer and with happenings that move the action towards the end (Görtz wins the king's trust in 2, the king sets off for Norway in 4). There are shifts between others' view of the king and moments that open up his inner life. Neither perspective is ever sustained or reaches resolution. There is something Brechtian in this alternation of distance and intimacy; it creates desolate space between Charles and others. For all his saying, "I am never alone,"[8] he always is, even—or especially—in company. Yet Strindberg, unlike Brecht, never self-consciously inserts *Verfremdung* between his protagonist and his theater audience.

Strindberg's contemporaries were baffled by this play with its weak narrative line and terse and muted dialogues—so different from the action-packed and rhetorically charged first series of history plays (*Folkungasagan, Gustav Vasa, Erik XIV, Gustav Adolf*, 1899–1900). Most reviewers of the first production were positive (if not exactly enthusiastic), but many in the early audiences were outraged by what they regarded as Strindberg's defamation of the king, an affront to their Swedish patriotism. Only when fidelity to documented history and fairness to the king's character and accomplishments were no longer issues in Strindberg criticism and historians no longer were split into an "old" school to whom Charles XII had done nothing right as a king and a "new" school (in the 1890s) to whom he had done nothing wrong (Hatton 13–14), could rehabilitation of the play begin. Walter Johnson set the tone for subsequent commentary in 1963 when he called *Charles XII* "a superb play" (Johnson 159).

Its stature in the canon seems assured, though we are still looking for arguments to justify it. But if there is no consensus on what its unique strengths are, at least we seem to have learned where to look. Ever since Steene described Strindberg's protagonist as "an expressionistic character in an otherwise Naturalistic drama" (Steene, *The Greatest Fire* 132), most comments on the play have been variants of genre criticism. In addition to Steene's naturalism/expressionism dichotomy, there are tragedy/history, thesis play/dream play, a play about character/metaphysics/Hegel's teleological view of history, Shakespeare/Maeterlinck, Pirandellian conundrum/Beckettian waiting in a world of pain and confusion.[9]

To join Strindberg in refusing to play the game of categorization is not very helpful. Besides, Strindberg himself sometimes put genre labels on his works. He didn't think of genres as restraint but as challenge and opportunity, something to play with and change and put together in new ways (Ewbank 42–43). But in recognizing that some kind of case can be made for every one of the suggested generic affiliations we run the risk of ending up with a potpourri. The play's generic mixture is an asset, but it defies dissection. Its constituents are distinguishable, not separable.

What Strindberg did in dramatizing the legend of Charles XII was to create, first, fictional circumstances, derived from, but not identical with, historical fact; and, second, a psychological climate he knew from his own inner experience. Together they account for the exhaustion and discontent of both king and people. We approve of the play's suspension of ultimate meaning. We can make of it, not anything we like, but a number of not necessarily compatible meanings that Strindberg, with deliberate precision, put into it. There is every reason to think that he knew, intellectually and artistically, what he was doing.

Ambiguities are everywhere in *Charles XII*. Is the skipper who failed to rendezvous with the king's ship a traitor in Danish pay or an innocent victim of wind and ice? Is Görtz a disinterested intriguer of genius or a sly pretender to loyalty to the king? A charlatan or a financial vizard, about to become a victim of judicial murder? Is The Man who seems real in Tableau 1 a dream vision of the king's in Tableau 2? Was he or was he not married to the Skipper's daughter? (And what about the Sailor, who also claims her as his wife?) Was his military number 73 (as in Tableau 1) or 58 (as in Tableau 2)? And is the discrepancy the result of careless revision on Strindberg's part, or another instance—we say, at the risk of sounding portentous—of his distrust of the "truth" of facts and figures? Is the Dwarf Luxembourg someone like Lear's Fool, at once vulnerable dependent and mordant conscience, or just another embittered victim of the king's neglect? Are Horn and Gyllenborg heralds of a new, freer, more democratic age in Sweden's political life, or contemptible opportunists? What is the significance of their sudden ideological disagreement in Tableau 5? Is it just Horn who says, "Thus Providence plays games with those who want to play Providence!"[10] or is the play, too, saying it? Is the death of King Louis XIV of France not just a signal of the end of royal absolutism but also a political judgment on Charles XII, another king-autocrat about to die? What about the king's libido? Is it repressed by his obligation to his duties as king? Just tepid? A bisexual's? Where did the final, fatal shot come from? Swedenborg points to Heaven—as a mystic would. (Which doesn't mean that the shot did not come from above.)

Three passages, two of them juxtaposed in Tableau 4, illustrate characteristics of the kind of play *Charles XII* is. In the first, in Tableau 2 (*SV* 47:43–49), the king asks his secretary Feif to ask Horn and Gyllenborg about Görtz, then he himself asks Horn and Gyllenborg about Feif (Feif now absent), and finally he asks Feif about Horn and Gyllenborg and Görtz. The answers he gets are all different and dubious. At one point, in rising but silent pain and anger, he recognizes himself in Horn's characterization of Görtz.

The second passage in this manner of unresolved ambiguity is the sequence of the king's confrontations with Emerentia Polhem, his sister Ulrika Eleonora, and Katarina Leszczinsky, the wife of Stanislaus, ex-king of Poland (*SV* 47:105–24). The third (interrupting that sequence, pp. 111–12) is the brief, sardonic exchange between the king and Feif on the topic of marriage, a passage that is a variant extension of the dialogue on misogyny between Hultman and the Professor earlier in the same Tableau. The king-Feif-Horn-Gyllenborg-Görtz configurations in Tableau 2 and the sequence of confrontations with the three women in Tableau 4 bear on dramatic modality, the Feif-king dialogue on epistemology.

After angrily dismissing Emerentia for what he perceives as her disloyalty to her fiancé, Swedenborg, and just before the arrival of his sister, the king asks:

> KING: Feif! You have been married?
> FEIF: Yes, Your Majesty!
> KING: And?
> FEIF: Well—
> KING (*smiles*): And?
> FEIF (*shrugs*): Well—
> KING: That's what you all say, but I never get to learn anything!
> FEIF: Nor do we!
> KING: Perhaps there's nothing—to learn!—

FEIF: Perhaps![11]

The inconclusiveness—nothing is certain, not even that there is nothing to be learned from the state of being married—marks a pause between the bachelor king's encounters with a young girl engaged to be married and with an already married woman. The scene is another wry example of what is the main cognitive mode of this and many other Strindberg plays: the unknowability of all human relationships, even the most intimate and presumably enduring. In the final, quiet ultimate of skepticism in the king-Feif scene, doubt turns back on itself. Self-knowledge is equally elusive. The formidably "learned" Swedenborg admits that he has never really known another human being, not even himself (*SV* 47:148).

The sequence of confrontations of the king and the women, which encloses the king-Feif exchange, moves in the direction of diminishing eroticism: the flirty, seductive girl Emerentia, the ambitious sister who'll soon be Queen of Sweden, the ex-queen of Poland accusing the king of abandoning her husband. The men in the lives of these women are all implicated, in more or less unflattering ways, in their women's encounters with the king. All three women are self-seeking hypocrites—siren, sympathetic and solicitous mother substitute, moral creditor—and none of them gets anywhere with the king. Emerentia and Katarina are curtly dismissed. With his sister the king falls asleep. The sequence furthers no narrative progress, does not cause any change in the king's conduct or feelings, and the pattern it makes hardly allows inferences about a womanly archetype or about the king's sexuality, sense of guilt, family feeling, or concept of kingship. Chekhov comes to mind when we realize that the very pointlessness of the sequence by the criteria of conventional dramaturgy is its point: just so random, at once trivial and revealing/concealing, are the incidents that make up the fabric of our lives. And yet—as in Chekhov—form has been imposed on the apparently formless.

My argument is that it is not critical defeatism to say that *Charles XII* is a play that leaves open the questions it raises about the accessibility of human souls, the relation between fate and individual responsibility, the uncertain dividing line between fantasy or dream and reality, political morality, the mystery of identity, the mystery of religion. Such substantive issues impinge on the play's genre, and because they do, its genre is indeterminate. We take to its ambiguities because we feel a commitment to deconstructing everything we read and because we are postmoderns attuned to multilayered meanings and the demonization of certainties. We delight in our inability neatly to package the play by genre, or by dramatic paradigm, or by ideology. We see it as one of Strindberg's proto-modern plays. Surely (we say) it is no coincidence that among its closest chronological neighbors in the canon is *A Dream Play*. Yet we hesitate calling it expressionistic. Its dream sequences are tentative and can be plausibly interpreted as historical and social and psychological realism. And the scenario doesn't have the conspicuous incoherence of the scenes in *A Dream Play*. The "strangeness" of *Charles XII* is a modern strangeness, its resistance to genre determination a symptom of a crisis in our culture that is both malaise and candor.

NOTES

[1] Alastair Fowler, *Kinds of Literature: An Introduction to the Theory of Genres and Modes* (Oxford, 1982), 20 (qtd. in Ewbank 39).

[2] "Sveriges fördärvare, den store brottslingen, slagskämpen, busarnas avgud, falskmyntaren" (Strindberg, *Open Letters* 259). All translations from Swedish in this article are the author's.

[3] "svårigheternas land" (*SV* 47:42).

Meaning Compounded 101

[4] "En helvetes karl var det i alla fall!" (*SV* 47:149)

[5] "Det står en grå dimdager kring honom, och han ger aldrig lösningen av sin gåta. Just genom att aldrig komma ut ur dunklet får han ett drag av storhet" (Lamm 287).

[6] "... Sorgenland och Smärtarike—" (*SV* 47:79).

[7] "... var dag är det nytt folk" (*SV* 47:37).

[8] "Jag är icke ensam, Feif, jag är aldrig ensam..." (*SV* 47:49).

[9] Articles that deal (mainly, or in part) with the issue of Strindberg and genre are listed below under "Works Cited and Consulted." The authors are: Ewbank, Jacobs, Lide, Printz-Påhlson (1990), Robinson (1991), Sjönell, Steene (1959, 1973, 1990), Stockenström (1988, 1988), Wirmark.

[10] "Så leker Försynen med dem som vilja leka Försyn!" (*SV* 47:139)

[11] KONUNGEN: Feif! — Du har varit gift?
FEIF: Ja, Ers Majestät!
KONUNGEN: Nåå?
FEIF: Tja!
KONUNGEN (ler): Nåå?
FEIF (med en axelryckning): Tja!
KONUNGEN: Så säger ni alla; men jag får aldrig veta något!
FEIF: Inte vi heller!
KONUNGEN: Kanske det inte är något — att veta! — — —
FEIF: Kanske! (*SV* 47:111–12).

Works Cited and Consulted

Brantly, Susan. "The Formal Tension of Strindberg's *Carl XII*." Steene, "Strindberg and History" 92–107.

Ewbank, Inga-Stina. "'Tragical-Comical-Historical-Pastoral': Strindberg and the Absurdity of Categories." Robinson, "History and His-Story" 35–47.

Delbanc, Sven. *Den svenska litteraturen*. Vol. 4. Uddevalla: Bonniers, 1989. 45.

Fowler, Alastair. *Kinds of Literature: An Introduction to the Theory of Genres and Modes*. Oxford, 1982.

Guillén, Claudio. *Literature as System. Essays Toward the Theory of Literary History*. Princeton NJ: Princeton University Press, 1971.

Hatton, Ragnhild. *Charles XII*. London: The Historical Association, 1974. Monograph no. G84.

Hatton, Ragnhild. *Charles XII of Sweden*. New York: Weybright and Talley, 1968.

Jacobs, Barry. "Advent and Brott och Brott. Sagospel and Comedy in a Higher Court." Robinson, *Strindberg and Genre* 167–87.

Jenkins, Michael F.O. Introduction. *Lion of the North: Charles XII of Sweden*. By Voltaire. Trans. Jenkins. London and Toronto: Associated University Presses, 1981.

Johnson, Walter. "Charles XII: Madman of the North." *Strindberg and the Historical Drama*. Seattle: University of Washington Press, 1963. 155–74.

Jonasson, Gustaf. *Karl XII och hans rådgivare.* Stockholm, Oslo, København, Helsingfors: Svenska Bokförlaget [etc.], Scandinavian University Books. Studia Historica Upsaliensia, 1960.

Lamm, Martin. *August Strindberg.* Stockholm: Bokförlaget Aldus/Bonniers, 1968.

Lide, Barbara. "Strindberg and the Modern Consciousness." Steene, "Strindberg and History" 85–91.

Ollén, Gunnar. *August Strindberg* (World Dramatist Series). New York: Frederick Ungar Publishing Co., 1972.

Ollén, Gunnar. *Strindbergs dramatik.* Kristianstad: Sveriges radios förlag, 1982.

Printz-Påhlson, Göran. "Historical Drama and Historical Fiction: the Example of Strindberg." Steene, "Strindberg and History" 24–38.

Printz-Påhlson, Göran. "'Passions and Interests': Anthropological Observations in the Short Story." Robinson, *Strindberg and Genre* 61–81.

Rinman, Sven. *Ny illustrerad svensk litteraturhistoria.* Vol. 4. Stockholm: Natur och kultur, 1967. 111–14.

Robinson, Michael. "History and His-Story." Steene, "Strindberg and History" 53–66.

Robinson, Michael, ed. Preface. *Strindberg and Genre.* Norwich (East Anglia): Norvik Press, 1991. 9–13.

Sjönell, Barbro Ståhle. "Strindberg's Mixing of Genres." Robinson, *Strindberg and Genre* 48–60.

Steene, Birgitta. "Shakespearean Elements in Historical Plays of Strindberg." *Comparative Literature* 11 (1959): 209–20.

Steene, Birgitta. *The Greatest Fire: A Study of August Strindberg*. Carbondale, Ill.: Southern Illinois University Press, 1973.

Steene, Birgitta, ed. "Strindberg and History: An Introduction." *Scandinavian Studies*, special issue *Strindberg and History* 62 (1990): 2–5. Rpt. as *Strindberg and History*. Stockholm: Almquist & Wiksell International, 1992.

Stockenström, Göran. "Carl XII as Dream Play." Stockenström, *Strindberg's Dramaturgy* 223–44.

———. "Carl XII as Historical Drama." Stockenström, *Strindberg's Dramaturgy* 41–55.

———, ed. *Strindberg's Dramaturgy*. Minneapolis: University of Minnesota Press, 1988.

Strindberg, August. *Karl XII. Engelbrekt.* Stockholm: Stockholms universitet, 1993. Vol. 47 of *August Strindbergs Samlade Verk* (*SV*). Ed. Lars Dahlbäck et al.

Strindberg, August. *Open Letters to the Intimate Theater*. Trans. Walter Johnson. Seattle and London: University of Washington Press, 1967.

Wirmark, Margareta. "Strindberg's History Plays." Robinson, *Strindberg and Genre* 200–206.

History Revisited and Rewritten: August Strindberg, Magnus Smek, and Heliga Birgitta

Matthew M. Roy

One of Birgitta Steene's many contributions to Strindberg scholarship has been her sparring with traditional views of Strindberg's misogynistic tendencies to present us with a new picture of Strindberg as ambivalent feminist. Strindberg did indeed struggle with the double-edged sword of feminist thought, leading him to admire certain women as individuals while at times despising them as a sex. One such woman is Heliga Birgitta [Saint Bridget of Sweden]. As an intellectual force in her day, Heliga Birgitta presented Strindberg with the problem of portraying an intelligent individual with what Strindberg considered to be imbecilic ideas, a conflict which colored his historic yet fictive character. When the fates of Heliga Birgitta and King Magnus Eriksson, otherwise known as Magnus Smek, become intertwined with Strindberg's own, the question of sympathy skews Strindberg's historic depictions further still. This article will show how Strindberg's changing perceptions of Magnus Smek and Heliga Birgitta parallel an event in Strindberg's own life, impacting his portrayals of them as historic figures.

King Magnus does not seem worthy of much respect in Strindberg's early works. Strindberg calls him "lättfärdig" [of lax morals] in *Svenska folket* and "usel" [vile] in both *Svenska folket II* and *Det nya riket*. It is not surprising that Strindberg did not offer King Magnus much respect when many historical sources did not do so either. In her own revelations Heliga Birgitta even accuses the king of attending mass in spite of his excommunication, robbing, and betraying the Scanians, while also making the claim that he had intercourse with men:[1]

> We have something to say to guard your soul, and as a confession we ask you to pay, and with more appropriate words than you feel is fitting. But such is the perception: You have the ugliest reputation in and outside the kingdom that a Christian man can have: that you have had intercourse with men. It seems to us to be true, for you love men more than God, or your own soul, or your own wife (Noreen 51).[2]

Instead of explicitly utilizing this passage in *Svenska folket I & II*, of which Strindberg was probably aware, he claims that Heliga Birgitta acted in a manner unbefitting when she wrote her sermons against the royal house, making public her accusations. Strindberg quotes one of these sermons, wherein Heliga Birgitta bemoans the way in which the king and queen, who once shone like the sun and the moon, have lost their sheen by changing their morals. They have also advanced a friend of "huggorms släkte" [viperous race] who trampled upon Heliga Birgitta's friends and the lord's servants. The friend refers to Bengt Algotsson, whom both the king and queen favored highly, and who is also the man with whom it was rumored the king and, according to some accounts which Strindberg consulted, the queen had sexual relations. While Strindberg does not quote from this passage in *Svenska folket*, he does often refer in subsequent works to the king's "fulaste frejd" [ugliest reputation], an obvious reference to Heliga Birgitta's admonition of the king's "fulastu frægð i rikeno og vtan" [ugliest reputation in and outside the kingdom], a reputation branded upon the king for his love of men according to Heliga Birgitta's revelations.

In *Det nya riket* Strindberg also states that saints are a fetish, resulting from the civilized human's unsatisfied evil lusts.

One can easily read this as a remark directed at Heliga Birgitta, who already in *Svenska folket* receives less than flattering treatment. Scrutinizing the circumstances of her canonization, Strindberg claims that it was no small task for Heliga Birgitta to achieve sainthood. The clergy of the time found her to be a little too liberal, religiously, politically, and even morally, since she broke her promise of chastity enough times to bring eight children into the world. As she reappears in various texts during Strindberg's authorship, her reputation seems to suffer from ever escalating attacks. King Magnus, on the other hand, undergoes authorial redemption as soon as we arrive at the writing of *Folkungasagan* in 1899.

In this play Magnus lives in a nest of conspirators where he alone innocently believes in the faith bestowed upon friends and family. His wife, Queen Blanche, has an affair with his best friend Bengt Algotsson, in the *dramatis personæ* listed as Queen Blanche's favorite, while his mother conspires for the crown with her lover and future husband Knut Porse. Heliga Birgitta sits as a member of his court where she meters out punishment to her maids and claims herself to lack all morals, the admission of which she believes one should count amongst her positive qualities. King Magnus makes it very clear that her motives are anything but divine by pointing out that her encouragement to the Pope to return to Rome from Avignon is neither new nor her idea, that she suffers from arrogance which leads to her desire to found an unnatural order, a cloister where women shall rule over men, and that her revelations are nothing more than "gamla goda sanningar" [good old truths] which have been told many times over. In one of her many prophecies, Heliga Birgitta foretells that all of the king's "dygder skola smutsas av de onda och kallas laster" [virtues shall be sullied by those who are evil and be called vices] (*SV* 41: 52). She also foresees the defiling of the king's name, which history has recorded as "Magnus Smek," when she says to the king "ditt namn skall gå sudlat i hävderna tills ditt rykte en dag blir upprättat" [your name shall go soiled into the annals of history until your reputation is restored one day] (52).

Strindberg discusses both King Magnus's ugly reputation and his nickname in *Öppna brev till Intima Teatern* (*SS* 50: 240–42). First he reminds the reader that the Norwegians, rather than demeaning the king by using an ugly nickname, referred to him as Magnus the Good, which was also one of the original titles of *Folkungasagan* in Strindberg's manuscripts. Contemporary historians such as C.T. Odhner had, at the time, washed this blemish from the king's reputation, which Strindberg claims was a result of the king's loss of Skåne. The debate as to the true origin of this nickname continues to this day, divided in two camps between those who take Smek to mean "convinced" in old Swedish, thus the king was convinced or talked into his evil deeds by other men, and those who take it to mean "caress," as in the king was sexually caressed by other men in his court. The books Strindberg consulted as sources for his historical drama also contain elements of both aspects of this debate. The importance of Strindberg's historical research as a relevant backdrop to the development of his character portrayal motivates a closer analysis of the ways in which historians had depicted King Magnus "Smek."

The works of Fryxell, Odhner, Starbäck, Hildebrand, and Afzelius seem to be the most influential works in Strindberg's creation of the literary King Magnus. Fryxell's name appears already in *Svenska folket*. In his *Berättelser ur svenska historien* he claims that the king most likely received the name "Smek" because of the "lättsinnig" and "liderlig" [lecherous] lifestyle he led in his court. Odhner writes in *Lärobok i Sveriges, Norges och Danmarks Historia För Skolans Högre Klasser* that the king's "lastbart lefverne" [depraved lifestyle] brought him a warning from Heliga Birgitta and later his infamous nickname. Hildebrand blurs the distinction by claiming that the nine points of discontent, which Albrekt branded upon King Magnus after being chosen king, were the cause of the nickname "Smek." The first of these points had to do with the king's "slemma lefverne," [disgusting lifestyle] whereas the rest had to do with his disobedience of the church and poor administration of the kingdom. In *Öppna brev till Intima Teatern* (*SS* 50: 242) and *En blå bok II* (*SS* 47: 541), Strindberg uses Hildebrand's *Sveriges historia* to wipe the slate of Magnus's reputation clean, since Hildebrand wrote that the first of the accusations had no grounds, especially considering the fact that the Church never condemned his lifestyle. Strindberg writes "sedan man förstört hans rykte med lögner och vanfrejdat honom, säger man: han har ful frejd" [after one destroyed his reputation with lies and dishonored him, it is said: he has an ugly reputation] (*SS* 50: 242). He continues by stating that Heliga Birgitta spread these rumors in her revelations because Magnus, as a man, did not desire to stand under Heliga Birgitta, as a woman. The king's son Erik, who also happens to snoop in Heliga Birgitta's diaries in *Folkungasagan* and find the same passage on the king's ugly reputation, among other accusations, exclaims that they constitute lies, each and every one of them (*SV* 41: 47).

Interestingly enough, Afzelius is the only one of the five historians who clearly claims in *Svenska folkets sago-häfder, eller Fäderneslandets historia, sådan hon lefwat och till en del ännu lefwer i Sägner, Folksånger och andra Minnesmärken*, as Strindberg does in *Öppna brev till Intima Teatern*, that the cause of the king's nickname was his loss of Skåne. Afzelius describes the origin of the name as follows "att förmana med swärd i hand eller med list och blod, det kallades den tiden karlavulet, men med mildhet och goda ord, det kallades 'Smek'" [to warn with a sword in the hand, or with cunning and blood, was called manly at that time, but with gentility and good words, that was called 'Smek'] (181). Strindberg often referred to these historical accounts to justify the choices he had made in writing his fiction, or similarly to justify the narrative account of a historic event. According to Gunnar Ollén, he dismissed the accusations of King Magnus's homosexuality by taking recourse in Starbäck's *Berättelser ur svenska historien* (*SV* 41: 478). Indeed Starbäck does dismiss these charges, albeit with a much more direct passage than the one Ollén quotes in his comments to *Folkungasagan*. First Starbäck states that if King Magnus ever bore the nickname "Smek" it was due to his "stora, måhända otillåtna och onaturliga kärlek till unga män, som han wisade, och hwarför han i synnerhet tadlades af S:t Birgitta." [great, perhaps forbidden and unnatural love of young men, which he showed, and which is why he in particular was criticized by St. Birgitta] (223), to which he adds "men äfwen denna grund för tillnamnet är otillförlitlig, enär Birgitta talade efter berättelser, som sannolikt kommo från konungens motståndare" [But even this basis for the surname is unreliable, since Birgitta spoke according to stories, which mostly likely came from the king's adversaries] (223). Of special interest in this citation is the way in which Strindberg selectively chose what suited him in the material and omitted what did not. In other words, he referred to Starbäck in order to disprove the king's homosexual tendencies while at the same time not granting credence to Starbäck's explanation of homosexuality as the origin of the nickname "Smek." In this way Strindberg doubly assures the reader that every aspect of the accusations leveled against the king lack credibility and cause.

One might rightfully ask why Strindberg, after having referred to the king as "usel" and "lättfärdig" in his earlier works, suddenly turns to his defense in 1899. Gunnar Ollén points out in his notes to *Folkungasagan* that Strindberg was not necessarily interested in portraying people based on historical fact, but rather that he in Magnus's fate saw a parallel to his own (*SV* 41: 481). Ollén's observation functions exceedingly well in the instance of Magnus's alleged homosexual inclinations parallelled with a similar experience in Strindberg's own life. One year prior to the publication of *Folkungasagan*, Strindberg depicts a scene in *Legender* where a character named Benoit in the French version and Martin in the Swedish version (a thinly veiled portrayal of Bengt Lidforss) finds himself accused of homosexual tendencies, a situation with which the narrator sympathizes. A closer examination of this story will reveal how Strindberg could sympathize in a similar fashion with the fate of King Magnus.

In *Legender* Benoit sits alone in the Grand Hotel's café in Oslo, whereby he allows a young man at an adjoining table to join him in conversation. After a while, Benoit felt suspicious of the young man, believing that he was not the person he claimed to be. While they talked, one of Benoit's Norwegian friends (a portrayal of Edvard Munch) appeared in front of his table, laughed, and pretended that the young man and Benoit had a relationship of unnatural intimacy. When the Norwegian assures them that they should not be embarrassed, that it is just a woman in disguise, the young man stands up and proves the opposite (by exposing himself according to a letter to Gustaf af Geijerstam written 15 November 1897). Later the young man asks Benoit to borrow money, which causes further embarrassment in that it would appear as if the young man was receiving payment for services rendered. In a conversation about this incident, Benoit complains to the narrator of the injustice in leveling such an immoral accusation upon him in front of a friend and an entire audience. The narrator answers from his own experience, telling of when a German author accused him of unnatural instincts. While the scene itself was inspired by an experience in Oslo involving Bengt Lidforss and Edvard Munch, the narrator's account of the German author stems from Strindberg's own life.

The German author was Otto de Joux. In his book on the third sex (i.e. homosexuals) entitled *Die Enterbten des Liebesglückes oder Das dritte Geschlect*, de Joux mentions Strindberg twice. Gunnar Brandell cites part of de Joux's work in his biography on Strindberg in which a German journalist describes Strindberg's appearance (Brandell II, 354). The real passage of interest concerning the accusation mentioned in *Legender* appears in the paragraph prior to the one Brandell mentions.[3] At first, de Joux describes an unnamed Scandinavian author who hates women more than Beelzebub. The way in which he makes monsters of even the most naïve women, portraying them as bizarre demons and scorning all things eternally feminine, can only be the product of a true Urning (i.e. homosexual) nature. He than claims that Strindberg is the same kind of author. According to de Joux, the less sophisticated man can not grasp the depths and significance of Strindberg's Uranian soul. Strindberg learned of de Joux's work through a friend, after which he wrote to his mother-in-law Marie Uhl in 1896:

> Yesterday my friend told me as a well-known fact that in the year 1893 a book from Vienna was published by one Paul Jeux (?) in which I was openly portrayed as a perverse Person. The book was unkown to me and I was asked to summon the author to court. Now after three years? And for what! If the thing was known, but when it has no basis, it belongs to my fate to bear it as well (Letter 3465).[4]

The problem of what Strindberg perceived as the unjust accusation of homosexual tendencies concerned Strindberg personally during the writing of *Folkungasagan* as evidenced in the portrayals of Strindberg in de Joux's book and Strindberg's letter. The reader should not find it surprising then that Strindberg rose to King Magnus's defence regarding his alleged love of men and in so doing revealed the accusation's implausibility and nefarious nature. Another tactic in debunking those same accusations was the systematic attack of the accuser's credibility, in the case of King Magnus, the accusation came from Heliga Birgitta. We have already briefly reviewed how Strindberg went about assailing her credibility in *Folkungasagan*, but the complete picture surfaces only when comparing the Heliga Birgitta in *Folkungasagan* with the Heliga Birgitta in *Hövdingaminnen*.

Karl Ulfsson och hans moder, the last of the stories in the first collection of *Hövdingaminnen*, also known as *Nya svenska öden*, takes the reader to Rome where Heliga Birgitta spent the last years of her life. Heliga Birgitta's son, Karl Ulfsson, scours the Italian countryside in search of his mother, hearing several unflattering details of her behavior along the way. The accounts he heard include details of how she was forced to move because she could not pay the rent. Then the reader is reminded that Saint Brigit of Ireland was the first to found a Brigittine order of nuns already in the 600's (long before the foundation of Heliga Birgitta's order in Sweden), and that both Katarina of Siena and Petrarca tried to convince the Pope in Avignon to return to Rome (making Heliga Birgitta's suggestions that the pope do the same simply one voice of many). To add to the damage done to Heliga Birgitta's reputation, a character named Doktor Laurentius goes off on a tirade after which not a trace of sainthood remains; all of her work means nothing for the country or humanity, her cloister is unnecessary as the country is already crawling with them, the style in her revelations comes from other sources such as the Bible, she did not even write most of them since she does not know Latin, and if she becomes canonized it will be due to her money and chivalry toward the other sex. Thus Birgitta's claims to fame lose credibility one by one, thereby discrediting most everything she says, including her chastising of the king for having the ugliest reputation in the kingdom.

The reason that Heliga Birgitta's son has attempted to find her, stems from his duty as the head of the family to dissuade her from further angering Sweden's king. Karl Ulfsson states that her writings have destroyed the king's good reputation and that he shall utilize every means necessary to stop her.

When Karl finally finds his mother, he confronts her by informing her that at home she is believed to be striving to win the crown for her relatives. They believe she is conspiring against King Magnus with her revelations in which she speaks of his ugly reputation, even though she is the only one who made that accusation (*SS* 43: 193).

In *Folkungasagan*, Heliga Birgitta does not deliver the lines which accuse the king of having an ugly reputation. Instead a crazy, possessed woman called "Den besatta", who later in the play turns out to be Bengt Algotsson's shunned wife, makes this claim indirectly. During the scene in which she uncovers many of the court's secrets, she states "Du ser endast kärlek och vänskap, trohet och dygder, där du sitter till halsen i falskhet och ondska, och där alla laster till och med Sodoms blomstra—" [You only see love and friendship, fidelity and virtues, where you are sitting up to your neck in deceit and evil, and where all vices, even Sodom's, bloom—] (*SV* 41: 35), where Sodom's vice refers of course to homosexuality. Ollén and other Strindberg scholars have maintained that the crazy woman is the incarnation of Strindberg's sister Anna. I posit that she can also represent another aspect of Heliga Birgitta's self on stage, a split image allowing the Heliga Birgitta Strindberg respected at times to exist side by side with the Heliga Birgitta he despised.

One reason for granting this position credence lies in the fact that it was indeed Heliga Birgitta who accused the King of dabbling in the sin of Sodom, not Algotsson's wife. Yet another is "Den besatta's" ability to look into the future and sense invisible beings in the room, which history recalls as some of Heliga Birgitta's own talents. It is therefore just as easy to imagine that Strindberg depicts Heliga Birgitta in *Varia* in 1899, rather than, or in conjunction with, "Den besatta" when he writes "en besatt kvinna stiger fram och profeterar straffdomar öfver land och förste."[5] The depiction of Heliga Birgitta in *Hövdingaminnen* strengthens the position that "Den besatta" is another incarnation of Heliga Birgitta's character. Karl Ulfsson's first encounter with his mother occurs on the street, when his horse and saddle suddenly become difficult to handle. The feeling that someone has bewitched him with an evil eye compels Karl and his company to avoid the witch begging at the church door. The witch turns out to be Heliga Birgitta herself, who at times speaks in riddles exactly like "Den besatta", can read others' thoughts, sense peoples' presence, and smell the outset of danger according to popular belief. "Den besatta" in *Folkungasagan* warns Magnus of the evil eye, is called crazy, an unclean spirit and a witch. All of these elements considered in combination suggest that Heliga Birgitta and "Den besatta" can act as double representations of the same individual. Of course another reason to support this interpretation can be drawn from Strindberg's frequent use of the technique of multiple-representations of individual characters in plays such as *Till Damaskus* and *Ett drömspel*.

Making a witch of Heliga Birgitta is the ultimate tactic in discrediting her claims, allowing Strindberg to wipe the slate of King Magnus's reputation clean in his own way. In doing so Strindberg redeems not only the King Magnus of recorded history, but also the King Magnus of the early Strindbergian pen. History revisited becomes history rewritten, offering both redemption and retribution through literature.

NOTES

[1] I would like to thank Jens Rydström for referring me to his as yet unpublished entry on Magnus Eriksson in Routledge´s forthcoming book *Who´s Who in Gay and Lesbian History*.

[2] Vi hafum nokot þæt sigia, þæt idra siæl varþa, oc sua sum skriptamal biþium vi idar þæt løna' och mæþ flerum orþum tilbyrlekum, æn idar þækkis. Æn sua ær sensus: 'I harin þe fulastu frægþ i rikeno och vtan, þæn kristin man ma haua: at i hafin hapt naturabland mæþ mannum. Os

þikkis þæt vara likt sanno, þy i ælskin mer men en Gud ælla idra egna siæl ælla idra egna husfru.

[3] The rare nature of de Joux's book makes quoting the passage Brandell leaves out a worthwhile endeavor. Brandell's quote picks up where the following quote leaves off:

"Er ist Skandinavier und aus demselben unseligen Stoffe gebildet, wie sein jüngerer Landsmann, ein hochbegabter, ungemein seltsamer Schriftsteller dessen Name einige Zeit hindurch auch in Deutschland auf aller Lippen war. Dieser Ausnahmsmensch hasst die Frau mehr als den Beelzebub und sagt ihr das Allerschlimmste nach. Seine Werke sind wie eine einzige, unendliche Anklage gegen das dumme, elende und verschlagene Geschöpf, das dem Manne den Verstand und alle kraft nimmt und gegen die Liebe, die entehrt und verthiert. Diese schmerzlich aufheulende Entrüstung, diese überplatonische Wut, welche selbst die einfältigsten Frauen zu ungeheuren und phantastischen Dämonen stilisirt und allem Ewigweiblichen eine schreckliche Bedeutung gibt, ist eben nur der Ausfluss einer echten Urningnatur. Ihre Ohnmacht und Verzweiflung, ihr Neid und ihre Disharmonie sind es, die diesen wilden hass gebären. Ein solcher Dichter ist auch August Strindberg. Seine Werke, so tief und gedankenreich sie auch sind, geben dem normalen Menschen kein Gefühl; Sie bleiben ihm fern und fremd und stum, weil ihre Stoffe immer aus einem gepeinigten Gehirn entspringen und durchaus unsinnlich sind. Der minder komplizirte Mann kann sich zu solchen ungewöhnlichen, bedeutenden Uranidenseelen in kein rechtes Verhältnis setzen; er merkt nur eine grosse und tiefe Natur, bleibt aber stets unbefridigt, verblüfft, ja beinahe betäubt, wie etwa beim Anhören einer grossartigen Dissonanzen-Apokalypse von Hektor Berlioz..." (de Joux 218-19).

[4] Vorgestern erzählte ein Freund mir als bekannte Thatsache dass im Jahr 1893 ein buch aus Wien erscheinen von einem Paul Jeux (?) in welchem ich als eine Perverse Person offen geschildert war. Das Buch war mir unbekannt und mann aufforderte mich den Verfasser vor Gericht zu laden. Jetzt nach drei Jahre? Und wozu! Wenn die Sache wahr gewesen, aber da es kein Grund hat, gehört es meinem Schicksal das auch zu tragen.

[5] See Gunnar Ollén's notes in *Samlade Verk* to *Folkungasagan*, page 475.

Works Cited and Consulted

Afzelius, Arv. Aug. *Svenska folkets sago-häfder, eller Fäderneslandets historia, fådan hon lefwat och till en del ännu lefwer i Sägner, Folksånger och andra Minnesmärken.* Stockholm: Zacharias Hæggströms förlag, 1865. (see pages 187–188)

Brandell, Gunnar. *Strindberg—Ett författarliv II.* Stockholm: Alba, 1985.

Fryxell, Anders. *Berättelser ur svenska historien (del 2).* Stockholm: P.A. Norstedt & Söners Förlag, 1900.

Hildebrand, Emil. *Sveriges historia (del 2).* Stockholm: Norstedt, 1903–1910.

Johnson, Walter. *Strindberg and the historical drama.* Seattle: University of Washington Press, 1963.

de Joux, Otto. *Die Enterbten des Liebesglücks oder Das dritte Geschecht. Ein Beitrag zur Seelenkunde.* Leipzig: Verlag von Max Spohr, 1897.

Lindström, Hans. *Strindberg och böckerna I och II.* Uppsala: Svenska Litteratursällskapet, 1977 and 1990 respectively.

Noreen, Erik. *Fornsvensk läsebok.* Lund: Gleerups, 1962.

Odhner, C.T. *Lärobok i Sveriges, Norges och Danmarks Historia För Skolans Högre Klasser.* Stockholm: P.A. Norstedt & Söner, 1880.

Ollén, Gunnar. *Strindbergs dramatik.* Kristianstad: Sveriges Radios Förlag, 1982.

Rydström, Jens. "Magnus Eriksson" to be published in the year 2000 in *Who's who in gay and lesbian history*. Routledge.

Starbäck, C. Georg. *Berättelser ur svenska historien. Fjerde delen. Medeltiden.* Stockholm: F. & G. Beijers förlag, 1876. (see page 207)

Strindberg, August. *August Strindbergs Brev.* Vols. 1–15 edited by Torsten Eklund. Stockholm: Bonniers, 1948–76. Vols. 16–20 edited by Björn Meidal. Stockholm: Bonniers, 1989–96.

Strindberg, August. *August Strindbergs Samlade Skrifter* [*SS*]. 55 vols. Edited by John Landquist. Stockholm: Bonnier, 1912–21.

Strindberg, August. *August Strindbergs Samlade Verk* [*SV*]. Edited by Lars Dahlbäck. Stockholm: Norstedts.

Film

Deep Staging and Light: Notes on Hasselblads and Georg af Klercker

Astrid Söderbergh Widding

> From the very first time I saw them, I was fascinated; this fantastic feeling of being at the source: this is cinematography and its beginnings. A time that has definitely passed beyond the horizon. . . . This, then, is what is absolutely primary: the image—which also has this remarkable quality. The images being still, the lighting, the costumes—the sets are so beautiful, staged in depth. If one wanted a close-up, if the acting was supposed to become more intimate, the actors had to approach the camera. And then the stories: elementary, wild, and completely childish!
>
> *Ingmar Bergman on the films by Georg af Klercker[1]*

In an article entitled *La Nouvelle Mission de Feuillade; or, What Was Mise-en-Scène*, David Bordwell notes that the traditional *découpage/tableau* duality in silent cinema has been recast by researchers such as Tom Gunning, Kristin Thompson, Richard Abel, or Ben Brewster. They attribute the rise of intrascene editing principally to filmmakers in the United States while positing that Russian, Scandinavian, and western European filmmakers elaborated an alternative system predicated upon depth staging. These scholars have suggested that while there are some continuities between the depth shot of the 1910s and the flat, distant, "primitive" *tableaux*, the differences may be significant enough to warrant considering the years 1909 to 1918 as not simply a prolongation of primitive cinema but instead a major transitional phase, perhaps even a distinctive stylistic period.[2] In the last chapter of his book on film style, *On Staging in Depth*, Bordwell returns to the same general idea, and examines among other things the deep staging during this transitional period in film history. He states that "the director of the 1910s could lay out the action in considerable depth. In a vast set (some were sixty feet front to back), the playing areas might be multiplied, with distinct zones activated in the course of a scene."[3]

In Sweden, this is true not least in the case of the Hasselblad company, which produced 29 fiction films between 1915 and 1918, all except one directed by Georg af Klercker. The Hasselblad studio at Otterhällan in Gothenburg, where most of the films were shot, was also more than sixty feet in length. The films produced by Hasselblads tend to rely on staging in depth rather than on cutting, and yet not without noteworthy exceptions. But in general, through a complex play with centering, creating a dynamic flux between stability and instability, af Klercker's films offer a clear example of deep staging cinematography. According to Bordwell, "in the absence of cutting-based stylistic norms, imaginative filmmakers took rough schemas from early film and developed them into a *mise en scène* displaying a range of emphasis, dynamism and refinement suitable to the new complexities of longer films."[4] Particularly interesting is the relation between this *mise-en-scène* and the lighting devices used in the films. In their discussion of pictorial staging in the theater, Ben Brewster and Lea Jacobs state that "Advances in lighting did thus make the depth of the stage more available as an arena of the action rather than a pictorial background."[5] In general, this seems to be true not only of theater, but also of cinema. However, and somewhat paradoxically, in the case of Hasselblads, the experiments of the company seem to point in the other direction, towards a lesser degree of lighting, whereas deep staging remains the central principle of spatial organization. Darkness also figures as a theme already in the title of several films from the company: *Nattens barn* (Children of the Night), *Mysteriet natten till den 25:e* (The Mystery of the Night before the 25th), *I mörkrets bojor* (In the Fetters of Darkness), *Nattliga toner* (Night Music). The critics regularly noted the sceneries in the Hasselblad productions, as in most Swedish films of the period, but their reception also offers a certain amount of commentaries to the lighting, one of the most noteworthy stylistic specificities in the company's productions, commentaries which are sometimes related to the discussion of the landscape. The Hasselblad films defy the idea, expressed among others by Fabrice Revault d'Allonnes, that a theatrical light should be characteristic of preclassical as well as classical cinema, and that it is only with modern cinema that more naturalistic lighting devices have become predominant. This is motivated by an empirical fact: that it was not until quite late in the history of cinema that the sensitivity of the raw film was sufficiently developed to allow a lesser degree of illumination, particularly if an image in depth is intended; today's 400 ASA should be compared to 10–20 ASA until the end of the 30s.[6] According to Revault d'Allonnes, the very possibility of depth in the image is directly dependent on a high degree of light. However, in spite of these limitations, af Klercker's films make little or no use of stage-like lighting. In their book *Theatre to Cinema*, Ben Brewster and Lea Jacobs offer a framework for such a re-reading of lighting in cinema, separately from the devices of the theater. They "reject the view that the history of the cinema is one of a steady emancipation from theatrical models. . . . Film lighting, for example, always owed more to still photography and painting than it did to theatrical lighting."[7]

Among the early light experiments is a scene from *Ministerpresidenten* (The Minister President), filmed during the summer 1916. Here, an entire sequence where the corrupt lawyer Alphonse Carrel commits burglary at the banker Leroux's place, in order to steal some documents from a safe deposit that would compromise the president and hero, Jean Bazard, is filmed with Carrel's flashlight as the only source of light. However, while this scene was successfully staged, little attention seems to have been paid to narrative continuity in the lighting particularly in the last reel. One critic of the period complained about this: "In one image, the electric light is on, in the next, occurring at about the same time, Our Lord's brilliant sunshine provides the lighting, and the next moment one reaches out for the electric again. Thus, it is not clear which time of the day is intended."[8]

I mörkrets bojor, released in 1917, contained a remarkable scene of burglary similar to the one in *Ministerpresidenten*. Here, a man having received a warning about the burglary sits in the dark in a living room waiting for the thieves. The maid switches off the ceiling lamp before leaving, and the man then goes on to switch off the lamp on his desk, so that the room becomes completely dark and his presence can barely be noticed. When the thieves arrive, however, one of them carries a flashlight which at his opening of the living room door is directed straight towards the camera. Deeds of darkness seem to inspire dark images. This preference for the darkened screen might be related to the critique of electric arc lighting on stage in the nineteenth century. Wolfgang Schivelbusch describes how the transformation of the stage by the new types of light carried new challenges and possibilities, but was met with skepticism in some respects: "The disproportionally strong and intense light ... washes out all the surrounding colors and because theatrical devices become crudely apparent in the bright light, it destroys all illusion."[9] Even though the problem with colors had disappeared in a cinematic context, the awareness of the artificiality of the set and the possibly destroyed illusion is equally true of the bright film image. Schivelbusch's claim that "darkness heightens individual perceptions, magnifying them many times" also motivates the Hasselblad option of privileging the shadows, which gives a particular intensity to the single source of light when it appears on the screen.[10]

Fången på Karlstens fästning (The Prisoner of Karlsten's Fortress) from 1916 is also especially interesting for its lighting, or rather its lack of lighting. The whole film seems to be constructed as a lighting experiment: the natural light dominates in the scenes from the fortress and its environment, where the interiors without exception take place in the shadows. As concerns electricity, only a small lamp on a table is used, together with a flashlight in one of the chasing scenes. In addition, there is a fire in another fortress interior. This makes the film as a whole rather dark. Still, there are several striking effects of light and perspectival play. When the heroine is locked up in the fortress by her kidnapper, she ends up in a cell where the light floods in from an opening to the left. The thickness of the walls distorts the perspective, so that the shadows of the window bars appear in fan-shape. In the already mentioned chase in the dark, there is a similar effect when the pursuers pass through a long corridor, where the flashlight creates light phenomena on the walls as well as strange perspective effects where space seems to be extended in all directions. Thus, no flatness of the image follows from the darkness. Similarly, in the scene where the heroine first arrives to the fortress, the image is structured in four different planes: a rather dark vault with an arch in the foreground, with another arch behind where the vault appears even darker, and then a third vault behind that, where there seems to be some kind of opening as the light floods in, and then finally a door in the background which is opened towards yet another dark space. The depth effect acquired in this way is quite amazing.

The lighting experiments in the Hasselblad productions with darkened images are thus often combined with a staging in depth in a way that seems to defy the conventions and even the technical requirements of the period. It is clear that Brewster's and Jacobs's statement which is generally true, that in Northern Europe as well as the East coast of the USA, the light for interiors involving deep staging (which were mostly studio-shot) was always boosted with arc or mercury-vapor lamps, is not valid in this particular case.[11]

Another example of deep staging combined with varying degrees of light is provided in *Mellan liv och död* (Between Life and Death), released in 1917, where a central location in the film is the medical laboratory, where doctor Brinck and his assistant Inger are working. All the shots from this laboratory are staged from one single perspective: a full shot with a working table with test tubes etc. in the foreground, and a skeleton in the very center of the image. Through variations in lighting, however, strikingly different effects are obtained within this identic framework. In the first reel, when Inger is working alone in the laboratory, the skeleton is brightly illuminated, which may seem strange. In the second reel, however, when Inger out of jealousy starts to prepare her poisoning of doctor Brinck's fiancée, the same bright light floods over the skeleton as an indication to the spectator that the work which is done in the laboratory is, indeed, mortal. Then suddenly, as if struck by an insight, Inger switches off the light totally, and then again switches on a small lamp directly above the working table. Later in the same reel, the skeleton remains in the shadows or is hidden by the actors. In the third reel, however, when doctor Brinck returns to the laboratory after a nightmare where his fiancée is lying on *lit de parade*, the skeleton is brightly lit, once again an efficient memento as to mortality. In the last part of the reel, when Inger turns out to be in the laboratory again, the skeleton is no longer brightly illuminated but it still remains perfectly visible in the background.

The differing degrees of lighting during the different parts of the story also seem to confirm that the Hasselblad lighting strategies were based not only upon the direct narrative effects that could be gained, as in the nocturnal burglary scenes where the sparse lighting clearly contributes to the overall atmosphere of suspense and threat, but that they were also used on the intradiegetic level, to emphasize certain thematic aspects of the narrative. In the skeleton scenes, lighting creates a dimension in the narration that comes close to the metaphorical.

This also clearly occurs in another scene from *I mörkrets bojor*, where Elinor Petipon, falsely accused of the murder of her husband and having lost all memories of the fatal night, sits in her prison cell in the dark. The prison chaplain and his son enters the cell, and suddenly there is a flood of light through the window, accompanied by the intertitle "I also had a son once." However, the light disappears again. For a moment, the light of memory seems to have dissipated the shadows of the past, but it only lasts for a few seconds. Then, again, darkness returns to the cell as well as to Elinor's mind.

A lost film from 1917, *Brottmålsdomaren* (The Judge), also seems to have contained interesting examples of nocturnal imagery with sparse lighting. One critic notes that "In the fatal scene where the wrongfully convicted goes for a walk through the shadows after his nocturnal love meeting, the lighting effects are especially striking, and the images from the coast are beautiful," which points in the same direction as the metaphoric light described above.[12] Some preserved production stills confirm the critic's impression.

Nattliga toner, released in 1918, contains a sequence which combines deep staging with the play of light and shadows. Baron von Meislingen, the villain, is awakened in his bed by a sudden remorse for having murdered the poet Peter Longhair in order to steal his magnum opus. After having lit the small lamp on the bedside table, he also switches on the ceiling light. He then leaves his bed, opens the door and enters the next room. When the camera changes position, it takes place far away from Meislingen, in a foreground that reveals two separate rooms in a suite. He then switches on the light in the room in the middle, the bedroom still being visible in the background plane of the image, and moves towards the foreground. Here, he pushes away a piece of drapery and then finally turns on the light in the third room where the camera is placed. After having poured a few glasses of wine and emptied them, he returns in the same direction, towards his bedroom, the camera remaining in the foreground plane of the image and watching his recession and his switching off of the four lights, one after the other. And the camera keeps its position during the whole sequence, even though this means that only Meislingen's feet remain visible when he returns to bed. The bedroom door, that was closed when he left his bed, now remains open. The deep staging effect thus obtained is impressive, even when the lights are put out and the suite of rooms are in the shadow, a scene probably filmed in daytime when the glass of the studio allowed a certain amount of light to pass through, even with the curtains drawn.

As was roughly outlined above, a double discourse is articulated in the critic's reception of the Hasselblad films, where nature is sometimes contrasted with the electric—as in *Brottmålsdomaren*, with darkness against light—and sometimes brought together with it, both on the side of light. Through the incessant contrasts between light and shadows, nature takes part in the visual doubleness created in the images, which also has to do with the general ambivalence towards modernity expressed both through the films themselves and their reception, which I try to show in a larger study on af Klercker.[13] The effects are paradoxical. Whereas the electric could be associated with modernity, with the New World, the shadows might seem to belong to the Old World. But the bright floods of light, that may be found in the Hasselblad films together with the obscure images, are on the contrary often associated with theatrical settings, and thus with the old aristocratic society and their drawing rooms overburdened with ornaments, whereas the dark urban settings, nocturnal decadence and crimes with their natural lighting for better and for worse seem to belong to modern society. Thus, there is a clear duality in the films, but with the frequent stagings in depth lacking lighting, they also bridge this gap between the theatrical and the modern.

NOTES

[1] Ingmar Bergman in an interview by Jannike Åhlund, in *Chaplin* 2 (1992): 30 f.

[2] David Bordwell in *The Velvet Light Trap* 37 (Spring 1996): 10.

[3] Bordwell, *On The History of Film Style* (Cambridge, Massachusetts/London: Harvard University Press, 1997), 179.

[4] Ibid., 198.

[5] Ben Brewster and Lea Jacobs, *Theatre to Cinema, Stage*

Pictorialism and the Early Feature Film (Oxford/New York: Oxford University Press), 150 f.

[6] Fabrice Revault d'Allonnes, *La lumière au cinéma* (Paris: Éditions Cahiers du cinéma, 1991), 22 f.

[7] Brewster and Jacobs, 214.

[8] *Nya Dagligt Allehanda* 1916–09–20.

[9] Wolfgang Schivelbusch [1988], *Disenchanted Night, The Industrialization of Light in the Nineteenth Century* (Berkeley/Los Angeles/London: University of California Press, 1995), 199, 202.

[10] Ibid., 221.

[11] Brewster and Jacobs, 186.

[12] *Dagens Nyheter* 1917–10–16.

[13] Astrid Söderbergh Widding, *Stumfilm i brytningstid, Stil och berättande i Georg af Klerckers filmer* (Stockholm: Aura förlag, 1998).

Maternal Gesture and Photography in Victor Sjöström's *Ingeborg Holm*

Mark B. Sandberg

Early in Victor Sjöström's 1913 film, *Ingeborg Holm*, the mother Ingeborg washes her youngest child. The unstudied, even ordinary gesture takes place in the foreground of the shot's playing space, in the intimate space of the child's bedroom. The movement is fresh and natural, of a piece with the opening sequence's unassuming scenes from the idyllic family outing, the meal together at home, and preparations for bed. The transparent camera observes each of the scenes in a single shot from a fixed point without intervention, giving each gesture continuity and duration in space and time. The film's famous reliance on deep-staging reinforces this sense that the depicted world is whole.[1]

The narrative events of the film waste little time in disturbing this sense of stability with a relentless trajectory of loss. A tragic chain of circumstances strips Ingeborg of every token of her identity as wife and mother: her husband dies of a stroke, his new grocery business fails without his guidance, Ingeborg falls ill and cannot work, the family declares bankruptcy and ends up at the poorhouse, and the children are fostered out to different mothers in the countryside one by one. Forlorn, Ingeborg Holm loses her sanity as well, ending up in the poorhouse asylum. During her free-fall from middle-class mother to childless pauper, simple gestures like those of the opening scenes—such as walking home together from the garden, or the slicing of bread for dinner, or the matter-of-fact washing of the child—come under increasing pressure. Actions that looked natural lose their meaningful context, and unmarked gestures become marked by displacement. By the end of the tragic course of events, Ingeborg can be seen in the asylum cradling not a child, but a flat wooden board, showing her "baby" to anyone who will look. What once was a mothering gesture is now one of the extravagant gestures of the insane.

It will be the assumption of this essay that gesture does more than "carry" the story in *Ingeborg Holm*. Within the self-imposed limits of a realistic (even if extraordinarily merciless and relentless) narrative, Sjöström's film explores different modes of performance by creating a story that is not only about a woman who loses her family and class standing, but her grounding in a gestural system as well. Ingeborg is a woman who loses the ability to move naturally and authentically in her surroundings. As her losses pile up, she finds it increasingly difficult to simply "be" a mother: she is left to "act" one instead, through maternal gestures that persist beyond their relevant context. Although the film on the most obvious level is about saving Ingeborg's sanity, the staging of that rescue so insistently in terms of competing gestural systems gives *Ingeborg Holm* special resonance with shifts in film acting in the early 1910s, more particularly with naturalist acting's interest in contextualized gesture. By identifying *context* with *origin*, and naturalist gesture with the bond between mother and child, Sjöström's film creates a powerful argument for naturalist aesthetics that gave film a new cultural standing.[2]

Research into silent-film acting suggests why a film made in 1913, especially one with *Ingeborg Holm*'s commitment to deep-staging and social realism, might convey a special awareness of gesture. A useful starting point is Roberta Pearson's examination of acting style which places a transition from "histrionic" to "verisimilar" codes in the Griffith Biograph films around the year 1912. Histrionic acting styles for Pearson are those that rely on a limited repertoire of theatrical gestures. Like those classified by Delsarte, these are gestures that can be isolated, held, and even repeated emphatically in an overtly performative style. Verisimilar effects are by contrast embedded in a narrative flow and motivated by milieu. If histrionic style is "digital" in its reliance on conceptually discrete movement units that can be frozen for effect, Pearson argues, verisimilar style is "analogic" in its conception of movement as continuous and unmarked.[3]

Ben Brewster and Lea Jacobs have pursued similar questions with admirable thoroughness in their recent book *Theatre to Cinema*, and present a comparative account of "pictorialism" on the nineteenth-century stage and in the early feature film. The wealth of detail they provide encourages a more nuanced conceptualization within early film history of binarisms like spectacle/narrative, melodrama/naturalism, as well as Pearson's conceptual pair histrionic/verisimilar.[4] Tracing concepts like "situation," "tableau," and "picture" through their varied uses in nineteenth-century theater and silent film, Brewster and Jacobs show that in the context of international style, there are no clear wide-scale, abrupt transitions in the 1910s (on the one hand, toward continuity editing, or on the other, away from the tableau), but instead an experimentation with what turn out to be very complex interrelationships between these various means of dramatic expressivity and emphasis. A particularly important contribution of their study is the recognition that a strong pictorial mode persisted well into the feature films of the 1910s, especially in Europe.[5]

A framework like that proposed by Brewster and Jacobs is especially helpful in this particular case, since *Ingeborg Holm*, like many other films in the early 1910s, was a stage play before it was a film. A play of the same title had premiered on Swedish stages six years earlier in 1907, written by Nils Krok, an educator and playwright in southwest Sweden who for a time was on the board of directors at the Helsingborg poorhouse. His experiences there led to his polemical call for reform of poorhouse welfare laws, couched in the drama of the fictional character Ingeborg Holm's fate in that system. Complicating the relationship between the play and film is the fact that Sjöström himself had directed a stage version of Krok's play in 1908, four years before he became a film director. Krok in turn reworked the script for film himself, and in 1913 when Sjöström decided to take it on as a film project (in order to give lead actress Hilde Borgström a project to fill out the remaining time on her contract), he rewrote the script again.[6] The particular facts of this adaptation suggest that the resulting film might reveal a particular self-consciousness about acting style.

Energy Conservation and Class

From a current retrospective view, it is perhaps difficult to appreciate the hard-won achievement represented by the "natural" gestures in the opening domestic scenes of *Ingeborg Holm* (fig. 1). Experimental naturalist theaters, such as André Antoine's Théâtre Libre in Paris, had already in the late 1880s discovered the difficult paradoxes involved in creating a natural-seeming dramaturgical system that was nevertheless legible to an audience.[7] At that time, an action as mundane as characters eating a meal on stage could carry quite a charge for a theater audience unused to seeing actions from everyday life. In its use of everyday space, action, speech and gesture, the naturalist theater constantly tested the balance between ordinariness and legibility by attempting to eliminate all of the traces of direct address while still preserving the audience's access to the depicted world.

The encounter between this theatrical tradition and film complicated matters further. As in other countries, the actors in early Danish and Swedish film were borrowed from the theater during its summer off-season, and in Scandinavia, that meant that early film acting overlapped crucially with the developing naturalist theater tradition. Naturalist drama's influence on stage practice was not immediate, of course; although Ibsen's and Strindberg's dramas made an immediate literary splash

Fig. 1. "Random" composition, "everyday" gesture from the opening family scenes of *Ingeborg Holm*. (16 mm frame enlargement)

throughout Europe, it took several years before directing, acting, and stage space changed to accommodate the principles of naturalist performance implicit in those plays (such as nuanced, contextualized gestures proceeding from inside a character, presented without acknowledging the presence of an audience). But by the time film production began in earnest, naturalism had become the dominant mode of theatrical performance in Scandinavia, and the training both actors and directors received at that time was largely in the naturalist style.

Such was the case with Gustav "Muck" Linden, the main director at Stockholm's *Dramaten*, when he was hired by Svenska Bio's producer Charles Magnusson to direct films in the summer of 1910. As film historian Bengt Idestam-Almquist relates, Linden had been trained by the great naturalist director Otto Brahm in Vienna and Berlin, and he brought to this film project all of his experience with and assumptions about naturalist staging. Like many newcomers to film, though, he underestimated the difficulty of adapting to the new medium, especially to the idea of the camera: could it simply record a theater performance without adjustments? According to eyewitnesses, Linden was surprised to learn that it could not, and panicked once the filming started. When confronted by the problem of wordless drama, he started shouting on the set, "Stora gester! Stora gester!" [Grand gestures! Grand gestures!], abandoning his naturalist training in order to compensate for the silence of the new medium.[8] As Linden himself recalled in an interview from 1930, "Tänk efter själv, hur det måste kännas för en teaterregissör, att plötsligt stå som ledare av en massa folk som inte hade något att säga annat än med gester och grimaser—jag minnes än i dag att jag fann denna begränsning av deras uttrycksmöjligheter högst fatal" [Just think how it must feel for a theater director to stand suddenly as leader of a bunch of people who didn't have anything to say except with gestures and grimaces—I remember to this day that I found this limitation on their possibilities of expression to be most disastrous].[9]

The accomplished realism of the acting in *Ingeborg Holm*, which was of course still faced with the same limitations of silence, seems all the more remarkable in comparison, since experiences like Linden's make clear that the creation of natural-looking gesture in front of a camera was an acquired skill, one that required actors to rein in compensatory reactions and develop a confidence in the eventual visibility of subtle movement. Even the charming, unaffected acting style of the three children would have required training in blocking (so important to picture composition in Sjöström's film, as David Bordwell has pointed out)[10] and instructions not to interact with the camera. One contemporary review hints indirectly at the paradox of the children's "natural" gesture producing aesthetic effects: "Och så äro ett par små aktörer så fulla av barnens naturliga behag och förmåga att plastiskt och mimiskt uttrycka känslor—ett par verkliga små premiäraktörer" [And then there are a couple of small actors so full of children's natural charm and ability to express emotions gracefully and mimically—a couple of real little opening-night actors].[11] Jan

Olsson has suggested an important thematic aim of especially the youngest child's visual prominence throughout the first part of the film—depicting vulnerability in order to establish the stakes for the tragic losses—but equally relevant is the way the use of children implies that all of the depicted gesture in these first scenes is as unstudied as we assume theirs to be.[12] When this same review claims, "Regien är också bäst där den skildrar familjeinteriörerna" [The directing is also best when it depicts the family interiors], it shows that the naturalism of the opening scenes set a the standard for the rest of the film.

Perhaps due to the strong impression of these first scenes, *Ingeborg Holm* is often regarded as a model film of social realism and naturalist style. A close look at other parts of the film, however, shows that there are in fact a variety of gestural modalities that compete for attention, especially after Ingeborg's losses start piling up. It is as if "natural" gesture is dislodged, even collapses as a system, when subjected to narrative pressure. In return, bits and pieces of other gestural systems make cameo appearances as the film progresses inexorably to its conclusion.

Pantomime, for instance, does not usually come to mind in connection with Sjöström's film, but when Ingeborg's nighttime escape over the poorhouse fence is discovered, we get a scene marked by just such gestural excess. In the scene, two workers approach the woodpile to gather wood and accidentally find the shawl Ingeborg has dropped on her way over the fence. They point off-frame left to her probable escape route, then gesture with the shawl, first to each other, then to the poorhouse director who enters the frame from the right. One of the workers then points back off-frame left to show the director, who in turn points at the place they found the shawl, only to be joined in the same gesture by the other worker. The other then points back at the poorhouse, as does the director, upon which the old woman from the poorhouse, Ingeborg's fellow inmate, joins the group from off-frame right. She takes the shawl, gestures with it gleefully, after which the director again points at the escape route off-frame left. The woman then joins in for yet another round of pointing—off-left, back at the shawl, off-left again.

If my account here belabors the act of monstration in this scene, it is because the scene's own insistent repetition foregrounds the gesture to an unusual degree for a "naturalist" film. One might simply account for this contrast in gestural styles by calling it evidence of uneven development, typical of a transitional phase in which the supporting players are not up to the verisimilar playing style established by the principals, as Pearson suggests was sometimes the case with the Biograph films. But I will argue that there is more going on here, that the shift to a more overt acting style here is tied narratively to the shift of milieu to the lower-classes in the poorhouse. In the poorhouse, histrionic style is the norm, and it contrasts sharply with the gestural system Ingeborg brings with her there.

When she first enters the space of the waiting room, for instance, she conveys middle-class propriety with careful, controlled movement into a space filled with the caricatured movement of the teeming lower classes. Arrayed in the film's characteristic deep-staging diagonally along a bench, the poorhouse's "rightful" inhabitants spit, push, shove, rock constantly back and forth, tussle with the uniformed guard. At the instant Ingeborg appears in the doorway, however, they form what is quite nearly a true theatrical tableau of surprise to see a representative of the middle class at the poorhouse. They pause long enough to watch her enter, returning to their chaotic bustle only after Ingeborg sits down uncomfortably on the bench.

The gestural contrast of the waiting room continues throughout the interior scenes from the poorhouse. Early on, one of Ingeborg's fellow workers offers her a swig from her hidden hipflask while Ingeborg goes about her work duties. Ingeborg's shocked, indignant response and willful maintenance of her poise, back turned, elicits both ridicule and abuse from the old woman, who runs through a variety of stock gestures: laughing, pointing, spitting, shaking her fist (fig. 2). An extra resonance of this scene comes when one realizes that Ingeborg's activity at the sink here is a continuation of the household gestures from the early scenes, as is the gentle mothering help she gives to the infirm old man at the start of this scene. She is in other words holding on to her gestural system—and her class identity as a middle-class mother—amidst the background noise of lower-class gesture. Ingeborg's determined maintenance of poise and posture in this context is perhaps best seen as an attempt to conserve gestural energy in a place where there is too much of it.

Opposed to the excess and variety of movement in general in the poorhouse are those moments of near-stasis when the composition approaches the status of a tableau, a contrast hinted at in the waiting room scene just described. In the nineteenth-century theater, the idea of tableau had necessary components of both prolonged stasis and compositional unity, a pictorial sensibility that

Fig. 2. Gestural contrast at the poorhouse. (16 mm frame enlargement)

Brewster and Jacobs see as the crucial link between nineteenth-century theater and cinema in the 1910s. As they point out, moments of true tableau are rare in feature films, but pictorial moments that underscore important dramatic events are quite common, especially in the European cinema of the time. When narratively motivated, pictorial moments can come quite close to the idea of tableau while remaining integrated in the dramatic flow of a film.[13]

Ingeborg Holm's deathbed scene early on certainly qualifies as such a moment, with the added contrast of oblivious background activity giving it a cruel twist, but also emphasizing the pictorial aspects of the wife and her dying husband in the foreground.[14] Several other moments in Sjöström's film would qualify as well. One is when the children are reunited with their mother after they are first brought to the poorhouse before being fostered out to their new homes (fig. 3). This shot shows the slight moment of pause when Ingeborg's face, framed carefully by the heads of all three children, turns upwards. The moment of recognizable composition we have here contrasts interestingly with the everyday sense one gets from the opening scenes, even taking into account the somewhat random isolation of pose in frame enlargements such as in figure 1.

Another clearly motivated pictorial moment occurs near the end of the film when Ingeborg's mind snaps. The scene depicts the foster mothers returning their charges to the poorhouse for check-ups, and among them is Ingeborg's youngest, who seems to be fine except for the fact that he no longer remembers her as his mother. She tries desperately to please him by making a toy doll out of her apron, but to no avail. After this, "lidandets sista droppe" [the last dregs of suffering], Ingeborg breaks out in insane laughter (fig. 4). The incessant movement of the other figures behind her, which has been staged once again at an angle in depth, suddenly ceases; all eyes are on her. On stage, this would indeed be a *coup-de-théâtre*, easily imaginable as a dramatic cur-

Maternal Gesture and Photography   141

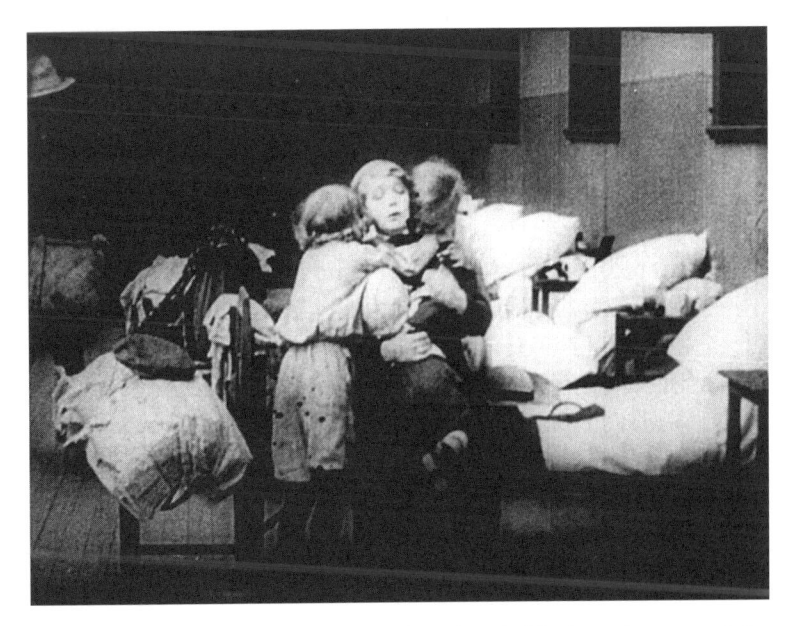

Fig. 3. Pictorial moment staves off the inevitable fostering out of the children. (16 mm frame enlargement)

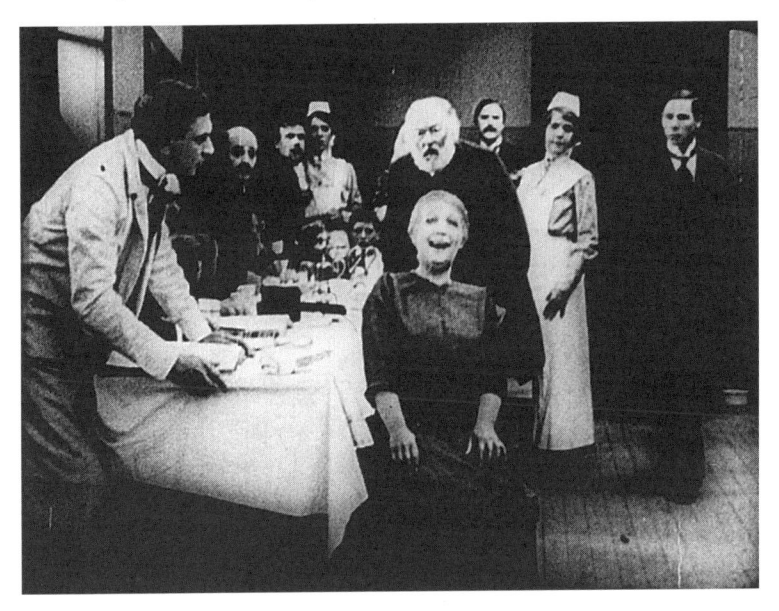

Fig. 4. A tableau motivated by Ingeborg's breakdown. (16 mm frame enlargement)

tain closer. But here it is a momentary pause only, justified only by the extreme surprise and lasting only as long as might reasonably be expected given the narrative situation. In the nineteenth-century theater, a frozen pose could last for minutes, straining the physical strength of actors and actresses. The goal of this exertion is usually assumed to be the achievement of an ordered compositional unity and beauty. But in deadline narratives (plays or films with unusually fraught forward motion), the tableau might also be seen as a stalling technique. In *Ingeborg Holm*, that is certainly the effect; if anything, the pictorial moments here seem like moments of reprieve. Since Sjöström's film relies so pointedly on a model of narrative entropy, forward motion necessarily entails loss. Each of the film's pictorial moments correspondingly serves to conserve "natural" gestural energy and resist its dissolution among the excessive gestures of the poor and the insane.

Photograph and tableau

A turn to contemporary writing about the pose in photography suggests that there may have been a more general currency to this idea of "rest" and the photograph. In Sweden's main journal of amateur photography, an essay from 1898 entitled *Den fotografiska posen* lays out a "fundamental theory" of pose that proposes the following laws of portrait photography:

> Hvarje pose får aldrig framställa ett moment af rörelse utan blott ett moment af hvila såsom resultat af en föregående rörelse. . . .
> Blott de ställningar äro vackra, som hafva framgått ur vackra rörelser.
> Blott de rörelser äro vackra, genom hvilka resultatet uppnås genom den minsta möjliga muskelansträngning af en normalt utvecklad människa.

[Each pose should never depict a moment of movement, but only a moment of rest resulting from a previous movement. . . . The only attitudes that are beautiful are those that have proceeded from beautiful movements. The only movements that are beautiful are those in which the result is achieved through the least possible muscle strain of a normally developed person.][15]

Since the photograph required only an instant of stasis, it could be taken from a stream of movement as a slight moment of relaxation, still bearing marks of preceding movement and hinting at movement to follow; in short, part of a verisimilar flow of movement. Unlike the theatrical tableau, it could avoid the idea of motion-defying exertion because its duration was that of the briefest pause. As a recording, however, the photograph could preserve the moment of rest in perpetuity, in an image frozen yet seemingly natural.

The paradoxical quality of the photograph when perceived in this way is helpful in an analysis of the portrait photograph hovering over the narrative developments in *Ingeborg Holm*. As Ingeborg sorrowfully packs her older son's belongings at the poorhouse the night before he is fostered out to his new home, she pauses and includes a photograph of herself, inscribed in the lower right with the words, "Till Erik, från Mor" [To Erik, from Mother].[16] Her pose is proper, with a respectable expression and erect bearing, and the inscription underscores its iconic value as a representation of motherhood (fig. 5).[17] The camera lingers on this photograph in point-of-view while Ingeborg considers placing it in Erik's box as a reminder of her and the life he is about to leave behind. The visual memory-trace of that photograph thus remains not only with Erik, but with the spectator during the ensuing events: the fostering out of the children, Ingeborg's escape to see her sick daughter, her recapture, and her eventual descent into insanity, all of which mark con-

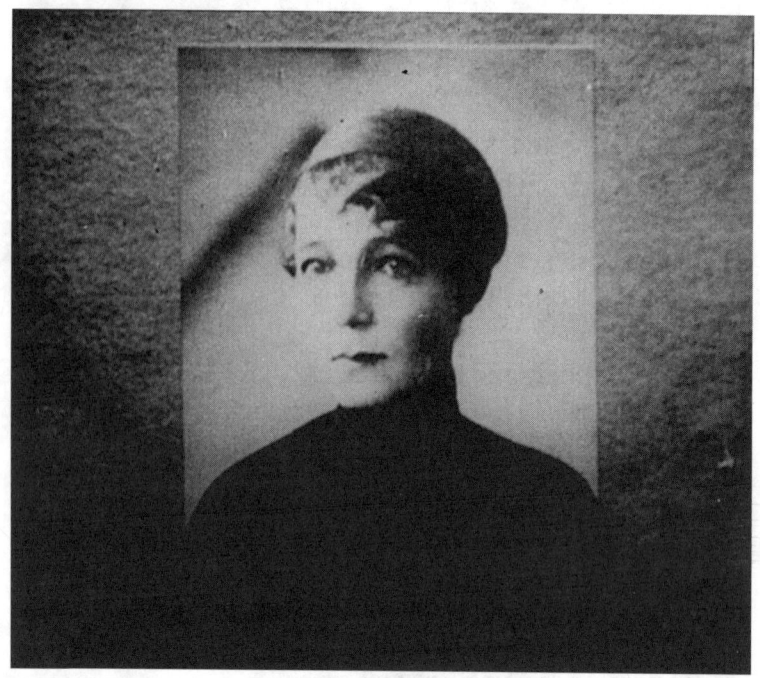

Fig. 5. The crucial photograph: Ingeborg as mother. (16 mm frame enlargement)

siderable narrative distance from the photographed mother and the film's point of origin. Late in the film, we see the photograph again in an identical point-of-view shot when Erik, now a sailor fifteen years later, pulls out the photograph and looks at it fondly as he returns to port. This visual reminder of the earlier moment sets up the shock of the following scene when Ingeborg wanders in greatly changed, white-haired and institutionally clothed, cradling a wooden board instead of a baby.

But there is also more going on here. The photograph not only helps measure the disparity between the lost iconic mother and the insane woman before us, but helps overcome it within the narrative as well. Devastated at the sight of his mother absorbed in her absurd cradling gesture, Erik forces her to look at the photograph she had given him years earlier (fig. 6). As she looks back and forth between photo of her former self and her grown son Erik, she recognizes in it and in him (or rather in the relation between the two of them) her initial identity as a mother. The board drops from her hands, and the mother touches her son's cheek, first hesitatingly, then lovingly as the displaced cradling gesture once again finds an appropriate context (fig. 7). Ingeborg has recovered, and true gesture—in the naturalist style—has returned as well.

The photograph, then, turns out to be the narrative pivot, the kind of outside help the closed system of this narrative needs in order to recover the inexorable losses of the main character. By setting up the strictly entropic trajectory, the film leaves open only two possible narrative solutions: stop the forward motion or force a return to a moment before the losses began. The appeal to the photograph accomplishes both; taken from a moment of fullness, when Ingeborg's identity seems most natural and given, it is first shown to us just prior to her fall into the world of the poor. When Erik shows her the photograph at the end, then, he is in effect returning her and us to the middle of the film. Another way of saying this, of course, is that the photograph performs a flashback function, albeit without the moving image, embedded narrative, or interiority of subjective vision usually associated with that narrative device in later film. But the still photograph does not "flash back" in order to explain the present state of affairs, but to contradict and cancel them out. Ingeborg is not *really* the crazy woman in white, the photograph proves; she has been the mother in the portrait all the time.

The stakes of the saving photograph increase, interestingly, when one discovers that it was not in Krok's stage version of *Ingeborg Holm* at all, but was one of several adjustments made to the story in the film adaptation.[18] The stage version concentrates on a tendentious exposure of abuse in the welfare system in which the character Ingeborg Holm is merely the victim; her case is more reported and discussed than depicted. Although she loses her reason in the stage version as well, she recovers it

146 Stage and Screen

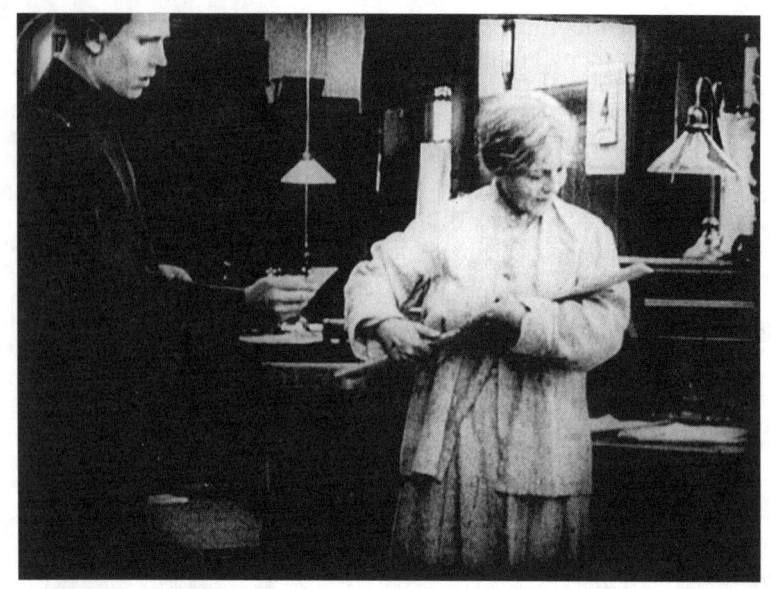

Fig. 6. Phototherapy: Erik shows Ingeborg the photograph. (16 mm frame enlargement)

Fig. 7. Photograph redeems gesture. (16 mm frame enlargement)

only after much resistance in a drawn-out conversation, and even then only because of the surprise re-appearance of her youngest child waiting outside. A photograph on stage would not be legible enough to perform the rescue, of course, since there it cannot be framed in close-up or point of view shot, but in film it can. The photograph in Sjöström's film does not merely perform the recovery more economically, it also does so by enlisting the aid of film's most basic medium, namely its photography.

Alan Trachtenberg has brought up this notion of meta-photography in early film by reminding that

> ... cinema consists of a linear sequence of *still* photographic images, each differing in slight degree from the next and together creating the illusion of motion. Movement out of stillness is the paradoxical fact of the medium. Moreover the illusion of motion succeeds because the individual photograph becomes invisible. The viewer cannot single out a particular still—a paradoxical and a well-concealed fact.[19]

But if the viewer cannot single out an image, the film itself can, at least if it incorporates a still photo as an object in the narrative. Any point-of-view shot of a photograph thus brings out the hidden still image that is the premise for all moving images. The conceptual layers of such a point-of-view shot are rich; although the strip of film is moving, the image does not appear to do so, but it can only remain still on screen by moving rapidly through the projector in multiple exact copies.

When early film isolates a still photograph as a significant visual object, Trachtenberg continues, it does so most often in order to arbitrate identity, with the portrait being the most common format. In cases of hidden or masked identity, the still photograph is often given the visual authority to sort things out, to cut through the moving image's deceptive possibilities by returning to a level of static objectivity and visual stability.[20] The addition of motion to the still photograph, these meta-photographic moments seem to indicate, opens the possibility for false identity, so that only by returning to the still photograph can identity be secured. (There is of course nothing necessary about this arrangement; it is easy to imagine a different scenario in which the motion picture's superior ability to capture characteristic individual gesture over time might be seen as more secure than the single pose of a still photograph.)[21]

The point to emphasize is that out of many possible characteristics of a photograph that *could* be foregrounded in a film—its infinite reproducibility, its drift in time and space, its excision from a larger visual context, the irretrievability of the depicted moment—early narrative silent film seems most inclined to inflect the still image with effects of presence and authority. It is easy to imagine other potential uses and meanings of Ingeborg's photograph, for example, simply by imagining it not as a singular, saving portrait, but as the multiple, identical copies that are in reality traveling through the projector in order to make the effect of stasis possible, or more whimsically, imagining it to be a portrait of an Ingeborg-impersonator, or perhaps a pathos-filled, ironic pose contradicting the reality of a sordid family life. Instead, Sjöström's film presents the photograph as an especially trustworthy, even therapeutic piece of evidence: the mother's signature in the lower right gives it a textual anchor, and the narrative situation when it is first shown frames its meaning significantly for the audience.

Another way of describing this "shoring up" of the still photograph is to see it as an effect of fetishization. This is relevant on the most obvious level: the photograph's power to heal Ingeborg flows crucially from the fact that it has apparently been carried for fifteen years in Erik's pocket. But there are more subtle fetishistic aspects to the use of the photography in *Ingeborg Holm*. For instance, it has the power to return Ingeborg to the moment *just prior* to her fall, a moment that achieves a retrospective fullness far greater than any meaning it has originally had. At first sight, the photograph seems quite ordinary after all, as unmarked as the "everyday" quality of the opening scenes; it is only after the narrative of loss is set in motion that the portrait starts to accrue both its concentrated meaning as Ingeborg's true identity and its power to save.

The arresting function of the stage tableau also seems relevant here, if only to underscore the particular fetishistic potential of the photograph. The frozen moments of stage tableaux have often been assumed to be anti-narrative in effect, but as Brewster and Jacobs point out, they can also be seen as a means of dramatic emphasis and narrative dilation.[22] In this view, the stage tableau slows the narrative flow in order to provide a gathered moment of supporting pictorial commentary. Some of the pictorial moments elsewhere in *Ingeborg Holm* certainly have that effect, and are closely tied to theatrical models. But a different case can be made for the photograph, largely because the idea of recording allows it to contradict the later unfolding of events with a persistent indexical image of a previous moment. It allows for a convincing effect of return for both Ingeborg and spectator, because as a recording it can be repeated exactly as it first appeared when it resurfaces late in the film.

This observation—that the photograph cancels out the forward motion of the last half of the film—has implications for the film's gestural systems as well. The portrait, that is, helps correct the gestural excess of the poorhouse by returning Ingeborg to natural, contextualized gesture of the film's opening, where we see the "real" Ingeborg instead of the later "theatrical" one. Nowhere is this more evident than in the asylum scene, with its extreme foregrounding of performative, decontextualized gesture. When she is brought into the asylum for the first time, her cradling gesture is placed in simple series with all of the other gestures of the insane (fig. 8). In the room is a megalomaniac, wearing a crown and commanding imaginary subjects, a woman pacing nervously back and forth like a caged animal, another compulsively raveling and unraveling an invisible ball of string, and another in the foreground trying to saw through the bedpost with her hand. Each of these gestures is recognizable, but repetitive and invariable. They lack not intelligibility, but meaningful trajectory and context.

The asylum gestures could be called histrionic in several important senses. They are gestures detached from meaningful milieu and performed in isolation. They are highly legible, stock gestures taken from the lexicon of the insane, written entirely on the surface of the body, seemingly unguided by any interiority. The gestures of the insane are "digital" in their extreme isolation and framing: each player repeats the same gesture again and again, much as a virtuoso actress might do with a particularly successful gesture on the nineteenth-century stage. The placement of

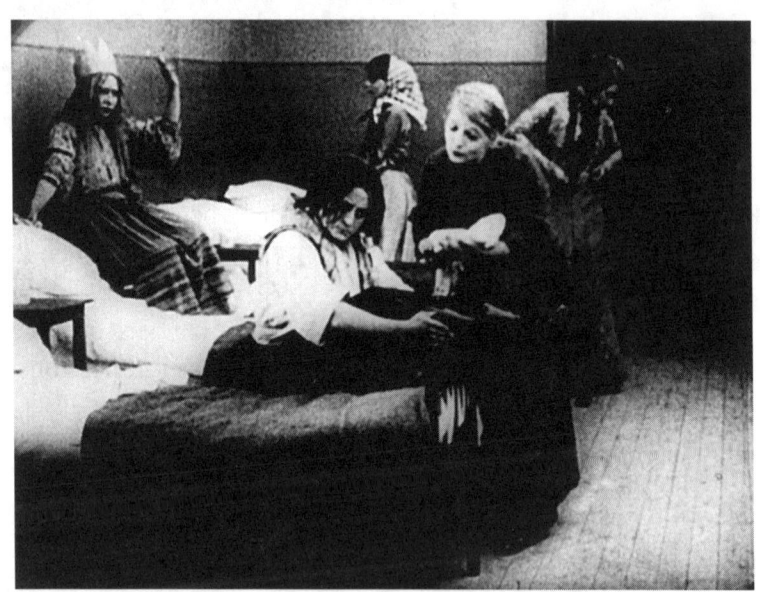

Fig. 8. Gestures of the insane. (16 mm frame enlargement)

Ingeborg's cradling motion in series with these other gestures makes clear that for realistic gesture, context is everything—without it, even the most natural maternal gestures can seem insane. The film plays out on the narrative level the naturalist credo of gesture proceeding from character and milieu, equating contextualized acting with true identity, and overt performativity with the poor and the insane.

An effective cultural strategy emerges from Sjöström's film then, one that makes clear why one contemporary reviewer could herald the arrival of *Ingeborg Holm* with the enthusiastic claim, "Film can be art!", and another could elaborate, "Hilda Borgström's performance adds perfection to this film, makes it of universal application, lifts it far above the impoverished everyday life in which it is set, and breathes the Life of Art into the whole piece, rendering it a masterpiece and a genuine *document humain*."[23] Naturalism was the currency of cultural legitimacy in the theater of Scandinavia at the time, and Sjöström had made a socially realist film that not only enlisted naturalist style, but made its principle of contextualizaiton key to the narrative developments. In winning sympathy for Ingeborg, the film also enlists support for "natural" context, for unmarked gesture, for the transparent and reliable medium of photography. It conserves gesture, recovers the stability of the middle class, and promotes the cultural legitimacy of the film medium.

Not that it does so without the loose ends typical of fetish construction, however. As mentioned, the first gesture unleashed by Ingeborg's recognition of the photograph is a simple, contextualized touch on the cheek. What follows immediately on its heels, however, is once again a pictorial moment approaching the status of a tableau, showing the mutual recognition of mother and son (fig. 9). The cathartic relief at their reunion distracts from some fundamental tensions in this sustained image. Even if the photograph has performed a recovery, that is, it cannot enact a complete return to the moment of prior recording. It cannot erase the marks of age, suffering, and loss (in other words, the elapsed time of the narrative). The "perfect" picture at the end still has Ingeborg clothed in the uniform of the asylum, and Erik resting his now-grown fame awkwardly against her shoulder. The natural gesture of the opening scene can only return with traces of the narrative events still marking the image with loss, making the photograph's recovery of the "real" Ingeborg quite willful indeed.

Further, there is something paradoxical in the fact that the motion that cinema has added to the photograph is a fundamental precondition for depicting the losses inflicted in *Ingeborg Holm*. There is no downward spiral possible in a still photograph, as there is in moving photography. In *Ingeborg Holm*, the entropic narrative ensures that the passage of film through the projector will be tightly calibrated to the increasing misery of the main character. The film's appeal back to the still photograph for grounding is thus in one sense a suppression of the motion that distinguishes cinema from earlier forms of photography. This is a familiar pat-

Fig. 9. Final tableau of mother and son. (16 mm frame enlargement)

tern from the early years of film, in which cinema makes a bid for legitimacy by becoming anti-cinematic, by claiming to be more like theater, painting, literature, or in this case, still photography. The naturalist gestural style in this film depends crucially on the metaphor of the still photograph. But in order to avoid unintended resonances of that equation (such as the photograph's lack of verisimilar flow—the fact that it shows a pose, not a full gesture), it is essential that both photograph and gesture be identified with origin, hence *Ingeborg Holm*'s tight connection between the naturalist and maternal gesture and the photograph's ability to recover both at once. Another image from the film can serve as a final emblem of this strategy. When Ingeborg escapes from the poorhouse to gain access to her sick daughter, she runs into the countryside where the daughter has been fostered out. Along the way, she stumbles exhausted into a rural home, asking for food and rest. There, in the intact sphere of a kind rural family, Ingeborg sees a cradle and a baby. She moves over to it, her face filled with longing. She sits sorrowfully at the side rocking the cradle, with a gesture that in some senses marks the midway point between her untroubled maternal gestures of the opening scenes and the insane cradling at the end of the film (fig. 10). Here, it is not her own child she rocks, but that of the woman behind her. Ingeborg has a "foster" relationship to this child, just as the other mothers have a foster relationship to her own children. If the scene is meant to convey the fullness of the intact family life that she has lost, her temporary intrusion into the scene underscores the fact that her gesture at the cradle can never be "natural." However tender her movement might be, it is still someone else's child.

The dissonance hovering around this image of Ingeborg at the stranger's cradle is a helpful reminder that the equation of naturalist gesture with origin is a strategy, one with cultural and institutional implications for the cinema in 1913. Given the response to the film, it seems to have been a successful strategy, since it created empathy not only for a character, but for an entire gestural

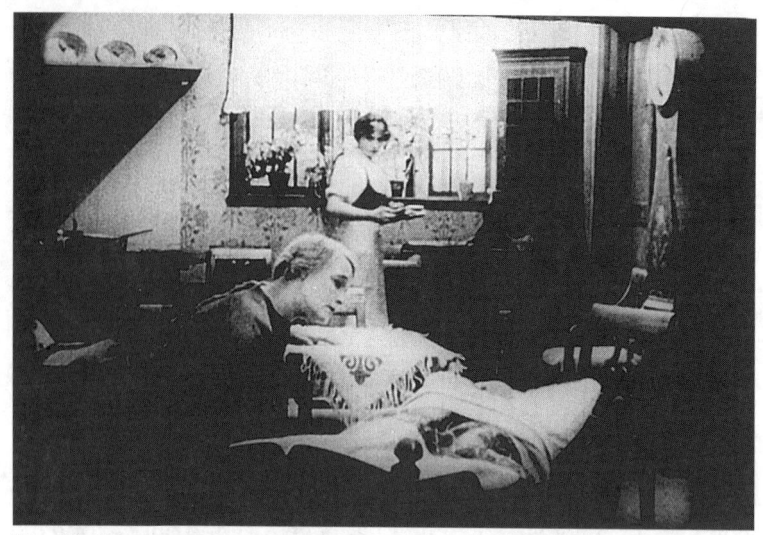

Fig. 10. Ingeborg at the rural cradle. (16mm frame enlargement)

system, a mode of naturalist performance that was to become a hallmark of Swedish silent cinema. *Ingeborg Holm* has been called one of the earliest examples of successful social agitation in the cinema, due to its incitement of a debate about welfare laws in Sweden.[24] I would add that by linking the fate of its protagonist to the idea of gesture, it agitates successfully for naturalism in film as well.

NOTES

[1] Histories of film style have frequently singled out *Ingeborg Holm* for its exemplary use of deep staging. Ben Brewster, Barry Salt, Kristin Thompson, David Bordwell, John Fullerton, and Tom Gunning all refer to Sjöström's film, some with extended visual analysis. For some, like Salt, the lack of editing in the film is seen as a developmental delay, but the consensus seems to be that *Ingeborg Holm*'s particularly accomplished deep staging should be seen as evidence of a mature stylistic alternative to American editing in the early 1910s. See Ben Brewster, "Deep-Staging in French Films, 1900–1914," in *Early Cinema; Space Frame Narrative*, ed. Thomas Elsaesser (London: British Film Institute, 1990), 45–55; Barry Salt, *Film Style and Technology: History and Analysis* (London: Starword,

1983), 113–19; Kristin Thompson, "The International Exploration of Cinematic Expressivity," in *Film and the First World War*, ed. Karel Dibbets and Bert Hogenkamp (Amsterdam: Amsterdam University Press, 1995), 65–85; David Bordwell, *On the History of Film Style* (Cambridge, MA: Harvard University Press, 1997), 191–95; John Fullerton, "Contextualising the Innovation of Deep Staging in Swedish Film," in *Film and the First World War*, 86–96; and Tom Gunning, "Notes and Queries about the Year 1913 and Film Style: National Styles and Deep Staging," *1895* special issue, "L'année 1913 en France" (October 1993): 194–204.

[2] Fullerton makes a similar claim that deep staging had in the public mind become associated with legitimate (naturalist) theater, so that when early Swedish feature films incorporated that technique of *mise-en-scène*, it would be read as a bid for cultural standing. "Contextualising the Innovation of Deep Staging," 91.

[3] Roberta E. Pearson, *Eloquent Gestures: The Transformation of Performance Style in the Griffith Biograph Films* (Berkeley: University of California Press, 1992), 18–37.

[4] Ben Brewster and Lea Jacobs, *Theatre to Cinema: Stage Pictorialism and the Early Feature Film* (Oxford: Oxford University Press, 1997).

[5] To be fair, it should be noted that Pearson also tries to complicate these categories after setting them up in opposition, noting that examples of a mixed style can be found both before and after 1912, reflecting the varying levels of acting skill among the performers. But her implicit assumption still seems to be one of forward progress *toward* a verisimilar style, while Brewster and Jacobs emphasize that pictorialism in feature films of the 1910s should be seen as an alternative, not a vestigial system of gesture. See Pearson, 50–51, and Brewster and Jacobs, 101–9.

[6] For a summary of Sjöström's directing experience with both play and film, see Bengt Forslund, *Victor Sjöström: His Life and Work* (New York: New York Zoetrope, 1988), 43–49.

[7] For a useful account of Antoine's theater and the paradoxes of realistic staging, see Jean Chothia, *André Antoine*, Directors in Perspective, ed. Christopher Innes (Cambridge: Cambridge University Press, 1991).

[8] Bengt Idestam-Almquist (Robin Hood), *Svensk Film före Gösta Berling* (PAN/Norstedts, 1973), 54.

[9] "Muck Linden berättar," *Filmjournal* 12.15 (1930): 30.

[10] *On the History of Film Style*, 194–95.

[11] X. X. [pseud.], "Ingeborg Holm—fattigvårdseländet på filmen," *Arbetet* (Lund), 11 November 1913, 5.

[12] Jan Olsson, "'Classical' vs. 'Pre-classical': Ingeborg Holm and Swedish Cinema in 1913," *Griffithiana* 50 (May 1994), 113–23.

[13] In the chapter of their book on "The Fate of the Tableau in Cinema," Brewster and Jacobs observe that "motivated tableaux" are the rule in cinema, which lacking the built-in structural pause of a curtain between acts rarely seems able to justify a complete freezing of action (48).

[14] Pearson mentions this effect of "modified tableau" as one means of adapting theatrical tableau to film (38–39), and Brewster and Jacobs add further examples of contrastive planes of action (51–52).

[15] Herman Hamnqvist, "Den fotografiska posen," *Fotografisk Tidskrift* 160 (April 1898): 87–88.

[16] This inscription is not visible in many of the 16mm prints I have seen, but was quite legible in the 35mm print from SFI shown at the 1993 Pordenone Silent Film Festival's retrospective on the films of the year 1913.

[17] Forslund mentions the interesting biographical detail that Sjöström, who lost his mother at age seven, remained deeply attached to her memory, and had a portrait photograph that he carried with him for years after (15, 24).

[18] Due to my difficulty in obtaining a copy of this now-obscure play, I am relying in what follows on a comparison of Krok's play and Sjöström's film in an unpublished paper on file at the Filmhuset library in Stockholm. See Sara Heldt, "*Ingeborg Holm*: Studie av en stumfilm," (1984), C-1 uppsats, 19–22.

[19] Alan Trachtenberg, "Photography/Cinematography," in *Before Hollywood: Turn-of-the-Century Film from American Archives*, ed. Jay Leyda and Charles Musser (New York: The American Federation of

Arts, 1986): 73.

[20] Ibid., 76.

[21] Trachtenberg brings up this possibility in his brief mention of *Photographing a Female Crook* (Biograph, 1904) when he suggests that in this and other films that problematize the status of photography, "The moving picture seems to be wresting authority from the still picture," 78.

[22] *Theatre to Cinema*, 28.

[23] *Göteborgs Aftonblad*, 27 October 1914, and *Filmen* (February 1914), both quoted and translated in Forslund, 45–46.

[24] For a summary of *Ingeborg Holm*'s role in this debate, see Erik Hedling and Anna Meeuwisse, "Filmen som agitator: Victor Sjöströms *Ingeborg Holm*," *Bokbox* 93 (December 1987), 15–23.

Desire Disavowed in Victor Sjöström's *The Phantom Carriage*

Tytti Soila

I'm going back to my room upstairs
and lie down on my bed . . .
that bed of pain my tears have streaked, year in,
year out[1]

"A poor little slum-sister was about to die"—these are the beginning words of Selma Lagerlöf's short story *The Phantom Carriage*, and the beginning of its 1921 film version directed by Victor Sjöström as well.[2] The poor little slum sister Edith has contracted a "fast acting and tough kind" of TB. Now the young sister has a short time left in this life. Her mother thinks it is good for her to die on the eve of a holiday—it is New Year's Eve—so no sounds from the city life will disturb her. But sister Edith cannot bring her mind to peace. She desperately wants to meet a man called David Holm before she dies. People are sent to look for him even if they resent the task. David Holm is a bad person, an evildoer and a drunk. Why does the saintly young woman beg to see this man, why is she bargaining with Death himself to get postponement of her fate, just to be able to meet him?

In spite of its beginning, the narrative focal point of *The Phantom Carriage* is inevitably on the character of David Holm (played by Victor Sjöström himself), a decent family man who has fallen into bad company, started drinking, lost his job and pulled his family including his younger brother into misery. His wife has abandoned their home, taking the children with her while he has been in prison. Back in freedom, David Holm has continued his miserable life, wandering about in the country looking for his wife in order to get his revenge on her. Unforgiving, he thinks that she has betrayed him by leaving him without letting him know first.

On this very New Year's Eve David is drinking with a couple of other bums in a graveyard, telling them the story about a driver whose task it is to collect dead souls in his carriage—the Phantom Carriage. He says that whoever dies accidentally as the last person of the passing year, he is condemned to drive this carriage for another everlasting year. Saying this, David gets into a fight with the bums, gets hit and loses consciousness. It seems as if his death is inevitable, since the Phantom Carriage approaches and the Driver climbs off his shaky vehicle to meet him. The Driver appears to be the very man, Georges, who had introduced David to the bad life. He now seems anxious to convert David's mind, to make him regret his wrongdoings and make amends. The miserable life story of David, especially his encounters with his wife and Sister Edith, is rolled up in front of his and the spectator's eyes.

David Holm had come exactly a year earlier to the town spending his first night at the Salvation Army shelter, where Sister Edith was working. While David was sleeping, Edith spent the night mending his coat in the chilly rooms, not minding the germs that the nasty worn out coat might have contained. In the morning, David Holm, in his meanness, rips off the patches saying he is used to having the coat that way. Edith tells him that she has prayed to Jesus for him, wishing that he would give David a good new year. She invites David to return the next New Year's Eve to tell her whether her prayer has been heard, and he gives her his promise.

The two meet several times, in the pub and at the Salvation Army temple. On one occasion Sister Edith finds out that David is planning to leave the town because he is in search of somebody. The discussion is witnessed by David's estranged wife who reveals herself to Edith telling that she is the very person David is looking for. Edith is shocked but controls herself. Later she tries to reconcile the couple, hoping that this would make David a better person. She even manages in her effort which however has disastrous consequences to the family. David takes his revenge by daily abuse of his wife, finally driving her to the verge of madness.

On this New Year's night David Holm is reminded of all his past when he, in the guise of a phantom, is able to visit Edith's death bed and even his own home where his desperate wife is preparing to poison herself and the children. The memories and the visits—and ultimately the love of Edith—bring David to a change of mind. Georges, who is tormented by his guilt, offers to continue driving the Phantom Carriage for another year. David is, thus, able to return to his body from the realm of twilight. He manages to get home in time to prevent his wife's deathly plan and in the final scene the spouses cry in each other's arms.

The film *Phantom Carriage* peaks the Golden Age of the Swedish cinema in the 20s. It is famous for its multiple expositions, photographed by Julius Jaenzon, depicting the ghostly characters on the screen during a period when many means of cinematic expression were still difficult to accomplish. However, as Bo Florin points out in his book *Den nationella stilen*, even if the film always is mentioned because of its intricate structure and its treatment of different time levels, it is seldom properly analyzed.[3]

Among the things Florin introduces in his in-depth analysis of the film is the confirmation of the crucial role that Sister Edith's love for David plays in his repentance and reform. It is my intent to look into the original version of the film and take a step beyond Florin's statement and point out ambiguities in the narration that establish the centrality of Edith's character. Among other things I will contend that it is her desire and will power that, in fact, sets forth, not only David's reform but also the trajectory of the narrative flow. This statement is supported by the fact that the relationship between David and Edith is quite central in the short story of Lagerlöf, even if most of the verbal evidence of it has been erased in the film script.

Instead, in the process of transferring the written story to cinematic discourse a gendered dichotomization has taken place: the verbal discourse and focus of action concentrates on the male character(s), whereas the emotionality and desire of a woman—Edith—is disconnected from verbality and transferred to a visual level. Florin describes the visual and spatial style of the film as "lyric intimacy"—something characteristic to other Swedish films of the period, too—and holds that this style among other things "creates a center around Edith's bed, an impression which is further reinforced by the manner the other characters move about in the room—they go to her several times, cherish her and talk to her."[4]

The bed is undoubtedly a locus of great importance for the story since that is where Edith sends for David and this is, finally, where the hands of the two meet giving Edith peace. When Edith sends for David, the scene centralizes her half-sitting in the bed, the two women on each side looking down at her, their hands outstretched towards her. The background props contribute further to the symmetrical *mise-en-scène* which indicates the importance of her person even more: she is framed by the headpiece of the bed; straight above her on the wall there is a painting with two photographs on each side. This *tableau-vivant*-like setting forms itself to the very image of her desire, opening up a void into which the narrative in *The Phantom Carriage* is gushing in a centripetal movement where the characters constantly return to her bedside.

Subsequently, the importance of Edith's character in the story is underlined by the fact that the film begins with an opening iris that makes the spectator aware, not only of her person but of her intentions. It is, however, notable that the English versions of the film lack certain crucial scenes, conveying her character into a mere coincidence in the life of David Holm.⁵ One of the reasons for disclosing Edith's part in the English versions may be that people in charge of distribution have considered the love story confusing for what they saw as the main plot.

Another argument may have been a moralistic one: love between the married David Holm and the slum sister may have been perceived as something that might offend the audiences. This was a time in film history when Hollywood was tired of scandals and the industry wished to regain the confidence of the wealthy middle class. Or to put it quite simply: woman in the margins and man in the center was/is the normative concept so it was only "natural" to follow it.

Whatever the reason, in the process towards exposition to larger audiences the character and intentionality of Edith's role became marginalized. Yet, in the original film version her feelings and their eventual disavowal are unmistakably at display. The two crucial scenes preoccupied with Edith's emotions take place after a service in the Salvation Army temple which David has attended (even if it only was to jeer a friend who has repented—and later will be a Salvation Army soldier).

David is on his way out when Edith reaches him, reproaching him as he humiliates a TB-smitten woman. He then tells Edith that he is just about to leave the town. She is upset, steps closer to him and lifts her hands to his breast with a plea: "No, you should not do that!" Looking like two white birds on a tree branch, her hands against his breast speak for her, too. Paradoxically, the contrast between the small white hands and the dark heavy mass of David's body emphasizes the bond between the two even more. And as Bo Florin points out, the fact that the two of them are being observed by a third person, underlines the intimate quality of their encounter even further.⁶

When David gazes at Edith, she removes her hands, looks

down and then up again: "I would like to struggle with you yet another while!" Edith means the struggle of wills, as she wishes to convert him to a better life—which in its turn could be a beginning of something else, too. The camera crosscuts between her entreating face and his spiteful glances while he retorts: "How tempting that might be, I still cannot stay!"

Before David leaves, Edith puts her hands once again on his arm and he stares at them in a slow movement of his head. As if embarrassed, she pulls them back and turns her face away, concealing it from his interrogating eyes. When he closes the door she looks after him through the glass doors and then turns around. Next cut will give the interior view she is looking at, indicating a future perspective. The room full of people demonstrates that Edith still will have obligations even if the man she loves will be leaving.

This scene, which relates to an impending farewell, is but a prelude to the eventual disavowal of her feelings, her love: the woman who has listened to the conversation between David and Edith approaches her. They withdraw to another room in order to talk undisturbed and as soon as Edith has closed the door, the stranger says that she's the person whom David Holm is looking for. Edith pulls her hand back in astonishment and when the woman—there's no name for her—says that she is David's wife. Edith breathes deeply and puts her hand on her heart. Framed in a close up, the woman tells Edith her story.

Edith, breathing heavily grasps her body with both hands as if wanting to keep herself together in one piece. Then she turns away and takes a few steps, looking for the support of a table. After another glance at the woman, she turns her eyes up as if she was praying, her hand still pressed to her breast. This is the moment of denouncement. She then hurries to the woman steering her to sit on a couch, saying, "You have to take David back. That's his only chance!" The woman shakes her head and Edith adds that certainly the woman need not make up her mind right away.

In this scene, Edith's body language expresses extreme emotional reactions and inner battle. After seeing the woman out—she leaves through the same doors as David Holm had—Edith remains, watches her. The film text: "she had overcome herself and did not ask for anything more of what belonged to this world" clearly expresses her state of mind. Her disavowal however concerns love "in this world", i.e. marital love and sexuality, not the Lagerlöfian "love of spirits."[7]

The spectator already knows from the beginning of the story that Edith's desire is stronger than that, and that she will still be calling for David on her death bed. Yet in order to sustain two contradictory discourses, the male center of the story and the power of Edith's desire, the latter must be disguised on the narrative level as something else: as a terminal disease. This displacement—the distorted, metaphoric form of the love between Edith and David—may be explained by the specific status of a woman's desire in melodrama.

According to psychoanalytically influenced feminist film theory, the male character is the sole dynamic instance of the classical narrative, and as such the one to forward its trajectory towards closure. The femininity is associated with space and matter which inevitably is said to deprive woman of subjectivity.[8] In a standard case such as Hollywood mainstream film, the body of a female character is positioned as an object of a (male desiring) gaze, and as such, as a resistance to the progress of a narrative: in its invitation to be looked at, the female body creates a lull that tends to stem the narrative flow.

Generally the driving force of a narrative is, then, masculine desire. A prerequisite of desire is lack, or a kind of distance originally created by the infant's separation from the mother('s breast and body) and, as Mary Ann Doane writes, "insofar as desire is defined as the excess of demand over a need aligned with the maternal figure, the woman is left behind."[9] In the same instance Doane, however, continues by stating that female desire still is a necessary basis for the structure of certain popular sub-genres such as Love Story.[10] She further points out that women in fiction are frequently associated with waiting and maintains that although waiting is not a "proper" subject of a narrative *per se*, it is still capable of producing narrative.[11]

Edith is impatiently, desperately, waiting for David Holm to appear, as she has been waiting for him to reform. At the same time she wishes to hold back her own death: "I cannot die, I can not! Give me but a few moments! You know that I love him, don't you. I have never loved him the way I love him today," she begs when the relentless Death is already standing next to her bed. Edith cannot give up the thought that whatever she has been trying to construct, it has been ruined by David Holm. Her situation is not much unlike Penelope's who waited for Odysseus, who kept her persistent suitors back by weaving during the day and undoing her work at night. The process of creating a void for waiting as a narrative strategy, is quite similar in both stories.

Mary Ann Doane links waiting and women's desire to weaving and sewing maintaining that needlework signifies a form of narrative power for the woman.[12] There is indeed a connection between these two phenomena in *The Phantom Carriage*, too, as Sister Edith mends David's coat on their first encounter. A signifying detail in this context is that, in rural Scandinavia there was a custom—still practiced in some places when Lagerlöf wrote the story—whereby a young bride-to-be would sew a shirt for her fiancé as a sign of their alliance.[13]

Edith's needlework, then, literally sews David and herself to each other. This figure gets slightly challenged by the fact that David's wife also sews while waiting for her drunken husband to come home at night. But as far as I can see, this does not weaken Edith's position but only underlines the shared experience of women, thus reinforcing the concept of waiting (for the husband/beloved one) itself. Further, it is obvious that Edith contracts TB from David—and by being smitten with the disease, she is smitten by love. In common fantasy, TB was imagined to be an aphrodisiac.[14]

At first glance a consuming, terminal disease seems to be a strange metaphor for love but still, a passage from this very factual illness to the expressions of love and spirituality did exist. The disease was common and everybody knew that TB, in reality, was (as it still is) a disgusting disease of liquids, phlegm, and hemorrhages. But, in popular fantasy, it was not depicted as such. Instead, it was seen as spirited and ephemeral. As Susan Sontag noted in her essay *Illness as Metaphor*, there are many imaginary junctions between tuberculosis and emotionality. In the context of *The Phantom Carriage* I would venture to maintain that the disease becomes a nodal point where several crucial meanings of the story accumulate in an extraordinary and intricate manner, creating a signifying net between love, death, religion, and, indeed, film making that condense in the body of Edith.

In popular fantasy the image of TB was paradoxical and its symptoms were depicted as deceitful—but the contradictoriness was exactly what also gave it its power as a metaphor. According to Susan Sontag, "Like all really successful metaphors, the metaphor of TB was rich enough to provide for two contradictory applications. It described the death of someone thought to be 'too' good to be sexual: the assertion of an angelic psychology. It was also a way of describing sexual feelings—while lifting the responsibility for libertinism, which is blamed on a state of objective psychological decadence or deliquesce."[15] Edith is depicted as the saintly young woman who had devoted her life to the salvation of the outcasts of society. At the same time her passion is presented as overwhelming and transgressive. The bond between Edith and David excludes David Holm's wife. There is no evidence of love between spouses which in a sense makes their relationship dispensable. The family as it is portrayed in the film represents at its best a working class idyll, not "real" love. David Holm's wife is an earthy woman, ready for action and ready to protect herself and her children. But within the frame of this story she is even left without a name. She could be anybody.[16] At the end of the story it stands clear that David sees his marriage as a duty and his plans for the future deal with raising his children and "making decent people out of them." The reconciliation between the spouses is just a prerequisite for such plans.

The emotional system of values of the film, then, revolves between two images of love or affection, which according to Lagerlöf's own words are on one hand a spirited, heavenly one, "love of the spirits"—and an "earthly" one on the other hand.[17] And the down-to-earth statement of the narrative discourse is that the spiritual affections don't always merge with the worldly ones. This kind of split might be explained against the actual background of Selma Lagerlöf, her situation as a lesbian who struggled to express her feelings and experiences in her fiction. In several stories she describes the dilemma of an "impossible" love and, as for example *Dunungen*, they may be read as descriptions of lesbian love in disguise.

In *The Phantom Carriage* a reason for the distortion of expression: love depicted as disease, is that the formal resistance towards elaboration of female subjectivity (always present in classical narrative) tends to produce adversities and contradictions within the narrative economy. The patriarchal discourse dominant in classical narrative supports the male position and in cases where the female discourse is strong enough to take place, there also exist elements capable of sabotaging it. Or, as Mary Ann Doane puts it: "The flaw of the Love Story is to posit the very possibility of female desire [which is the] reason it often ends badly."[18]

One of the ambiguities of *Phantom Carriage* is that it does not always follow such rigid narrative laws. Consequently, Edith's death is not depicted as a punishment: this is particularly clear in the Lagerlöf novel where death above all suggests the future unification between David and Edith. The touch of their hands by Edith's bed seals the promise. "He is overwhelmed by love, love of the spirits, of which the love between the earthly people is but a feeble imitation," as Selma Lagerlöf writes about David.[19] In her version of the story Edith's spirit accompanies David, encouraging him on his way to repentance and to saving the life of his family. And David knows that after fulfilling his duties in this life, "he would be allowed to go to his beloved, to his longed for."[20]

The film's inherent moral codex, then, does not "condemn" Edith for loving a married man. Generally, the moral universe of the bourgeois melodrama is conservative and "punishes" such transgressions. When for instance Susan Sontag mentions *The Phantom Carriage* in her essay, she underlines the punitive role that the disease plays in this story. In fiction a fatal illness is a test of moral character, she claims and, comparing Edith with Fantine in *Les Miserables*, presents her case as an example of redemptive death of a fallen woman.[21]

True enough, Edith dies, but throughout the story she is looked upon with reverence by the other characters. In the end it is clearly indicated that crowds of angels come to carry her to Heaven on her death. When David leaves Edith's room in the Lagerlöf version he "believes he sees the room being instantly filled by illuminated figures. He seems to meet them in the staircase and on the street, but he is taken away in such a haste that he has not time to distinguish much."[22] In the film Georges simply states: "We do not have anything to do here anymore. Those who will take care of her will soon be here." Also, the Carriage Driver's final words to a dying person: "You, prisoner, step out of your prison" are slightly altered when Edith's time comes to an end: "You prisoner, you loveable, step out of your prison!"

It also might be reasonable to remind any secularized person at the end of the 20th century that less than one hundred years ago, death was seen as the passage to eternal life by a far larger number of people than today. Letting go of life and worldliness was believed to lead to the eternal life. In Sweden, a religious revivalist movement was one of the three strong folk movements which had powerful impact on the lives of people at the turn of the century. Ecstatic religious experiences were by no means uncommon and belief in the salvation of the repenting souls was strong. Death was understood as inevitable but not necessarily as a punishment. Instead, glorification of death and the dead was common. Richard Dyer writes about the concept of "bright beauty of the deathbed" as something very remote to our present society—pointing out that about one hundred years ago dead bodies within Western art often were seen as objects of beauty—as "sight[s] of veneration."[23]

As already stated, in a standard melodrama (mainstream film) the female body cannot "mean" anything else than to be an object of a visual (sexual) pleasure. However, Mary Ann Doane refers to psychoanalytic writings about the case of hysteria, where repression of a feeling or event gets its expression in a bodily symptom. She observes that in films with Medical Discourse a female body, carrying symptoms of a disease, also appears to signify depth and not only surface, i.e. "to-be-looked-atness."[24] A symptom on a woman's body refers to the fact that there is a cause: a story, a past, reinforcing thus the narrative potential of the female.

According to the mythology of TB there is generally some passionate feeling which expresses itself in a bout of TB: it was thought to come from too much passion, affecting the reckless and sensual—but it was also regarded as a disease of repression or frustration.[25] In *The Phantom Carriage* Edith's love for David is being suppressed both by herself and the narrative of the story. However, it is painfully there. In the original novel, she says to the Driver of the Carriage: "You must understand that I am under a great distress when I'm saying this. It is not easy to confess that I love but that man. It has been such a shame to think that I really have fallen so deep, that I could love someone who is bound to another. I have struggled and I have fought against it. I have thought that I, who wanted to be a guide and redemptor of the miserable, have become worse than the worst among them."[26] These contradictory emotions are engulfed and mirrored in the single metaphor of TB. The mere symptoms of the disease—such as white pallor and red flush—involve extreme contrasts easily understood as signs for opposing feelings of affection, shame, hope, and desperation.[27]

TB-sufferers may have been represented as passionate creatures, but the disease has also been celebrated as an illness of born victims, of sensitive, passive people who are not quite life-loving enough to survive. Another contradictory feature attached to the image of TB is that even if it was seen as a disease of the delicate and sensitive, in the late 19th century it was also connected with social problems, such as alcoholism. Interestingly, one central polarization in *The Phantom Carriage* is concentrated around the progress of the disease: the illness that consumes Sister Edith so fast, does not seem to have much effect on David Holm. The anamnesis of the two of them, then, pictures the saintly, unearthly Edith at one and the wretched but big and strong David at the other end of the same scale, making it possible for them to be unified within this single metaphor.

Together, yet apart. The saintly young woman and the vile man. Light and darkness. Edith is associated with brightness from the very beginning of the film. Even when she is wearing the dark salvation army uniform and hat, her face and hands are strikingly white, and the murky color of her clothes only accentuate this whiteness. Also, the contrasts between her and the characters by her bed who wear dark clothes, not only draw the spectator's eyes on her but create a qualitative difference between her and the others. Edith's shining bedsheets, the whiteness of her gown, and the halo around her blond head (accomplished by a carefully set lightning) tend from time to time to depict her as dissolved in light.

Richard Dyer maintains that the extreme instance of translucence in cinematic representation is the angelic white woman. At the other extreme of a continuum there is the "criminal, insane, disabled white person"—a dark and husky (male) figure. The image of a darker man—such as the unshaven David with his shabby clothes—together with the shining white woman is a basic configuration to represent heterosexual love in cinema. It is also the representation of the idea of white superiority *par excellence*. Interestingly, Dyer also observes that it is the combination of translucence and substance—not translucence alone—which really defines white representation.[28] The intimate scene between David and Edith, with Edith's hands leaning against the mass of his breast, her face bent up towards his, is one such image. Among other things, then, *The Phantom Carriage*, in its classical appearance is one of those films that has contributed to the idea of white superiority in Western culture.

However, as Dyer observes, apart from being one of the most powerful representations in cinema, this figure depicting white heterosexual unity is far from being unambiguous. He holds that it is not just the matter of two different ways of distributing light on different sexes that constitutes the dynamics of this image, but also the way light constructs the relationship between men and women. Therefore, a significant feature is that the man is being illuminated by the glow of the woman—something that connotes his yearning for her (light). And Dyer concludes: "there is a frightening, disfiguring darkness to the sexuality that, moth to a flame, yearns towards the pure light of desirability."[29]

Worth noticing is that in this respect the heterosexual dichotomy created and supported by Edith and David is different: it lacks the "darkness of sexuality." In the basic configuration the darkness of man signifies sexual desire but David does not show any such feelings towards Edith. His gaze on Edith in the scene at the Salvation Army Temple is intimate—curious perhaps—but not desiring. There does not seem to exist any destructive features in the final relationship between the two. The object of David's abusive and dark side (including his eventual carnal desires) is the nameless wife. David's desire to join Edith—especially in the novel—is to join her in light, as light. And in a sense this is being realized, too, at Edith's bedside, when their hands meet. She, permeated by light, is reaching to grab David's hand. He, in the guise of a phantom, is on his knees, face lifted up to her, and he is transparent, too. They are in harmony with each other—and the question is whether disavowal of desire is a prerequisite of such harmony.

Finally, it is not surprising that a major cinematic and cultural enterprise such as *The Phantom Carriage*, would communicate and reflect upon its basic conditions within its own visual/textual body. As David and Edith momentarily hold each other's hands, they become a symbol for transgressivity in this film where characters dwell on the borderline between life and death, are able to see ghosts, leave their bodies, walk in and out through walls; where time is elastic and where a carriage travels on the waves of a sea as well as on the dirt road. When a film is being projected on the silver screen, the light shines through the film strip. There is a need for light but also for transparency. It is not only the lives and bodies of Edith and David on the bedside which are ephemeral, the projected image is, too. In this single frame the two of them come to manifest the different elements of the film itself, its ideology, narrative and it's technical conditions.

NOTES

[1] Homer, "Stranger at the Gates," Book 17 in *The Odyssey* (New York, 1996), 357.

[2] Still another version of the story was made in the 50s by Gustav Molander.

[3] Bo Florin, *Den nationella stilen, Studier i den svenska filmens guldålder* (Stockholm, 1997).

[4] Florin, 182.

[5] Among them the scene described later in the text, the scene of disavowal of her love.

[6] Florin, 183.

[7] Selma Lagerlöf, *Körkarlen* (Stockholm, 1940), 78.

[8] Teresa de Lauretis, *Alice Doesn't: Feminism, Semiotics, Cinema, The Woman's Film of the 40s* (Bloomington and Indianapolis, 1984), 118–119.

[9] Mary Ann Doane, *The Desire to Desire* (Bloomington and Indianapolis, 1987), 11–13.

[10] Doane, 112. A discussion of genre is somewhat complicated when it comes to Scandinavian film, the genre system being far lesser developed there than in the Anglo-Saxon countries. Especially at this time there hardly existed anything between comedy and melodrama, and sub-genres such as Women's Film or Love Story did not existed. The audiences in Scandinavian countries have always been so small the industry has had to address to a more homogenous public than Hollywood has done. Nevertheless, I think it is appropriate to apply some of the thoughts concerning genre film from later periods than *Phantom Carriage* in my discussion.

[11] Doane, 109.

[12] Doane, 110.

[13] Thus for instance a popular ballad in Finland witnesses of a young woman who sews a button in a man's shirt, also sew her heart in it.

[14] Sontag, 13.

[15] Sontag, 25–26.

[16] This is even more extraordinary because the character is being played by a then famous actress Hilda Borgström.

[17] Lagerlöf, 78.

[18] Doane, 118.

[19] Lagerlöf, 78.

[20] Lagerlöf, 15.

[21] Susan Sontag, *Illness as a Metaphor and AIDS and Its Metaphors* (New York, 1990), 41.

[22] Lagerlöf, 76.

[23] Richard Dyer, *White* (London and New York, 1997), 208–209.

[24] Doane, 39.

[25] Sontag, 22.

[26] Lagerlöf, 65.

[27] Sontag, 11.

[28] Dyer, 116.

[29] Dyer, 134–135.

Realism Refined and Retouched: Alf Sjöberg's *Bara en mor*

Rochelle Wright

Ivar Lo-Johansson's novel *Bara en mor* (1939; *Only a Mother*, 1991) is often cited as a milestone in Swedish literature because it is both a psychologically convincing portrait of an individual woman, Rya-Rya, and a painstakingly faithful depiction of the environment that formed her. The narrative proceeds chronologically from Rya-Rya's eighteenth year, shortly after the turn of the century, to her death some twenty-five years later, with only one brief flashback to a scene from the youth of her mother. Though the focus is on Rya-Rya, considerable attention is also devoted to the milieu and to the thoughts and actions of important secondary characters, in keeping with Lo-Johansson's intent to depict an entire social class, the *statare* (estate-workers). The strength of the novel lies precisely in the author's epic approach, the manner in which he shapes the story through the cumulative piling on of telling detail.

This technique, effective though it may be in realistic prose fiction, is less successful in a film, both because of time constraints and because it is the antithesis of dramatic action. When Alf Sjöberg adapted Lo-Johansson's 450-page novel for the screen in 1949, he needed to find a visual vocabulary that would allow him to compress or eliminate much of the specific subject matter of the source without doing violence to its spirit.

Some of Sjöberg's structural and stylistic choices reflect the realistic underpinnings of the film. He retains the straightforward chronology of the novel rather than incorporating flashback sequences or allowing the past and present to occupy the same physical space, as he did in his adaptation of *Fröken Julie* (*Miss Julie*, 1951), and his camera techniques and use of lighting frequently, though not always, suggest a concrete here-and-now rather than the shadowy, expressionistic landscape, both mental and physical, of *Hets* (*Torment*, 1944). Sjöberg shared with Lo-Johansson a socialist political orientation and a fondness for theorizing about his own work. These similarities notwithstanding, their approaches to the material differ significantly. Sjöberg's goal is not strict documentarism, but to illustrate the theme articulated in the printed text that introduces the film—"Hur långt är inte avståndet från människa till människa!" [How great a distance is there not from one human being to another!]—and to examine interpersonal alienation in the context of collective versus individual identity.

Though the social framework of Sjöberg's film is scaled down vis-à-vis the novel, the director establishes the importance of the collective and Rya-Rya's position within it in the opening credits sequence. Because the estate-worker system had been abolished in 1945, Sjöberg can claim to offer, as Lo-Johansson could not, a retrospective analysis of a vanished way of life. As the film begins, a voiceover provides background information on the estate-worker system as well as a generalization about their situation that subsequently acquires added significance because it can be applied specifically to Rya-Rya: "De levde fatalistiskt, aldrig fria, aldrig sig själva, instängda i ett omedgörligt öde där ingen fick vara annorlunda" [They were fatalists, never free, never themselves, constrained by an unyielding destiny decreeing that no one was allowed to be different].[1] During the voiceover, the camera slowly pans across a row of unsmiling estate-worker faces staring straight ahead; the title *Bara en mor* appears precisely when Eva Dahlbeck, who plays the lead, is in the frame.

A quick cut to a photographer now reveals that the estate-workers are posing for a group picture, a circumstance that lends added resonance to the narrator's earlier comment that we are viewing "bilder från en stor folkklass som nu försvunnit" [pictures/ images from a large social class that no longer exists]. Together they comprise a collective, but as they face the camera, Sjöberg's own as well as that of the photographer, they are apparently oblivious or indifferent to the presence of others. The lack of interaction among the estate-workers, though appropriate to the specific situation, underscores the earlier reference in the printed text to existential isolation. When the camera pans back across the row of faces to Eva Dahlbeck, her name appears in the credits, once again differentiating her from the group.

Then, suddenly, the static pose dissolves and the group disperses in all directions as everyone rushes off to work in the fields. By his own account, Sjöberg's intent in this scene was "att visa den elementära kraften i arbetarstammen, hela den inneboende styrkan" [to show the elemental force of the worker stock, all its innate strength].[2] The opening sequence also functions rhythmically, shifting suddenly from stasis to rapid movement. In the immediately following montage of the workers haying, the tempo heightens, then gradually slows as the sun beats down and they grow tired. Though the sequence is masterful from a cinematic standpoint, Lo-Johansson, who was present during much of the filming, raised strenuous objections, arguing that it was unrealistic because estate-workers never *hurried* off to work; their pace was slow and plodding. Similarly, the author was upset that the estate-worker barracks (called "Bakvänt" [Wrong Way Round] in both novel and film)[3] that became the set for many important scenes were actually located in the province of Uppland, rather than in Sörmland, where the novel takes place. Though Lo-Johansson's reservations may seem minor or petty, Sjöberg's decision to ignore them is paradigmatic of his approach: he is not aiming at a strictly accurate representation of reality, but rather at a distillation that highlights salient features.[4]

The verbal reference to pictures/images and the on-screen presence of a photographer may nevertheless be an allusion and indirect tribute to Lo-Johansson's own efforts to document the lives of the estate-workers, not only in his fiction but also in reportage. During the late 1930s and early 1940s, together with the photographer Gunnar Lundh, he traveled around his home province of Sörmland in search of typical faces and places that would serve as a record for future generations. Lo-Johansson's endeavor to chronicle and publicize the circumstances of this impoverished rural proletariat were specifically aimed at social reform, at the abolishment of an entrenched system of agricultural labor he regarded not only as mind-dulling drudgery but as virtual slavery. *Statarna i bild* (Images of the estate-workers), the joint effort of Lo-Johansson and Lundh, was published in 1948, just a year before the premiere of Sjöberg's film.

As the credit sequence implies, the film version of *Bara en mor* places Rya-Rya squarely in the foreground; Sjöberg reduces the number and significance of minor characters and the importance of the collective as a whole. In contrast to the specificity and detail of the novel, he highlights only a few major events or episodes in her life. Because the main character is present in nearly every scene, however, the film does not seem episodic in the negative sense of the word. The director also relies on several visual and narrative strategies to provide coherence and connection. One such technique is to create parallel action within the same scene, which allows for counterpoint and dense, multifaceted use of the frame. Another is to arrange contrasting scenes in a sequence whereby they comment on each other and throw each other into relief.

In both the novel and the film, a single impulsive act on Rya-Rya's part—swimming naked in the lake on a hot summer day—causes her to be ostracized and forever changes the course of her life. A comparison of the way this event and its aftermath are narrated in the respective media illustrates how Sjöberg departs from Lo-Johansson in order to bring out drama and conflict. In the novel, Rya-Rya's dip, related in a laconic line or two, takes place some distance away from her fellow workers and is witnessed only at a remove. In the film the bathing scene is expanded into a dramatic episode in which the entire crowd of estate-workers drops their pitchforks and rushes to the water's edge to point, laugh, and jeer at Rya-Rya, a change that underscores their collective condemnation. As a contrast to Rya-Rya's act, the novel describes, in much greater detail, a group outdoor bathing scene in which all the estate-worker women, old and young alike, egg each other on to remove their clothing and take the plunge. Thus Rya-Rya's transgression is not the act of bathing naked in itself, but her refusal to pay attention to and obey the law of the herd.

This juxtaposition is lacking in the film, which instead individualizes the conflict by offering a contrasting indoor bathing scene in which Berta (Margareta Krook), soon to become Rya-Rya's competitor for the affections of Nils, is silhouetted behind a screen while submerged in a tub. Though Berta expresses the viewpoint of the female collective when she rhetorically asks Rya-Rya, "Har du inte vett att gå för dig själv när du ska ställa med din kropp?" [Don't you have sense enough to go off by yourself when attending to your body?], the film underscores her personal rivalry with Rya-Rya rather than her representative function. Moreover, Berta's self-appointed role as a guardian of public morality is undercut visually; when she arises from the tub the audience clearly sees the contours of her body. In the skinny-dipping scene Rya-Rya's nakedness is shown only in long shot, while in close-ups only her head and neck are exposed.

In the film, the effect of the swim on Rya-Rya's state of mind is suggested by two contrasting scenes in which she stands at a mirror. Immediately after returning home, she smiles happily at her reflection and combs out her hair with an admiring glance, letting the light shine through it. At this point she seems secretly pleased with herself and confident that her act will have no long-range consequences. Cut to a close-up of Rya-Rya lying in the grass at "Varma Backarna" (Warm Slopes), talking to Nils (Max von Sydow, in his first film role), who is off-camera, about the idyll she envisions their life together will be. Suddenly the camera shifts to Nils, an unresponsive, hulking figure who then gets up and leaves without a word as Rya-Rya cries out his name. Cut back to Rya-Rya at the mirror, filmed in extreme close-up, her face in the shadow, with an expression of stunned pain. Off-camera, her mother is singing a hymn. The expressionistic shadows of the background gradually dissolve into a room filled with dancing couples and the music switches to a polka, while the camera remains focused on Rya-Rya's face. This sequence suggests that as a result of the shock she has undergone, Rya-Rya is in a trance-like state, only partly aware of her surroundings. Like a sleepwalker or dreamer, she is unable to exert her will, and it follows that when Nils rejects her again, this time in public and while dancing with Berta, she will submit to the lustful impulses of Henrik (Ragnar Falck).[5]

The following scene illustrates how Sjöberg uses parallel action to provide commentary and explication. It is constructed in two tiers. On the lower level, Rya-Rya and Henrik lie down on the grass at Varma Backarna. At a higher elevation, two young men are engaged in fisticuffs. Their violent encounter is a stand-in for the sexual act taking place off-camera, and when the victor in the fight stomps on the hat of his opponent, the connotation is that Rya-Rya loses her virginity. There is no such parallel action in the novel.

Visual counterpoint within a scene also is used, for instance, to suggest Rya-Rya's relatively privileged position on the estate after her marriage, but simultaneously to hint at its precariousness. Rya-Rya is first shown surreptitiously purchasing cloth for a dress from a peddler. The camera then follows her into another room, where we see a thin arm in the foreground, hanging down and banging rhythmically against a chair. The rear view of a shadowy figure is glimpsed to the left of the frame as a woman's voice begs Rya-Rya to take over her milking chores. The image of the arm, its gesture and the accompanying sound, call to mind the repetitive task that has brought on the woman's disability and simultaneously evoke her pain and despair. When Rya-Rya refuses to help her—because of Henrik's intervention, she has been spared the obligation to do the milking—the other woman speaks of suicide. Rya-Rya is apparently unmoved, but after the visitor leaves she is overcome by nausea. This reference to another unplanned pregnancy reminds Rya-Rya and the audience that childbearing, too, can be debilitating and that Rya-Rya's privileges are not secure. In the novel, there is no associative connection between the visits of the peddler and the milking-woman.

Similarly, Sjöberg illustrates, through scenic juxtaposition, Rya-Rya's internal conflict between her maternal obligations and commitment to family on the one hand and her longing for love from a man on the other. On Midsummer Eve, she has left her husband and his drunken companions (or, more accurately, been thrown out by them) and is wandering around on the estate. Stopping at the water's edge, she catches sight of Edvard Hammar (Ulf Palme) on the other side. At that instant a child's scream is heard and Rya-Rya rushes home to discover that her daughter Margaretha has swallowed a coin, tossed to her in a maudlin gesture of generosity by the hapless Henrik. The baby chokes to death. The visual link between the appearance of Hammar and the child's death implies Rya-Rya's sense of guilt: because she was not eternally vigilant, because her thoughts strayed, she allowed the tragedy to take place.

In one important instance, Sjöberg arranges the sequence of events within a scene so as to explicate a matter that is not overtly stated in the novel. Though Lo-Johansson's narrative makes it clear that Rya-Rya is unfulfilled and unhappy in her marriage and that she craves both affection and romantic love, no plausible explanation is given as to why Hammar in particular exerts such a powerful attraction on her. The film, in contrast, suggests an association with her previous love for Nils. In Sjöberg's version, Rya-Rya, hearing that Nils plans to marry Berta, writes a letter asking him to come see her. After waiting anxiously and in vain for Nils to appear at the appointed hour, she discovers Hammar sitting in a dark corner of the adjacent room. It is as if her unconscious mind had conjured him up from the shadows as a replacement for the one she cannot have. (This is not the only instance in the film when a figure seems to appear out of nowhere at Rya-Rya's bidding; in an earlier scene, the camera shifts to reveal Erika Rost standing in the doorway just as Rya-Rya and the Inspector are discussing her.) In the novel, Hammar's initial visit takes place while Rya-Rya is pregnant with her first child and elicits no strong reaction from her except annoyance.

Scenic counterpoint further underscores the contrast between Hammar as an embodiment of Rya-Rya's romantic longing and her actual marital situation with Henrik. While Rya-Rya watches out the window as Hammar departs in the rain, Henrik returns home and demands sex from her. When she resists, he forces himself on her. Henrik's act of violence takes place off-screen and is revealed only by Rya-Rya's scream. The rain, foregrounded on the windowpane as the camera peers in from outside, is a visual allusion to her pain and unhappiness.

In the film, Hammar's speech and demeanor are far more mysterious, suggestive, and poetic than in the novel. He is a romantic loner and outsider who seems to exert a hypnotic force on Rya-Rya; his animal magnetism is underscored by Ulf Palme's mellifluous voice and compelling screen presence. The novel demystifies Rya-Rya's lover by introducing his wife and daughter in the cast of characters, and her brief encounter with him is seen more as a temporary aberration than as an expression of subconscious desire.

Sjöberg's film was criticized by some reviewers for not being realistic enough, for eliminating the dirt and grime, for minimizing the abject poverty in which Lo-Johansson's characters live.[6] Though the charge that the film prettifies the estate-worker environment and the workers themselves is a valid one—the characters even sweat attractively, and Rya-Rya never loses her beauty as she does in the novel—what is more important is that Sjöberg shows us how the protagonist herself tries to cling to a vision of reality that is distorted because it is retouched and refined. The photographic image becomes an important vehicle within the film narrative for conveying this vain attempt. Just as the stiff posture and expressionless stares of the estate-workers in the opening sequence when they are posing for the photographer bear little relation to their everyday demeanor, Rya-Rya discovers that pictures and the reality they supposedly represent sometimes can be poles apart.

When Rya-Rya and Henrik go into town to buy wedding rings, Rya-Rya stops at a photographer's studio to admire a picture of a well-dressed, smiling mother with two cherubic children that is on display in the window. Henrik is unimpressed, asking, "Vad gör du? Står du här och drömmer nu igen?" [What are you doing? Standing here dreaming again?] But this is the image that Rya-Rya is striving to attain, and a couple of years later, wearing a new dress and with her own two children in tow, she secretly goes back to have their picture taken. A brief shot of the same family portrait she had noticed on her previous trip reminds the audience of Rya-Rya's intent and goal.

The outing is not a success; the studio is crowded, the photographer harassed, and moreover the younger child cries continuously. The image that eventually is recorded for posterity is hardly one of family happiness and harmony: Rya-Rya stares blankly at the camera as the baby struggles in her arms. The painted backdrop, a stylized representation of classical antiquity, complete with a grove of trees and the pillars of a temple, could hardly be further removed from her everyday reality and is a jarring contrast to the countrified appearance of Rya-Rya's plaid dress and the straw hat of her son.

Henrik, hearing from others that Rya-Rya has been to the photographer behind his back, reacts angrily, unaware that she intends the picture as a present for him. His ire, moti-

The awkwardness and discomfort captured in the studio portrait do not correspond to Rya-Rya's idealized internal image of family bliss. (*From Svenska Filminstitutets Bildarkiv. Reproduced with the permission of Svensk Filmindustri.*)

vated by insecurity and the need to feel he is in control, is symptomatic of the communication gap and lack of mutual sympathy and understanding that characterize the marriage and also suggests that he does not share Rya-Rya's unspoken goal of family unity. By the time the picture arrives in the mail, however, it no longer represents the actual family constellation at all, but rather becomes an acutely painful reminder of what has been lost, for moments before little Margaretha had died. Rya-Rya, wailing like a child herself, cannot bear even to look at the photograph and thrusts it into a bureau drawer.

The picture subsequently represents an unfulfilled image of family togetherness, in part bitterly ironic, since it has been shattered, in part idealistic, since it is still a goal. Some years later, as Rya-Rya is preparing the Christmas meal, Henrik bursts in and berates his wife for having taken on housecleaning responsibilities at the Inspector's, a job that he assumes includes sexual favors. Striking her, he rushes out as the children circle around to comfort their mother. Before Rya-Rya and the children sit down to Christmas dinner without him, she reaches into the drawer and places the picture on the plate originally intended for Henrik.

It is important in this context that Rya-Rya does not, as Gunnar Lundin claims, put the photograph at a place set for her deceased daughter;[7] there are six plates and six living family members. Also significant is that Rya-Rya and the children, but not Henrik, appear in the picture. The substitution of the studio portrait for the actual presence of Henrik becomes an emblematic gesture: as Rya-Rya becomes increasingly alienated from her husband, she turns instead to her children for affection and validation. After the brief episode of passion with Hammar, she retreats completely into her maternal role and projects her longing onto them.

That Rya-Rya's search for fulfillment now will be solely through the younger generation is underscored verbally as well: during an argument, she bursts out to Henrik, "Jag har bara ett att leva för nu" [I have only one thing to live for now]. An immediate cut to Rya-Rya taking her two youngest children to school establishes

The photograph replaces the absent Henrik at Christmas dinner. (*From Svenska Filminstitutets Bildarkiv. Reproduced with the permission of Svensk Filmindustri.*)

conclusively that it is they who lend meaning to her life. When the children subsequently outshine their peers on the final oral examination—a scene that borrows elements from another Lo-Johansson novel, *Godnatt, jord* (1933; *Breaking Free*, 1990)—Rya-Rya glows with pride and happiness. In her deathbed scene, filmed beautifully and lingeringly but without excessive sentimentality, Rya-Rya is concerned for her family, not herself, and finally rests content when the children reassure her that they will manage. As in the novel, she asks Henrik to forgive her, and he does. The film ends with a lovely silhouetted shot of Rya-Rya's face in peaceful repose.

The audience may nevertheless recall the printed text that introduces the film: "How great a distance is there not from one human being to another!" Rya-Rya has achieved inner harmony and reconciliation with her nearest and dearest, but it is impossible to escape the implication that this came about only through the sacrifice of her own personal happiness. She was able to bridge the abyss only once, with Hammar, and that step, like the fateful dip in the lake, shattered her life. Especially in the deathbed scene, the individual images of Sjöberg's film are so artful, so aesthetically pleasing, that they embellish the reality being depicted and hence deflect the underlying pessimism that lies at the core of both novel and film. Here, Sjöberg partially undercuts his own stated intention of focusing on interpersonal alienation; psychological realism takes a back seat to the film convention of providing a resolution that is emotionally satisfying to the audience. On the whole, however, Sjöberg's arrangement of the material and his focus on parallel action, counterpoint, and scenic juxtaposition serve to highlight Rya-Rya's story in a manner that is both filmic and faithful to the source.

NOTES

[1] Translations of voiceover and dialogue from the film are my own.

[2] Lundin and Olsson, *Regissörens roller*, 66–67.

[3] Here and elsewhere, English-language place names follow the published translation of the novel.

[4] Sjöberg discusses Lo-Johansson's criticism in Lundin and Olsson, *Regissörens roller*, 66–67, but emphasizes that the author's overall assessment of the film was positive. Sjöberg's own stance toward the material is further explicated in "Bara en mor. Reflexioner kring en ickedokumentarisk film" (*Biografbladet* 1949:3, reprinted in Häggbom, *Bara en mor*, 16–17, and Lundin and Olsson, *Regissörens roller*, 124–126).

[5] Sjöberg provides a detailed analysis of this sequence in "Omskakning i bildsinnet," originally published in *Biografbladet* (1949–50:4) and reprinted in Lundin and Olsson, *Regissörens roller*, 127–129.

[6] Reviews of the film are available on microfiche at the Klipparkiv of Svenska Filminstitutet. A summary of critical response may be found in *Svensk Filmografi* IV, 746–747, and in Lundin, *Filmregi Alf Sjöberg*, 98.

[7] Lundin, *Filmregi Alf Sjöberg*, 95. The published script describes the scene as follows: "Henriks stol är tom. Rya kommer bortifrån byrån med porträttet från fotografiateljén. . . . Hon sätter ner det framför Henriks plats" [Henrik's chair is empty. Rya comes from the bureau with the portrait from the photographer's studio. . . . She puts it down in front of Henrik's place]; Ettrup et al., *Bara en mor*, 68–69.

Works Cited

Bergström, Lasse. "Maskspel med ödets avsikter." In *Skott i mörkret*. Stockholm: Wahlström & Widstrand, 1956.

Ettrup, Lise, Flemming Kurdahl, and Mette Weisberg. *Bara en mor*. Læs en film series. Copenhagen: Gjellerup & Gad, 1987.

Häggbom, Råland. *Bara en mor. En kommentar.* Uppsala: Kursverksamheten vid Uppsala Universitet, 1965.

Lo-Johansson, Ivar. *Bara en mor*. Stockholm: Bonnier, 1939.

———. *Breaking Free*. Translated, with an afterword and notes, by Rochelle Wright. Lincoln and London: University of Nebraska Press, 1990.

———. *Godnatt, jord*. Stockholm: Bonnier, 1933.

———. *Only a Mother*. Translated, with an afterword and notes, by Robert E. Bjork. Lincoln and London: University of Nebraska Press, 1991.

———, and Gunnar Lundh. *Statarna i bild*. KF:s bokförlag, 1948.

Lundin, Gunnar. *Filmregi Alf Sjöberg*. Lund: Wallin & Dahlholm,

1979.

———, and Jan Olsson. *Regissörens roller. Samtal med Alf Sjöberg*. Lund: Cavefors, 1976.

Åhlander, Lars, ed. *Svensk filmografi*, vol. IV. Stockholm: Svenska Filminstitutet, 1980.

Cross-Dressing and Subjectivity in the Films of Ingmar Bergman

Marilyn Johns Blackwell

Since clothing articulates sex roles in a given society, instances of cross-dressing can serve to challenge the ideology in that society. The extent to which clothing and ideology are complicit is suggested by Kaja Silverman, who points to the historical shift in men's clothing from a designator of rank and privilege to a signifier of "the solidarity between one male subject and all others. Male clothing [has also come] increasingly to signify allegiance to a larger social order, and man's privileged position within that order" (25). Thus, almost always gendered, dress usually reinforces the gender of the body beneath it, but cross-dressing undercuts this equation and has the potential of calling into question dominant ideology. As Annette Kuhn points out, by drawing attention to the artifice of gender identity, cross-dressing effects a "wilful alienation" from the fixity of that identity (54).

To a society that aligns gender difference with power, cross-dressing appears as threatening and subversive. Art works that represent cross-dressing have, then, the potential of resisting dominant ideology by problematizing gender fixity, of repudiating a world-view that would define women solely in terms of their biology. Within this framework, it is significant that Ingmar Bergman creates in his production three separate instances of cross-dressing, in *Ansiktet* (1958), *Tystnaden* (1963), and *Fanny och Alexander* (1984).

For Bergman, as for many other artists who take up this motif, cross-dressing is frequently associated with performance, practiced by people whose life is in the theater or the allied performance arts. Such a connection can emphasize the constructed nature of gender, the idea of gender as performance rather than biology. Thus Aman/Manda in *Ansiktet* is the assistant in a magician's show, and Johan in *Tystnaden* is clothed in a girl's dress by a traveling troupe of acrobats. The association between cross-dressing and performance underscores the notion that clothing itself is performance. If gendered clothing does not absolutely equate with the gendered subject, if the wearer is in some sense performing, this performance, as Kuhn suggests, "poses the possibility of a mutable self, of a fluidity of subjectivity . . . . As a means to, even the substance of, a commutable persona, clothing as performance threatens to undercut the ideological fixity of the human subject" (52–53). Cross-dressing constantly points to the distance between the "real" gendered self and the infinitely varied performances or personae through which the human subject expresses him- or herself. It is in this sense of cross-dressing as performance and performance as an intimation of the fluidity of the subject, that Bergman's interest in the issue can be located, for his entire production is dedicated to an exploration of the constitution of human subjectivity. If a fixed subjectivity and a gendered subjectivity are perceived to be one and the same, then the collapse of one entails the dissolution of the other, and Bergman's production consistently examines this ideological equation.

That cross-dressing is put to different uses by male and female artists is not surprising. For instance, Janet Todd notes that when Emma in *Madame Bovary* adopts male dress, "masculinity . . . becomes the mirror of her social-moral vacillations. When she dons a male costume at the end, the final disintegration of her personality is accomplished" (8). The parameters of this difference (ones that are helpful in defining Bergman's position) have been charted by Sandra Gilbert. Examining the motif of transvestism in three major male modernists (James Joyce, D. H. Lawrence, and T. S. Eliot) and three major female modernists (Virginia Woolf, Djuna Barnes, and H.D.), Gilbert finds that in the male tradition false costume is portrayed as either unsexed or wrongly sexed, while true costumes are properly sexed, thus reinforcing the "rightness" of gender appropriate clothing and of gender fixity as truth. She discovers in these authors a suggestion that "a departure from gender fixity implies disorder and disease" (405). In the female authors, however, she finds a tendency to treat costumes with ambiguity, a refusal to distinguish between mask and self. "On the contrary," she argues, "many literary women from Woolf to Plath see what literary men call 'selves' as costumes and costumes as selves" (394). For them, costumes, like selves, are fluidly interchangeable, not fixed and immutable: "just as male modernist costume imagery is profoundly conservative, feminist modernist costume imagery is radically revisionary, . . . for it implies that no one, male or female, can or should be confined to a uni-form, a single form or self" (394). While the male modernists seek to relocate a sense of self shattered by the cataclysm of World War One within a myth that reifies gender difference (thereby replacing historical "truth" with mythical "truth"), the feminists seek to define a gender-free reality beyond myth, to reveal the pure sexless (or "third-sexed") being behind gender and myth (412).

On the most elementary level, Bergman's treatment of cross-dressing differs from that of the androcentric tradition. Since cross-dressing is perceived in that tradition as an opportunity to reassert the masculine order or to allow the male to absorb the realm of female experience so that he can better rule, it is hardly surprising that most cross-dressers in the Western tradition are male, women largely denied this subjectivity-expanding experience since they are, after all, seen as possessing gender identity rather than human subjectivity. It is noteworthy, then, that Bergman's first cross-dresser is a woman. The Aman/Manda character in *Ansiktet* is an early acknowledgment by Bergman of the mutability of the self. This figure with her, as he puts it, "oavlåtligt skiftande sexuella identitet" (*Bilder* 180) is clearly central to the film; he asserts "själva navet i historien är naturligtvis androgynen Aman/Manda. Det är kring henne och hennes gåtfulla person som allt rör sig" (*Bilder* 167).

Significantly, we as viewers do not "know" that Aman is actually Manda, a woman. Many cross-dressing narratives, because of the threat that transvestism constitutes, go to great lengths to explain away the rejection of gender-appropriate clothing. Such is not the case in *Ansiktet*; although Aman does not look very "masculine," we do not learn that she is a woman until midway through the film. We know no more about the sexual identity of this figure than do the suspicious and threatening representatives of the official social order who interrogate them. Even the names of this character, Aman and Manda, are a kind of reversal of each other, a male-female mirror reflection. Thus, Aman functions, to a certain extent, like the feminist narratives Gilbert examines, to problematize the fixity of gender. And once we are given an explanation as to why Manda is disguised as Aman—because they are wanted by the police—the explanation seems flimsy indeed; given the physical profile of this troupe (one wizened old woman, one chubby, jolly man, one tall man with angular features, and one young woman) it seems unlikely that the police could be put off simply by Manda's disguise. And, one wonders, if they are wanted by the police, why does Vogler have his name emblazoned across the carriage? Thus a plausible excuse for the cross-dressing seems lacking. Rather one might speculate that Manda is dressed in gender-false clothing precisely so that Bergman can speculate on the genderedness of the artistic subject.

We note here that it is the cross-dresser Aman/Manda who articulates the dilemma of the artist both in the carriage and later when she tells the man of science and reason (evil as always in Bergman): "vår verksamhet är bedrägeri från början till slut .... förfalskning, falska löfter, dubbla bottnar ....

Cross-Dressing and Subjectivity   197

eländig, rutten lögn alltgenom.... Ingenting är sant." It is also he/she who is in discursive control when they are examined by the representatives of officialdom in the library, explaining that their magic is "ett spel, ingenting annat.... Vi använder apparater, speglar och projektioner. Det är mycket enkelt och fullkomligt ofarligt." While her husband sits mute, Aman/Manda expresses the truth of their artistry, her cross-dressing providing the distance between mask and self requisite to full awareness. Significantly, Vogler is also masked through much of the film, in false whiskers and eyebrows and a wig, but his disguise is sexually "appropriate" and thus does not allow him to achieve the same awareness as his wife. The verbal prominence of the cross-dresser is reinforced through camera technique. During the interrogation, Aman is usually located closest to the camera or at the center of shot compositions as a comment on the centrality of the cross-dressing experience to the film's locus of meaning.

But once Aman is unmasked, the film abandons its problematizing potential and moves forward toward an essentially conservative conclusion. Back in "correct" dress, Manda becomes a loving wife, consoling her husband in his artistic crisis, physically positioned behind him. Although she dons male dress once again to lock the attic door so that her husband can perform his art on Vergerus, when she unlocks the door out of pity for him, she is again in woman's dress. Compositionally too, she is now subordinate; while the policeman reads the decree from the king of Sweden summoning them to come and perform at the castle, Vogler is centered in the shot, while she stands behind him. The patriarchy is reaffirmed; the king saves the day and Vogler proceeds to his command performance with his loving and supportive wife by his side. The equilibrium between the sexes is restored; man is dominant, woman submissive, all within a divinely (or at least royally) sanctioned hierarchy of meaning. But this mechanical ending is almost completely unmotivated within the text and abandons the central issue of the film, the issue of the artist's relationship to his or her craft and the relationship between art and the human subject.

Although Aman/Manda's cross-dressing is an implicit acknowledgment of the lack of gender and subject fixity, it is also an attempt to infuse masculine artistry with the generative qualities associated with the female and is, as such, still a conventional and ideologically compromised representation of cross-dressing. Bergman's abandonment of the cross-dressing issue in favor of a *deus ex machina* affirmation of the patriarchy at the end of the film, however regrettable both artistically and ethically, is, one suspects, the only possible solution for an artist still so engaged at this point in his career in a quest for God, the ultimate patriarch.

But by the time Bergman makes *Tystnaden* in 1963, he has acknowledged the pernicious present/absence of God with all that that entails in terms of a dissolution and corruption of the patriarchy and its values. Indeed, this film marks the beginning of major changes in his work. Male protagonists engaged in quests for the supernatural are replaced by female protagonists trying to come to grips with their position in a patriarchal order that marginalizes them into nonexistence. This is also the first of two films to position a child as the central consciousness. It is this child, Johan, who is the second cross-dresser in the Bergman canon. Traveling with his mother and his aunt through a hostile foreign country that is relentlessly male (there are almost no women in the train or the teeming street scenes) and whose language he does not speak, Johan finds himself in an old hotel wandering seemingly endless corridors seeking amusement. While thus wandering, Johan espies a dwarf who tips his hat at him as he passes by. After staring for a time at a Rubenesque painting of a nymph and a satyr, Johan comes upon an open door and peers in to discover six dwarfs sitting about the room, reading the newspaper, playing cards, and repairing theatrical props amidst a great clutter of trunks and baggage.

He pretends to shoot them with his toy pistol; they play along and dramatically "die." Then, laughing and smiling, they put a girl's dress on him, and all of them stand about watching one of the troupe who is wearing an ape mask do acrobatic tricks. This play is, however, interrupted when the man from the hallway enters, yells, orders the dress taken off Johan, and then shows him to the door. The scene is followed by a shot of the boy rebelliously urinating in one of the corridors.

The prevalent critical position on this scene is that it demonstrates an incursion into Johan's life of the same distorted and fragmented sexuality that plagues the lives of Anna his mother and Ester his aunt. Such a reading gains credence from the fact that both women meet the dwarf troupe at times when they experience their own sexuality as degraded (Anna watches them onstage while a couple next to her copulates animalistically, and Ester sees them parade down the hall just after leaving her sister, who is having a meaningless tryst with a barman). This view is also supported by the fact that Johan's visit with the dwarfs is intercut with shots of his mother bathing her breasts, getting dressed, and putting on make-up in preparation for cruising a local bar. In the context of the rest of the film, then, such an interpretation seems warranted.

But a closer examination poses some problems for this reading, for there is no sense here that Johan experiences this cross-dressing as in any way threatening or distasteful. On the contrary, the introduction of the male dwarf in the hallway seems unusual but certainly not threatening; after all, he smiles and tips his hat pleasantly at the little boy. And when Johan looks in the room, he finds these men engaged in completely "normal" everyday activities. They are furthermore photographed in long shot, placing them at a safe distance from the little boy. They play along with his "shooting" them, and their facial expressions are friendly. Too, the screenplay does not refer to these people as "dvärgar," but rather as "små mänskor" or "små varelser," as if consciously refusing to use the word "dwarf," which in the literary tradition has come to be associated with debased humanity and the truncated self (this is especially true in Swedish literature, one of whose classics is, of course, Pär Lagerkvist's *Dvärgen*, with its unspeakably malevolent title character). In the filmscript, Bergman explicitly describes Johan's reaction at having this dress put on him as "lite generad, ... men inte alls rädd" (133).

Johan's cross-dressing occurs, then, among people whose lives center around performance, people who are doubly marginalized—once by their low-status profession and again by a society that sees them as biological freaks. The dwarfs seem freakish and perverted only to those who are already ideologically compromised. Perversion, the film argues, is a culturally assigned designation, the burden of which is placed on those who accept genderedness as absolute. Thus, Johan's experience of cross-dressing diverges from most dominant cinema transvestite narratives, in which the cross-dresser is motivated either by sexual perversion (thrillers like *Psycho*) or by a need to hide his or her true identity (musical comedies such as *Some Like It Hot*). In either event, both genres still reinforce the idea that subjectivity is gendered and that a departure from gender fixity is a violation of the normal order.

But Johan's experience is also greatly dissimilar from that which Gilbert finds in Joyce's Nighttown episode (which together with Lawrence's "The Fox" and Eliot's Tiresias form a kind of paradigm of the male modernist experience of transvestism). She points to how threatening and degrading the experience is for Bloom, to the fact that it is a woman, Bella, who so emasculates him, and to the element of sadism involved in this transvestism (394). These elements are all absent in Johan's experience. On the contrary, the fact that Johan's transvestism is interrupted and terminated by a male authority figure would seem to connote precisely how threatening gender fluidity is for the patriarchal hierarchy.

Joyce's Bloom further undergoes a kind of "ritual sexual

inversion" that Gilbert designates as a "Feast of Misrule" (399), from which the male regains strength for "proper" rule in order that the hierarchical principle of an order based upon male dominance/female submission may be recovered from transvestite disorder. By experiencing reality as a female through transvestism, the male incorporates into himself female experience the better to rule over both realms. The burden of the Nighttown episode is, then, she argues, a recovery of male potency, a reclaiming of the masterful male self, as exemplified in Bloom's emotional bonding with his "son" Stephen and his ordering his wife to bring him breakfast the next morning. But again, Johan's experience is different. The film cannot even remotely be said to portray the reemergence of the patriarchal order from transvestite disorder. On the contrary, the film ends with Johan intently reading a message from his aunt, a female legacy that points to the importance of identifying with women and of transgressing boundaries. By chronicling the boy's mental and emotional development as he tries to learn from and balance within himself the emotional lives of the two older women and by incorporating into itself a scene of cross-dressing that does not designate Johan's experience as degraded, perverse, or threatening, the film challenges the dominant ideology of gender and subject fixity.

Unlike *Ansiktet*, *Tystnaden* does not indulge in textual closure. At the end of the film, the boy continues on his journey. Kuhn finds a direct relationship between the denaturalizing potential of a cross-dressing text and its openness. She points to Barthes's contention that closure itself is "a mark of culturally dominant narrative forms, forms whose trajectory is always towards resolution, the closing over of gaps" (56). The closed form of *Ansiktet*, then, is motivated by Bergman's desire to align himself with the patriarchal hierarchy, whereas the more open ending of *Tystnaden* reinforces the film's rejection of that hierarchy and acknowledges its bankruptcy.

But it is not until Bergman's last film, *Fanny och Alexander*, that he creates a character who embodies what Gilbert calls the "visionary multiplicity" of gender. The climactic scene that presents this vision occurs, significantly, in the home of Uncle Isak, whose Jewishness distinguishes him (in Bergman's view) from the oppressive patriarchy of late nineteenth-century Lutheranism and who is connected to Alexander through the boy's grandmother. Thus Bergman stages Alexander's epiphany in an environment that challenges both religious and gender orthodoxy.

The person who facilitates Alexander's epiphany is Ishmael, played by an actress wearing "male" clothing and with a male name. Significantly the credits for the film do not indicate who plays what role; thus the viewer is even further hindered in his or her attempt to ascertain the sex of the actor. Ishmael is referred to by Aron as "min bror," and yet he/she speaks with a higher register, woman's voice. As in *Ansiktet*, the filmscript consistently refers to Ishmael as male, and yet the visual and aural evidence posit this person as female. Thus, the viewer is left with an impression of uncanny dual-genderedness, the "third sex" that Gilbert locates in female modernist texts. Significantly too, as spectators we are deprived of the "view behind," according to which we would know this character's "true" gender and thus be able to locate him/her in the patriarchal hierarchy.

Ishmael's gender amorphism points to Bergman's perception of the great human potential that lies beyond genderedness, an interpretation that Bundtzen intimates when she argues that Alexander's exposure to Ishmael forces him "to acknowledge and assume responsibility for his passions and their all-too-real consequences when projected by his imaginative power" (108). The boy, like Gilbert's male modernists' protagonists, seems to need the experience of gender amorphism or cross-dressing in order to achieve full subjectivity at the same time that the ending indicates that his "mastery" is aligned not with patriarchal but with female values. But Ishmael is more than a representation of the androgynous self; Bergman depicts this person as a mentor to Alexander in his artistic apprenticeship. For, in Bergman's view, society is hostile to both art and gender amorphism, linked as they are in their implicit affirmation of the mutability of the human subject. Society, then, needs to shut away both so as to quiet the voice and obscure the visions. The artist is outside the mainstream of society and threatens social convention. This interpretation is supported by Ishmael's statement, "Jag anses farlig. Därför är jag inlåst," and when asked why he/she is dangerous, Ishmael replies that he/she has "obekväma talanger." Thus, the film also represents gender amorphism as a threat to society; Ishmael's room is a kind of prison with locks on both the doors and with boarded-up windows. It is not accidental that Aron's sibling is named Ishmael, for like his/her biblical namesake, Ishmael has been exiled.

But Ishmael is threatening to little Alexander as we see in the sexual tension in the scene. When the two males first enter, Ishmael tells Aron that he needn't be afraid, that he/she won't "äta upp" little Alexander, "fast han ser mycket aptitlig ut." As Aron prepares to leave, he approaches his "brother" and gives him a long, passionate kiss. And later, while Ishmael is reading Alexander's mind, he/she lowers the boy's nightshirt and places his/her hand on his chest. These elements all posit gender amorphism as threatening to the male subject. But this text differs from the male modernist texts in Gilbert's study by positing the transgression of gender boundaries not as personal pathology but rather, however threatening, as an enriching component in a full human and artistic life as well as by implicitly rejecting the patriarchy in its ending.

The identification process between Alexander and Ishmael is documented both visually and diagetically with a variety of techniques. After reverse close-ups, Alexander, on Ishmael's instructions, writes his own name only to discover that he has written Ishmael's instead. That he has done so unconsciously is evident from the fact that he stumbles over the pronunciation of the last name. This identity mergence becomes explicit when Ishmael says, "Kanske är vi samma person; kanske har vi inga gränser; kanske flyter vi genom varandra, strömmar genom varandra obegränsat och storartat."

As the scene continues, Ishmael begins to read Alexander's thoughts ("Du bär på förfärliga tankar. Du bär på en människas död") and, as the camera moves into a close-up on Ishmael's face next to Alexander's ear, his/her voice recounts what the boy is thinking. As Ishmael reads Alexander's mind and as the visions stored there are articulated and released, the editing accelerates with rapidly intercut images from the bishop's home, images that will culminate in the evil stepfather's death. To quote Jacqueline Rose, "The uncertain sexual identity muddles the plane of the image so that the spectator does not know where he or she stands in relationship to the picture. A confusion at the level of sexuality brings with it a disturbance of the visual field" (226). The bishop, we note, has the same last name as the scientist in *Ansiktet*, Vergerus, a name Bergman reserves in his canon for spiritually bankrupt, ideologically corrupt male rationalists, and he is also, of course, an officer of the church with all that that implies in terms of his complicity with the patriarchal hierarchy. Throughout his career, Bergman reuses the same names in different films, most notably Vogler and Vergerus, underlining his vision of the mutability of identity and undermining the fixed, phallic aspect of language, according to which the power of naming is the power of possession, of the usurpation of the identity of the other.

That it is Alexander, empowered by Ishmael, who is responsible for the bishop's and his aunt's deaths is clear from Ishmael's statement: "Har du hört talas om att man gör ett beläte av nån man tycker illa om och sticker nålar i belätet? Det är en ganska klumpig metod när man betänker vilka snabba vägar de onda tankarna kan gå." Their deaths are represented as a direct result of the mergence of Ishmael and Alexander and of Ishmael's empowering gender amorphism. By articulating these images, Ishmael compels Alexander to a realization of his own power and his own responsibilities, even as the boy repeatedly voices his reluctance and fear of acknowledging this power. Both gender amorphism and the death of the patriarchy's representative are rendered as frightening, threatening, and yet as fostering a richer and more creative subjectivity.

Again, then, but in more radical form, Bergman does not present us with images of "ritual sexual inversion" whose "sexually compensatory transvestism" is intended to allow the male to reassert patriarchal dominance. On the contrary, the ending of the film depicts the death of the patriarchy and the emergence of a kind of matriarchy. With his biological father and his stepfather both dead, Alexander's mother takes over management of the family theater together with his grandmother (one of the few unambiguously positive characters in the film). The final image of the film, then, is of Alexander with his head in his grandmother's lap while she reads from the preface to August Strindberg's *Ett drömspel*: "Allt kan ske, allt är möjligt och sannolikt. Tid och rum existera icke; på en obetydlig verklighetsgrund spinner inbillningen ut och väver nya mönster." But if Helena had continued on in Strindberg's text, she would have read: "Personerna klyvas, fördubblas, dubbleras, dunsta av, förtätas, flyta ut, samlas" (7). This vision of the mutability of subjectivity reflects a view of reality implicit in Aron's earlier statement to Alexander: "Farbror Isak, han påstår att vi är omgivna av verkligheter, den ena utanför den andra. Han säger att det vimlar av vålnader, andar och spöken, själar och gengångare, änglar och djävlar," and both these statements are juxtaposed in the strongest possible terms with the bishop's rigid view of an immutable human reality, grounded in the destructive patriarchy to which he has dedicated his life. Instead, Isak's mystical, cabalistic reality and Helena's Strindberg-inspired vision of the multiplicity of human subjectivity prevail.

Quite explicitly, then, Bergman leaves his narrative open, as a female voice articulates, "Anything can happen." Female authority is asserted at the conclusion of this open narrative even if the words this authority articulates come from the pen of one of Western culture's most famous misogynists. Bergman ultimately affirms the insight to be gained from cross-dressing and gender amorphism, the insight that the concept of gender and subject fixity is and remains fundamentally false. During his career, then, Bergman develops an increasingly radical vision of the implications of cross-dressing. Like the female modernists Gilbert cites, he suggests that costume and mask, not anatomy, are destiny. The consciousness mergence implicit in gender amorphism is posited as both enriching and yet an act of appropriation threatening to the male self. Reluctant though he may sometimes be, ultimately Bergman does acknowledge that gender and subject fixity are false constructs that art in general and his art in particular can help contest.

Works Cited

Bergman, Ingmar. *Filmberättelser I: Såsom genom en spegel, Nattvardsgästerna, Tystnaden.* Stockholm: Pan, 1973.

Bundtzen, Lynda. "Bergman's *Fanny and Alexander*: Family Romance or Artistic Allegory," *Criticism* 29:1 (1987): 89–117.

Gilbert, Sandra. "Costumes of the Mind: Transvestism as Metaphor in Modern Literature," *Critical Inquiry* 7 (1980): 391–417.

Kuhn, Annette. *The Power of the Image: Essays on Representation and Sexuality.* London: Routledge, 1985.

Rose, Jacqueline. *Sexuality in the Field of Vision.* New York: Verso, 1986.

Silverman, Kaja. *The Acoustic Mirror: The Female Voice in Psychoanalysis and Cinema.* Bloomington: Indiana University Press, 1988.

Strindberg, August. *Ett Drömspel.* Edited by Gunnar Ollén. Volume 46 of *August Strindbergs Samlade verk.* Edited by Lars Dahlbäck. Stockholm: Norstedts, 1988.

Todd, Janet. *Gender and Literary Voice.* New York: Holmes and Meier, 1980.

Ingmar Bergman and the Mise en Scéne of the Confessional

Maaret Koskinen

Religion as art, art as religion

It is well known that Ingmar Bergman, in interviews as well as in his published articles, often has referred to art in terms of cult and worship. In *Det att göra film* from 1954, for instance, he writes about his longing to be an anonymous craftsman among others:

> I want to be one of the artists in the cathedral on the great plain. I want to carve a dragon's head, an angel, a devil or perhaps a saint out of stone. It does not matter which. Regardless of whether I believe or not, whether I am a Christian or not, I would play my part in the collective building of the cathedral.[1]

Thus Bergman quite obviously sets up an analogy between (Christian) religion and art as such: both are expressions of cult. This is expressed even clearer in a note written for the premiere of *Through a Glass Darkly* (1961):

> The creative artist performs an action of cult, similar to the priest, and the stage or the podium is the place of the cult.[2]

However, this relationship between art and religion is not unproblematic by any means. Quite the contrary, the act of cult for Bergman is seldom merely an expression of faith. More often than not it is performed with doubt and uncertainty, or at least in a context characterized by an oscillation between faith and unbelief, trust and doubt. For instance, in the previously mentioned text from 1954, Bergman stressed that:

> Regardless of my own faith or doubt . . . it is my opinion that art lost its basic creative drive the moment it was separated from worship. It severed an umbilical cord and now lives its own sterile life, generating and degenerating itself.[3]

Later, this sterility of art became the main theme in his acceptance speech *The Snakeskin*, written when receiving the prestigious Erasmus prize in 1965. Here again, the notion of faith vs doubt clearly encompassed art as well as religion. "Religion and art," Bergman wrote, "are kept alive out of purely sentimental reasons, out of a conventional politeness to the past."[4] In an interview from 1969 this was expressed in no uncertain terms:

> When it comes to god . . . an immense feeling of hesitation has always announced itself. On that score, a sense of trust has never revealed itself. . . . Faith has always been parallell with faithlessness and devotion to mocking. And finally, with regard to art . . . I have always been doubtful. . . , I have felt both inside of it and excluded from it.[5]

This notion of art as cult or extension and incomplete *Ersatz* for religion is, of course an important aspect not only of Bergman's theoretical declarations but of his films as well, especially those concerned with the theme of art and the artist. In *The Magician/The Face* (1958), for example, the film focuses on a kind of "dual faith and doubt-theme" involving two opposing systems of faith. On the one hand, the old fashioned art of magic and sorcery, on the other a new and growing ideology of science. As Granny (Naima Wifstrand) drily comments: "One sees what one sees and one knows what one knows." Thus she seems to acknowledge that seeing is not the same as believing, as the empirical-positivist scientist Vergerus, with his staunch belief in observation as the tool of truth, would have it. Granny, on the other hand, knows that sight is deceiving. As does, of course, Vogler the magician, whose entire career is based on the powers of illusion. With his Christlike makeup he is the very embodiment of the faith versus doubt-theme in the film, conflating its religious aspects with the artistic, as Vogler's "magnetic theater" is obviously also a metaphor for art (and film).[6]

In the 60s, after the so-called trilogy when Bergman had, as he himself put it, dispensed with "that heavy religious superstructure,"[7] it is interesting to note how the pendulum faith-doubt quite simply seems to shift from the domain of religion to the domain of art. This is perhaps best seen in *Persona*—Bergman's most artistically (self-)reflective film—where the actress Elisabet's relationship with, and silence towards, nurse Alma in many ways is similar to the silence of that god that the Knight prays to in *The Seventh Seal*: whereas one party talks and talks, confessing and asking questions, the other remains aloof and silent. As Maria Bergom Larsson has pointed out, in Bergman's later work, art is as silent as god was in his earlier films.[8]

Thus, it is possible to discern a developmental pattern in Bergman's films: questions concerning religious faith and doubt have simply been replaced by similar questions in the domain of art. In the latter case, questions about the need for art in the first place, and the role of art in a world that does not much need what art has to offer. Indeed, it may well be said that this pattern is characteristic of Bergman's entire *oeuvre*, that is an intellectually probing attitude, which continuously moves between opposites rather than securing a fixed position. It is for instance interesting to note how a similar pattern recurs when Bergman in the latter part of his career, in the early 70s, in turn abandons the theme of art and artists, now shifting his focus towards supposedly more ordinary people: a doubt or outright indifference towards matters of art and artists is replaced by an (albeit) tentative faith in everyday humanity, in what Bergman later has called "människans helighet".[9] To summarize: God was banished from Bergman's films[10] and so too, the theme of art. His view of art, however, as basically an act of cult remained. It became, to borrow the title of his TV-play from 1969, a ritual—an act of cult without god. As he himself put it at the time:

> The practice of art as sorcery, as ritual action, as prayer, as reciprocal gratification of needs—this I have always felt very strongly.[11]

What better proof of this idea than the fact that in his TV-play, *Larmar och gör sig till* (screened on Swedish television in 1997), Bergman manages not only to fuse film with theater, i.e. the two main areas of his professional life (the play is about a bizarre premiere of "the world's first silent talking picture", which, due to electrical failure brought on by a blizzard, instead turns into a play, a staged version of the film). He also draws on characters known from his previous fictional work, for example, Märta Lundberg, the schoolmistress, the widowed Karin Persson, and the church janitor Algot Frövik from *Winter Light* (1963), as well as his autobiography: Uncle Carl, his maternal grandmother Anna Åkerblom, his mother Karin. Even her two "little boys" are included. But more important is the fact that the staging of the play (within the play) is *organized, staged, and acted by the audience itself*, that is the very people who dare the blizzard to see the silent film, but now instead end up on stage themselves, while drinking hot coffee. What happens here is essentially that the play turns into a kind of profane communion, or as Bergman himself has put it, when commenting on the fact that he consciously used the audience from *Winter Light*: "they should be given a chance and commit a more earthly and concrete act of communion that stormy night in Grånäs."[12] What better proof of the idea of art as an act of cult without god?

The Confessional

However, there is good reason to believe that although religion as subject and theme vanished from Bergman's films it never vanished as a pattern of thought, or in a generalized sense, as cinematic language or style. Bergmans post-religious films quite obviously disclose a deep affinity with a Christian conceptual world. One example out of many is that illuminating and at the same time inexplicable light that suddenly, and with otherworldly grace, breaks forth, flooding over someone who suffers or is downtrodden. Bergman uses it in *Winter Light* when the parson is beset by doubts in the existence of that god he prays to every day, in *A Passion of Anna* (1969) where the fisherman has been beaten to death, and in *Cries and Whispers* (1972), at the very moment Agnes dies. This phenomenon has been described as a kind of lingering religious "hangover" or the remains from a fallen world.[13]

One particular facet of this fallen world in Bergman's cinematic *oeuvre* is crystallized in what could be called the confessional, or perhaps better, *the mise en scene of the confessional*. Naturally, the confession is normally related to Christian religion, and more specifically to Catholicism rather than the Protestant tradition to which Bergman belongs. What is stressed in this context, however, is the structural affinity between confession and prayer, that is the monologous character of both: *someone talks, someone listens*. Worth noting in this regard are the close links that exist between Christianity in general and pre-Christian cult rituals. Most important in this context is the fact that cult constitutes the roots of art and drama. In this context Bergman's definition of the ritual as "the practice of art as sorcery, as ritual action, as prayer, as reciprocal gratification of needs" is interesting, to the degree that *it also describes a similar pattern in the confession(al) act*, that is, that it is structured in a similar fashion to that of the artistic act of cult. Be it a Greek or a latterday theater *someone talks, someone listens*. In this case, it is the actor and the audience. Thus the confession is a part of that which is at the very core of drama, both in terms of what happens between the *dramatis personae*, on stage or screen, and what happens between the characters and the audience. It is located on the very border of the religious and the secular, being an act with roots in both religious and artistic cult ritual. Defined as such, the confession harbors much of what seems to be important to Bergman as an artist. He seems to have found a place and a stage and an unbuilt *mise en scene*, the confession as a kind of *Ur-scene*.

It is possible to find numerous examples of this in Bergman's early and decidedly prereligious films that are structured in terms of a confession of sorts. Perhaps one of the most obvious occurs in *Port of Call* (1948). Because this particular film is based on a book by Olle Länsberg and is considered a working class drama, it is usually referred to as an uncharacteristic Bergman film. But it is not uncharacteristic in its stylistic choices. Thus, in one of the film's pivotal scenes Bergman has Berit, the female protagonist, telling her boyfriend about an episode from the past, a harrowing experience with her mother. The camera slowly closes in on her face as she blankly looks towards the camera while starting her monologue, followed by a double exposure which slides her story into a flashback.

As such, Berit's introspective reminiscening delivered as a monologue, as well as her blank inward stare, seem at first to indicate that she is talking to herself, as if caught in a scrutinizing self-examination. However, here as almost always in scenes like this in Bergman,[14] there is someone who sits beside the person talking, often in the background, quietly listening, represented in this case by her boyfriend. Thus Berit's monologue is at the same time very much a kind of confessional directed to someone else and, as such, expresses a *fundamental faith in that someone is in fact listening*. Indeed, it is hinted that this "someone" may very well be more than only another fictional character. It is for instance interesting to note how Bergman has Berit speak straight into the camera, in the direction of the audience. This is, on the one hand, a venerable and conventionalized way in classical fiction film for entering into flashbacks, signalling that the character does not necessarily look so much at the audience as into some undefinable space beyond.[15] One the other hand, that space is still undeniably one that we share with Berit, and her look into the camera seems to beckon at another presence, acknowledging a basic trust that that other presence will in fact listen and be just as interested in her story as her boyfriend. What we see, then, may be described is a kind of secular prayer or confession directed at a basically benevolent, albeit unknown presence, perhaps the audience, out there in the dark.

In this light it is especially ironic that when Bergman later turned from secular themes to expressly religious ones, the context from which the idea of the confession emanates in the first place, the intimacy expressed in *Port of Call* seems to have evaporated altogether. The foremost example of this is of course the above mentioned scene in *The Seventh Seal* where the Knight goes to the confessional in a small country church and, after having poured out his innermost thoughts, discovers that the hooded monk behind the grid of the confessional booth is Death himself. So he is, in fact, betrayed by god or, since this god chooses in his inscrutable wisdom to remain silent and aloof, by a pitiful, albeit frightening, emissary and henchman for whom the Lord's ways are just as inscrutable.

An interesting variation of this theme of betrayal can be

found in *The Magician/The Face*, in the scene where Mrs. Egerman (Gertrudh Fridh) sneaks into Vogler at night and literally confesses everything that is in her heart to him, a perfect stranger. Significantly, she does so while standing right beside his *laterna magica* and the curtains he has prepared for the performance the next day. "I recognized you immediately", she whispers melodramatically and naively. He is obviously a kind of blank projection sheet for her, potent in his Christ-like demeanor. But, in reality he is reduced to listening to her in helpless disgust and self-loathing, for he knows only too well that his looks are fake. Here, the confessional is reduced to melodrama and religion to hack theater. Or to quote Vergerus, the cynic of the piece: "God is silent while people prattle."

The idea of religious faith as bad theater is stressed even more in *Winter Light,* particularly in the excruciatingly lengthy introductory sequence where the parson, Tomas (Gunnar Björnstrand) administers the communion to his parishioners. That this is nothing more than one long, meaningless ritual is made quite clear through Bergman's intercuts of the few parishioners, obviously bored and distracted.

Given the expressly religious theme of this film it is no surprise that it contains "real" confessionals, as it were, such as the fisherman's visit to Tomas. However, there are other scenes in this film that perhaps do not immediately strike one as being confessions. The most obvious one is the famous, extraordinarily long take of Ingrid Thulin as Märta Lundberg reading her letter to Tomas. It is as if Tomas has conjured forth her face while reading the letter for, with the exception of one brief cutaway, this scene consists of her face in close-up, staring at Tomas (and the audience), while pouring forth what is in her heart. As such, this take is, of course, a confession of sorts, and interestingly the recipient of that confession remains visually absent during that entire take, which he is also in a deeper sense. If nothing else, this is indicated by the nervous and clumsy way in which Tomas tries to jam Märta's thick letter back into its envelope. Thus, Märta's confession doubles the "real" confession scene in the film, where the fisherman walks away from his distracted confessor, who instead of listening to him, talks mostly of himself and his own problems. If in *The Seventh Seal* there was an absent and silent god, there is now a distracted and absent confessor, unable to help or reach out to the people closest to him.

Put somewhat simplistically, then, it is as if the absence of god, or his indifference, in earlier films like *The Seventh Seal* had infected the relations between people in Bergman's films of the 60s. It is in a way subtley logical that this should be expressed in the *mise en scéne* of a confessional where someone speaks and speaks and speaks, but no one listens.

It is obvious as well that in *Winter Light* Bergman involves the viewer in a dilemma similar to that of his characters, again through the look of a character. For while Märta's gaze is directed at Tomas, who is the main recipient to her confession, it is undeniably, just as in the case of *Port of Call*, directed at the viewer. Thus the audience is put into Tomas's shoes but, at the same time, our patience is also put to a test, and very consciously so. At least it is clear from the film's reception that one found the very length of this take almost unbearable (paralleling the other, above mentioned consciously long and boring scenes in the film).[16] It is as if the audience is asked: if god doesn't listen, if people don't listen to each other, do you as a movie audience have the energy to listen to what this film is trying to say?

As we know Bergman took one step further in this direction in *Persona*, a film which in its outright self-reflection also puts the audience to a severe test. Interestingly this film is structured in its entirety around a confession of sorts. One character talks, the other is silent and listens, or rather seems to be listening. Later when Elisabet betrays Alma's confidences (by revealing them in a letter to her doctor), resulting in the famous shot of Alma that seems to spontaneously combust and melt to the point where the entire film seems to break down. Thus, just as Alma's language in the end of the film fails her, the words come out in the wrong order, in a seemingly meaningless mess, the narrative potential of the film itself seems to falter. It is as if the growing suspicion between the characters is paralleled by a growing suspicion in the implied narrator toward the audience.

Language as a lie

This ambivalence towards the communicative tools we have at hand, gestures, masks, words, images, language, is also central to *Passion of Anna* (1969). Although it was made at a time when Bergman supposedly had left the problems of the artist behind, instead turning his interest towards so-called

Alma in *Persona*.

ordinary, everyday people, the interrogation of those communicative tools still included film language as well. This is particularly interesting when considering the outright disbelief that manifests itself toward spoken and written language in this film that words and language are used to hide and betray as often as to clarify. Or, to borrow a quote from Strindberg in "Spöksonaten" which Bergman has cited more than once, that "words hide thoughts."

This manifests itself on a number of levels in the film, and particularly in the scene where Anna (Liv Ullmann) suddenly starts telling Andreas (Max von Sydow) about her former marriage and how happy she and her husband (who is now dead) were.[17] "Of course, we had our conflicts," she admits, "but the words between us were never bitter or harsh" thus seemingly underlining that, like all married couples, they had their share of problems but nothing that shook the basic bond between them. However, at this point in the film a few hints have been introduced that seem to contradict her view, especially a letter from Anna's husband that Andreas has found, which speaks of violence, both "mental and physical." Thus, the viewer cannot be sure what to believe, especially since much of what people up to this point in the film have said seems to be contradicted by what they do.[18] It is precisely this uncertainty of character motivations, indeed the whole film seems to question the idea of "identity" as such, that Bergman uses in this particular scene.[19] He has chosen to convey Anna's confession in one long, mesmerizing take of Liv Ullmann's face in close-up. This is significant as the close-up of the face normally connotes "truth" in main-stream fiction film. As soon something is about to be revealed, such as confidences poured out, someone's true character unveiled, almost invariably there follows a facial close-up as a kind of visual corroboration that this is in fact so. Indeed, through time and use the facial close-up seems to have become the bearer of truth; in and of itself it is the visual figure of truth *par preference*.

Bergman, interestingly, uses these built in connotations for opposite purposes, to create ambiguity or to further the ambiguity already present in the narrative, and to deceive Andreas and perhaps more so, the viewer. For if language hides thoughts, as we have reason to believe in this case, so does the face. The face in close up, and in the able hands of a very good actress placed in a confessional situation, is the best kind of mask, the best kind of lie. To put it another way, this interrogation of spoken and written language is expressed in the very act of interrogating visual language.

In this context it is interesting to compare this close-up of Anna with the photograph shown earlier in the film that Elis Vergerus has taken of his wife, smiling radiantly. However, he tells Andreas, at that very moment she was beset by a migraine attack, and he adds:

> I don't pretend that I can reach the inner depths of the human soul with my photography, hell no. I can only register an interplay and opposite play between thousands of forces, large and small. When you look at the picture and fantasize . . . Everything is nonsense, playing, make-belief. You cannot read any person with any kind of claim of certainty. Not even brutal physical pain gives a reading.[20]

Again, these words seem to point to the difficulty in interpretation as such, and the possibility of knowing the truth in some meaningful sense of the term, especially with regard to people. In this context it is also interesting that Bergman has chosen to represent the letter from Anna's husband in the form of scrutinizing pans, back and forth, as though reading a text. Furthermore, these pans are taken in extreme close-up, so that the whole screen becomes filled with the individual words of the letter. As this shot returns a couple of times in the film, in such a way that it cannot entirely be linked to the point of view of one particular character, it is as if the implied narrator or the camera itself is trying to point to what is at stake here: that we can never be sure of what "the truth" is, or whether it exists at all, however close we seem to get. Thus, the tools we have at hand, images and, not the least, words, tend to fail us. Language, as Bergman once put it, is "terribly devious, many-layered. Slippery, secretive, false... it is hard to find absolute truth."[21]

Private Conversations

> Don't say the word 'God'! Say The Holy One. The Sanctity of Man. Everything else is attribute, disguise, manifestations, tricks, desperation, ritual, cries of despair in the darkness and silence.[22]

With all its shortcomings, language is necessary, it is all we have at our disposal. What better proof of this than the fact that Bergman in the latter part of his career has returned to the written word, and therefore also to the roots from which his career as a whole has sprung. In this context it is of particular interest that one of his literary works alludes to the confessional already in its title, *Private Conversations (Enskilda Samtal)*. Bergman notes, in the first few pages of the book, that it is a misconception that Luther did away with the confession. He "recommended what he called 'the private conversation'" instead.[23] At the same time, Bergman has returned to the figure of the parson, and with him almost necessarily to religion as a theme. Finally, also of interest is that one of the main themes deals precisely with the elusiveness of language and its paradoxical necessity in human relations.

This story about marital infidelity is woven around two interlocking themes or movements in time. One deals with how Anna, the heroine of the novel (based on Bergman's mother) tells her confessor, Uncle Jacob, about her infidelity, whereupon he admonishes her, in a Greger Werle-like fashion, to tell her husband everything and to speak the truth at all costs. "The truth, Anna! You're entangled in a skein of lies."[24] This part, then, deals with Anna as a grown and married woman. The other movement, however, recurs both in the present and in the past, and deals with the question of whether Anna should go to communion. Uncle Jacob asks her during their first conversation, and the issue returns at the end of the book, this time set in the past when Anna is a young girl.[25] Here she seeks him to tell him that she does not want to go to her first communion but, when he insists she should, she replies with words that by now seem so familiar in a Bergman context, that it would amount to a betrayal. "If I was to take part in that," and here she pauses and looks for words, "ritual, then I would be acting."[26]

The question of infidelity is played out in the chapter called *The last conversation*. "And now, Anna, now we're *face-to-face*. Now the time has come," he says, turning his eyes towards her. At precisely this moment Bergman chooses to make an authorial comment: "'Well,' then Anna lies, quietly and with no special emphasis."[27] Wherupon Anna goes on to say that everything went well. She and her husband talked, resolved things without animosity or bitterness, something which obviously makes Uncle Jacob very happy. "You see, Anna!", he exclaims.[28] In other words, here the confession or private conversation is reduced to an outright lie, although it is clear that Anna does it in order to protect Uncle Jacob because she knows her lie will make him happy. This is, of course, quite a pragmatic position to take, a kind of admission that we often feel forced to lie, just as we are, for social and psychological reasons forced to wear masks for another. The implied question then seems to be: is the act of de-masking always that necessary?

If this is indeed the question asked here, then it signals a most definite change in the late Bergman, compared to the early one, where lying, especially when manifested in the domain of personal relationships, was almost invariably presented as a problem. Now it seems to be regarded with greater tolerance. Just as there is no point in fighting about whether God exists or not, or whether art is an illusion, there seems no longer to be any point in wrestling with the nature of language. Because language exists, lies exist. Or formulated as an imperative, language exists, therefore I lie. As Vogler, the director, says in *After the Rehearsal:* "Nothing is, everything represents."

To get to the other main movement of the novel, the question of Anna's going to communion or not, the book ends with a kind of flashback to a similar situation that occurred in Anna's youth. In order to convince her, Jacob told Anna about what he calls the miracle, referring to when the disciples went out spreading their message after Christ's death, in spite of the doubt they felt. As Jacob puts it, "there is grace in the act itself."[29] Indeed, the book ends with the young Anna going to communion. That her mother promised her a trip to Italy if she did, suggests a recognition of the need for pragmatism in human relations. Regardless of whether it seems meaningful or not, true or not, you shall partake of the communion, you shall perform your rite, and above all, you shall confess![30]

Thus, to conclude, the idea of the confessional seems important to Bergman for many reasons. It captures the basic constellation in human as well as metaphysical communication. Someone talks, someone listens; someone acts, someone reacts or that someone does not listen, or sort of listens and sort of reacts. Inspite of this, and despite doubt, the important thing is not to stop trying. As was pointed out above, the confessional shares this structure with the performing arts as a whole, not the least being the importance of the presence of an audience on the listening end, so to speak. For as I have pointed out elsewhere,[31] Bergman is fond of reminding us of the presence of the audience and of "ritual" (to use his own words) that plays itself out between the performer/artist and the audience. In this vein, it should come as no surprise that Bergman often lets his authorial voice break forth in his literary work as well, with comments or outright questions: was it like this, does my memory serve, did the light fall like this, or like that?

Indeed, from such a perspective one can ask to what degree all of Bergman's work in some sense is a confession of sorts. The audience is more or less defined as the listening part, that is the other and necessary part on the receiving end of a communicative act. More often than not this thematizes the (im)possibilities of such an act! In that case, it is ironic that it has often been said that Bergman prefers to ally himself with a godlike creator who shapes and molds a world mainly for his own purposes while remaining silent, aloof, and oblivious to our reactions. In the light of the above I would turn this constellation around entirely. It is Bergman in the speaking part, the one who in some sense confesses to an audience. In that case it is we, the viewers and the readers, who are sitting in the confessors seat, with godlike powers to administer judgements or absolutions.

As Uncle Jacob, that stubborn but intensely likable parson in *Private Conversations* puts it when commenting on Martin Luther's idea of the private conversation replacing the catholic confessional proper: "But our splendid reformer was no great expert of the human heart." He continues:

> It becomes hard with daylight and face to face. Then it's clearly better with the magical half darkness of the confessional booth, the mumbling voices, the fragrance of incense.[32]

Given those terms, what better place for a confession than in a movie theater?

NOTES

[1] This translation can (except for one minor change by the author) be found in Charles B. Ketcham, *The Influence of Existentialism on Ingmar Bergman: An Analysis of the Theological Ideas Shaping a Filmmaker's Art* (Lewiston/Queenston, 1986), 54. Original in Ingmar Bergman, "Det att göra film," *Filmnyheter*, 19–20 (1954): 9. "Jag vill vara en av konstnärerna i katedralen på den stora slätten. Jag vill vara sysselsatt med att ur stenen hugga fram ett drakhuvud, en ängel, eller kanske ett helgon, sak samma vilket. . . . Oavsett om jag tror eller inte, oavsett om jag är kristen eller hedning så arbetar jag i det gemensamma byggandet av katedralen därför att jag är konstnär och hantverkare."

[2] Ingmar Bergman, *"Såsom i en spegel,"* program note for Svensk Filmindustri, dated October 16, 1961.

[3] Translation in Ketcham, p. 33. Original in "Det att göra film," p. 9. "Oavsett min egen tro eller mitt eget tvivel . . . är det min åsikt att konsten förlorade sin livgivande betydelse i det ögonblick den skilde sig från kulten. Den skar av navelsträngen och lever ett egendomligt sterilt andrahandsliv, avlande och degenererande sig själv."

[4] Ingmar Bergman, "The Snakeskin," in *Persona and Shame. The Screenplays of Ingmar Bergman*, trans. Keith Bradfield (London: Calder & Boyars, 1972), 14. For original, see "Ormskinnet. En betraktelse skriven till utdelningen av Erasmuspriset i Amsterdam 1965," in *Persona* (Stockholm: Norstedt & Söner, 1966), 11. "Religionen och konsten hålls vid liv av sentimentala skäl, som en konventionell hövlighet mot det förflutna."

[5] Bo Strömstedt, "Vad tyr du dig till, Ingmar Bergman?", *Expressen* 16 February 1969. "När det har gällt gud har . . . alltid en kolossal tveksamhet anmält sig. Där har aldrig en tillit uppenbarat sig . . . Tro har alltid varit helt parallell med otro och hängivelse med begabbelse. Och vad slutligen konsten anbelangar, så . . . har jag nog varit lite tveksam . . . , jag har känt mig både inne i den och utanför."

[6] See eg Paisley Livingston's chapter on the film in *Ingmar Bergman and the Rituals of Art* (Ithaca and London: Cornell University Press, 1982).

[7] See e.g., Björkman et al., eds., *Bergman om Bergman* (Stockholm:

Norstedts, 1970), 237: "den tunga religiösa överbyggnanden."

[8] Maria Bergom Larsson, *Ingmar Bergman och den borgerliga ideologin* (Stockholm: Norstedts, 1976), 123.

[9] In an interview on his staging at the Opera in Stockholm of *The Bachae*: "Stycket blottlägger något som jag kallar 'människans helighet,'" in Tore Carsson, "Operan hoppas på Bergman," *Dagens Nyheter/På stan*, 1–8 November 1991.

[10] In this light it is interesting to note that if god was banished from Bergman's films, he/she/it has since returned with a vengeance in his work in the theater, which of course is as it should, as the theater has its origins and roots in the cult. I am thinking here of course of *The Bacchae*, where both at the opera and at the Royal Dramatic Theatre, that dialectical conflict—god vs man, religion vs art, faith vs scepticism played itself out once again. Significantly, however, not in Bergman's films: in *Fanny and Alexander*, god was summarily and literally reduced to a puppet on strings in the hands of an able magician.

[11] Translation in Livingston, p. 58, original statement in Stig Björkman, Torsten Manns, and Jonas Sima, "Ingmar Bergman: 'Man kan ju göra vad som helst med film!'", *Chaplin* 10, 79 (1968): 45. "Konstutövningen som besvärjelse, som ritualhandling, som förbön, som ömsesidig behovstillfredsställelse—det har jag alltid upplevt kolossalt starkt."

[12] "Det är självfallet medvetna plock från tidigare sammanhang, särskilt publiken från *Nattvardsgästerna*—att de skulle få vara med och begå en mer jordisk och konkret nattvardsgång den där stormiga natten i Grånäs," in *Dramat. En tidskrift utgiven av Dramaten*, 1 (1998): 18.

[13] See e.g., Torsten Bergmark, "Ingmar Bergman och den kristna baksmällan (Ingmar Bergman and the Christian Hangover), in *Dagens Nyheter* 6 October 1968. Reprinted in Gunder Andersson et. al., ed., *Motbilder. Svensk socialistisk filmkritik* (Stockholm: Tidens, 1978).

[14] As Livingston so eloquently put it, when writing about Bergman's love for mirrors: "In Bergman's films, identity is never established in isolation, but is the product of a basic, inescapable reciprocity .... Thus, whenever Bergman sends one of his charcters to a mirror, he includes in the scene those who mediate the vision of the self," p. 51. See also

Maaret Koskinen, *Spel och speglingar. En studie i Ingmar Bergmans filmiska estetik (Plays and Mirrors. A Study in the Cinematic Aesthetics of Ingmar Bergman)* (Stockolm: Norstedts/Stockholms universitet, 1993).

[15] Marc Vernet, "The Look at the Camera," *Cinema Journal* 28, 2 (1989): 55.

[16] See Vilgot Sjömans book on the production of the film, *L-136. Dagbok* (Stockholm: Norstedts, 1963), 29 and 207.

[17] Koskinen, especially pp. 241–50.

[18] For instance, we are kept in the dark of who is guilty of the violence committed against animals that plague the small island community in the film. Given how little we know about Andreas and his background, at the same time that we understand that he is a deeply troubled man, it is implied that he as well as anyone else may be the guilty one.

[19] See Koskinen, 242 f.

[20] Author's translation. "Jag inbillar mig inte att jag når in till människosjälen med det här fotograferandet, tro inte det för fan. Jag kan bara registrera ett samspel och ett motspel av tusentals stora och små krafter. Sen ser du på bilden och fantiserar. . . . Alltihop är nonsens, lekar, dikter. Du kan inte läsa någon annan människa med något som helst anspråk på visshet. Inte ens brutal fysisk smärta ger alltid utslag."

[21] "Språket är fruktansvärt lömskt, mångtydigt, undanglidande, hemlighetsfullt, förfalskande . . . man har svårt att hitta den absoluta sanningen," 2 December 1983 during a visit at the Department of Cinema Studies, Stockholm University.

[22] 36: "Säg inte ordet 'Gud'! Säg 'Det Heliga'. Människans Helighet. Allt annat är attribut, utklädslar, manifestationer, tilltag, desperationer, ritualer, förtvivlade rop i mörkret och tystnaden." Ingmar Bergman, *Enskilda samtal* (Stockholm: Norstedts 1996), p 36. Most English citations are taken from Joan Tate's translation, *Private Confessions: A Novel*, (New York: Arcade Publishing, 1997).

[23] Ibid., pp. 22–23.

[24] Ibid., p. 32: "Sanningen, Anna! Nu är du insnärjd i en härva av

lögner."

[25] Ibid., p. 16.

[26] Ibid., p. 160: "Skulle jag vara med om den där—ritualen så skulle jag spela teater."

[27] Ibid., p. 143: "Och nu, Anna, nu är vi här *ansikte mot ansikte*. Och det är dags. /—/ Ja, och då ljuger Anna, lågmält och utan särskilda betoningar."

[28] Ibid., p. 144: "Så började vi tala med varandra . . . Det var en så märkvärdig kväll och jag tänkte på vad farbror Jacob hade sagt om att ge Henrik möjlighet att mogna. Inga förebråelser, inget hot, ingen bitterhet.—Ingenting ont.
—Ser du! Anna! Ser du!"

[29] Ibid., p. 16: "Men det finns nåd i själva handlingen."

[30] cf. *Bergman om Bergman*, p. 189 f. and Sjöman, on the often told story of how Bergman's father insisted on keeping sermon, at any cost.

[31] *Spel och speglingar*.

[32] *Enskilda samtal*, p. 23: "Det blir svårt med dagsljus och ansikte mot ansikte. Då är det avgjort bättre med biktstolens magiska halvmörker, de mumlande rösterna, doften av rökelse."

"This is my hand."
Hand Gestures in the Films of Ingmar Bergman

Egil Törnqvist

The human face in close-up is, more than anything else, the signature of a Bergman film. This has often been recognized, not least by Bergman himself. But in addition to the face there is the hand. The first idea for *Persona* (1966),[1] Bergman has said, was of two women comparing hands.[2] A film title like *Beröringen/The Touch* (1971) points in the same direction. Deliberately ambiguous, it reflects a two-fold personal urge; in Bergman's words:

> I have an enormous need to . . . touch other people both physically and mentally, to communicate with them. Movies, of course, are a fantastic media [*sic*] with which to touch other human beings, to reach them, either to annoy them or to make them happy, to make them sad or get them to think. To get them started, emotionally. That's probably the truest, deepest reason why I continue to make movies.[3]

As this indicates, the film characters' need to be physically in touch with each other not only mirrors the director's *physical* needs, it is also a sign of his need to touch his audience *mentally*. For who can remain indifferent to a caressing or slapping hand?

Hand gestures[4] appear of course constantly in all films as one of the most important expressions of body language or kinesics. We usually do not pay much attention to them, because directors do not focus on them. But occasionally we are struck by a gesture, because the director has made it prominent. This can be done in a number of ways. A gesture can strike us as being unusual in itself or it can appear unusual in the context in which it is shown. The dialogue can draw attention to it—compare the title of this paper. Or it can be surrounded by a 'telling' silence, encouraging us to pay increased attention to it. These are all devices applying both to theater and film. In film, gestures can, in addition, be made prominent through striking camera distances, camera movements and camera angles.

Gestures can be categorized in various ways. We may differentiate between those gestures which "are used in processes of communication and interaction" and those which "serve to fulfill an intention," between those which "accompany language" and those which "substitute for it."[5] We may distinguish between national, social, and individual gestures. Gender and age may be linked with gestures. Deictically, we may separate gestures directed towards oneself from gestures directed towards others. Psychologically, there is a broad spectrum: gestures may be experienced as tender, enthusiastic, theatrical, shy, authoritarian, aggressive, pacifying, etc.—either by another character in point-of-view shots (subjective gestures), by the viewer (objective gestures), or by both.

The danger of categorization, especially if it limits itself to one or two of the indicated possibilities, is that it easily leads to simplification, that each signifier is seen as an image of the same signified. Although we tend to associate a clenched fist with aggressiveness, it can express many other things depending on the context. In a work of art—a film in our case—not only the immediate context but also the more distant context is of importance. Opening and closing shots, for instance, often show an overall correspondence which makes small divergences significant.

"This is my hand," says the Knight in *Det sjunde inseglet/ The Seventh Seal* (1957), thereby verbally drawing attention to the hand he and we are watching. He has just discovered that Death, disguised as a confessor, has betrayed him. "I can move it," he continues, "feel the blood pulsing through it." As he says this, he looks smilingly at his hand, turns it, clenches it into a fist and opens it again. The hand is literally a *pars pro toto* for his body which, though threatened by Death, is still alive. The momentarily clenched fist, which was earlier seen when the Knight held out his hand containing the chessmen to Death, "becomes the living symbol of something indomitable (and foolhardy) in Mankind."[6]

A more cryptic verbal reference to the signifier 'hand' figures in *Tystnaden/The Silence* (1963). One of the few words Ester learns from the unintelligible language spoken in Timoka is *kasi* meaning 'hand.'[7] In a world where God is dead[8] and verbal communication is unreliable, "only the hand—the communion—remains. And the music."[9] The long, initial sequence showing Johan's, the young boy's, hand against the window emphatically proclaims the hand as a key metaphor in the film. Before she dies, Ester writes a few words in the foreign language on a piece of paper, which she gives to Johan, her nephew, as a spiritual testament. The film ends with a sequence showing Johan and his mother Anna in a train compartment on their way home to Sweden. They have left Ester to die in the hotel. Johan picks up the paper she has given him. Anna reads it indifferently, then moves away from him to the window. She opens it and lets herself be cleansed by the rain outside. Bergman then intercuts between the boy reading Ester's 'testament' and his mother, uneasily looking at him while narcissistically busying herself with her own body. The final shot is a frontal extreme close-up of Johan, trying to spell out the words he is reading. The spatial separateness between mother and son, the latter engrossed in the aunt's message, suggests that the communion which *kasi* stands for now exists only between Johan and the far-away Ester.

The clenched fist appears as a marked symbolic gesture in

Persona. Elisabet has suddenly stopped speaking in the middle of a performance and has now refused to speak for three months. When her psychiatrist asks Alma, a nurse, to take care of Elisabet, Bergman resorts to a brief flashback showing the moment on the stage that signifies a turning point in Elisabet's life.[10] We see her, in *Electra*,[11] turning her head away from the theater audience so that she comes to face us, the film audience. At the same time she raises a clenched fist. The gesture combined with the two audiences—both invisible—indicates her protest against the two forms of presentation involved; against acting as a meaningful activity; and against speech as a meaningful form of communication.[12] When Alma is informed about Elisabet's silence—but not about the raised fist—we see her nervously fidgeting with her hands, respectfully held behind her back. The contrast between the determined actress and the insecure nurse is, in other words, initially indicated in their gestures.

Left alone in her room in the hospital, Elisabet watches a political feature program on TV, showing how a man, somewhere in Asia, burns himself to death, while near him another man, his hands folded in prayer, is crouching. Horrified at what she sees, Elisabet moves away from the TV set to the far corner of the room, putting one hand to her mouth as if quenching a scream.[13] Literally cornered, she sees how the suicide, raising a clenched fist, repeats her own gesture of protest. But while hers was merely a theatrical gesture, his is real. Compared to him, "she is only a coward hiding behind an assumed mask of silence."[14]

At no moment in life has joining hands such a ritual significance as in the wedding ceremony. When the violinists Stig and Marta in *Till glädje/To Joy* (1950) get married, we see in a close-up how their ringed hands join. A little later they are seen playing together in a Mozart flute quartet. The harmonious music, by candle light, continues as they kiss in their new home. Then their hands are seen, in silhouette, joining each other while pressing the palms against a window covered by ice-ferns, warning us that their marriage will eventually turn frosty.

A variation of the male hand joining the female is found in *Sommarlek/Summer Interlude* (1951) when Marie, a prima ballerina, and Henrik, a student, have spent their first night together. Their bliss is expressed in the form of a close-up of their hands, up in the air, constantly changing positions in relation to each other. Their 'dancing' together recalls the *pas de deux* we have seen Marie dancing at the dress rehearsal of *The Swan Lake* in the beginning of the film and anticipates the one we see at the premiere of this ballet at the end of it. On the latter occasion, Marie's ex-partner David is standing in the wings looking at her. When she discovers him, she momentarily leaves the dancing and approaches him—a symbolic move. In a close-up, we see his shoes close to her ballet shoes. When her shoes tiptoe, we realize that they kiss and that this is the beginning of a new *pas de deux*.

Gestures indicating husband-wife relations appear early in the TV series *Scener ur ett äktenskap/Scenes from a Marriage* (1973). Marianne, a lawyer, is visited by Mrs. Jacobi, who wants to divorce her husband after many years of married life, because "there is no love in the marriage." At the time Marianne is forcing herself to believe that she herself has an ideal marriage. Mrs. Jacobi, who appears much more mature and balanced than her legal advisor, hiding behind spectacles, undermines Marianne's frail self-confidence. This is indicated not least in their gestures. When Mrs. Jacobi states that she goes around with a mental picture of herself that does not tally with reality, we see Marianne, in close-up, put a finger to her mouth. Marianne asks her client whether she thinks that love . . . The question is not completed. There is a pause during which Marianne moves a finger to her forehead, positioning the thinker and revealing her two rings indicative of her married state. When Mrs. Jacobi claims that she believes that she has the capacity for love, a tilt down to her clasped hands makes us glimpse her wedding ring. When she goes on to explain that her love is shut in a locked room, she opens her hands and holds them separated, the palms turned against one another, visualizing, as it were, at once a locked room and two separated marital partners. She goes on to say that her senses are letting her down. "I can say that this table is a table," she remarks. "I can see it, I can touch it." At this moment her ringless hand—alone, separated—is seen touching the table next to her. "But my sensation is"—quick pan to extreme close-up of Marianne—"thin and dry. Do you understand what I mean?" After a telling pause Marianne answers: "I think I do." During the following speeches the camera significantly stays with her. The visitor has undermined Marianne's illusory feelings of her own conjugal happiness and initiated the process of self-examination. And the gestures have helped to cue us to the fact that the lawyer has more in common with her client than she wants to admit.

Shaking hands is normally a sign of a formal-to-friendly attitude. But when Isak Borg in *Smultronstället/ Wild Strawberries* (1957) in his nightmare witnesses how his alter ego, the corpse in the coffin, clasps his hand to pull him into the coffin, the gesture is a vampiric foreshadowing that Isak's days are numbered. The sequence is an imaginative variation of two vampiric handshaking sequences in world drama, that between the Old Man and the Student in Strindberg's *Spöksonaten/The Ghost Sonata* and, even closer, that between Don Juan and the Governor, whom he has killed, in Molière's *Don Juan*,[15] a sequence visualized in *Djävulens öga/The Devil's Eye* (1960).

Film can effectively isolate hands from their owners and thus make them anonymous. Such an anonymous hand appears early in *Törst/Three Strange Loves* (1949). Bertil and Rut have a problematic marriage. On their way home from Italy, they are now in a hotel room in Basel. We see Rut's sad, pensive face in the somber morning light. There is a dissolve, indicating what is on her mind, to a white sailing boat moving across a sunny strait. A low angle shot of mast and sail appears

"This is my hand" 235

to be a shot from Rut's point of view when, in the next medium close-up, we see her lying on the deck in a bathing costume, a satisfied smile on her lips. Next to her a male arm, the hand of which touches her shoulder and cheek, in a slightly brusque but friendly way. We are led to believe that Rut reminisces happy bygone days with Bertil in the Stockholm archipelago. But in the next shot we see, in close-up, a male face that is not Bertil's. Surprised, we discover that what Rut is reminiscing is the relationship with another man, Raoul, an army captain. In the following shot the hand becomes more assertive, pulling Rut's nose and commandingly patting her cheek. Retrospectively—for we have not seen much of Bertil yet—we understand that Raoul is the macho antithesis of the soft aesthete Bertil, whom we later see polishing his nails. And that Rut is emotionally torn between the two. Gestures prove indicative of two highly contrasting mentalities.

The anonymous hand returns in *Höstsonaten/Autumn Sonata* (1978). The internationally famous pianist Charlotte—who would be more concerned with hands?—has neglected her daughters Eva and Lena. Her guilt feelings come to the fore in a nightmare. It begins with a close-up of Charlotte's face and hand. Suddenly a woman's hand caressingly creeps into hers. The hand remains unidentified since, figuratively, it is both Eva's and Lena's hand. The hand caresses Charlotte's cheek. Moving behind her head, it suddenly begins to tear at her hair. Charlotte wakes up screaming. By means of contradictory gestures, Bergman visualizes Charlotte's experience of her daughters' love-hatred for her.

One of the most striking, and most enigmatic, gestures in Bergmanian cinema is the-hand-against-the-window, the significance of which in *The Silence* I have already touched upon. Let us look a little closer at this significant gesture. Anna, Ester and Johan—the latter at once Bergman's alter ego and his 'camera'—are on their way to Timoka. Johan, sitting by one of the windows in the train corridor is holding his right arm raised, his palm pressed against the window. He, and we, "see the landscape flashing by . . . like moving pictures on a screen"[16]—as though the demarcation line between fiction and reality had been blotted out. Keeping his hand still like a shield, Johan quickly moves his head back and forth, as if he were counting the tanks flashing by outside the window. With their cannons, all pointing in the same direction, the tanks have a threatening phallic appearance. Johan's gesture may be seen as a child's self-protective resistance to the hostile world outside, marked by aggressiveness and sexual urge. Or it may be seen—and here the objective close-up from outside of his face and hand is especially relevant—as a contrast between the child's unguarded openness and the masked, hostile world (the hermetically closed, phallic tanks) of the grown-ups.

Johan in *The Silence* has a counterpart in the nameless boy in the pre-credit sequence of *Persona*. Both are of about the same age and both are played by the same actor. Moreover, Johan's gesture returns, with significant variation, in that of the nameless boy, arguably the most complex of all Bergman's filmic gestures. The nameless boy reaches out first towards us, then towards the huge female face, vaguely divined behind a transparent screen, which alternately carries the traits of Elisabet and Alma. The boy's exploring gesture can be seen both as a psychological gesture related to the film (a son in search of his mother) and as a meta-filmic gesture (the director in search of his audience; the viewer in search of the significance of the screened images). In either case there is a point to the fact that the boy in vain tries to touch what he and we see. His hand seems to express curiosity combined with a groping longing for communion. Psychologically, the boy represents Elisabet's neglected and Alma's aborted child. As such he incarnates their repressed feelings of guilt. In the film proper he appears metaphorically as the little Jewish boy in the famous photo from the Warsaw ghetto, a photo that Elisabet contemplates at length. With both his hands raised above his head, the boy, evidently on his way to death in a concentration camp, makes the sign of capitulation to the surrounding German soldiers. Bergman intercuts between Elisabet looking at the photo and a sequence of shots, picking out various faces and hands in the photo—like a film director editing his movie.[18] In the culminating extreme close-up Bergman isolates the Jewish boy's face and raised right arm to provide a link with the nameless boy of the pre-credit sequence, a link supported by the gradually louder electronic sound accompanying both sequences. In addition, the archetypal gesture of the Jewish boy provides a link between the two guilty mothers of the film on one hand and on the other the audience which can hardly avoid feeling guilty when watching the defenseless boy.[19]

Once more Bergman shows a young boy—his alter ego—with his hand pressed against a window. In the pre-title sequence of *Fanny och Alexander/Fanny and Alexander* (1982), we get a close-up of the transparent flowers embroidered on a window curtain—a synecdoche of the idyllic life of the Ekdals, fully visible at the flower-decked reunion in the epilogue. A slow down-tilt reveals the ice-ferns on the window behind the friendly curtain—the chilly Vergérus's world—and Alexander's left hand pressed against the window.[20] A slow pan right brings the boy's face into frame. Through the iris he has breathed in the window, he looks out on a square where twigs with colorful feathers indicate that it is Easter time. A horse-drawn carriage, piled with old furniture, moves by. A man in bowler hat and long beard and a woman in a kerchief sit on the box, behind them a couple of children. The seemingly homeless family passing by the 'Christian' twigs looks Jewish. What Alexander is watching from his privileged position in his grandmother's upper-class apartment are the pariahs of society. Soon he himself, when homeless, will be taken care of by the Jewish Jacobi family. The shot *in petto* suggests the three environments, and life conceptions, Alexander will be involved with. At this moment, he is still watching two of these environments from a distance, as through a camera, and he is shielding himself from them.[21]

The most extreme example of a synecdochic use of a hand we find in *För att inte tala om alla dessa kvinnor/Not to Speak of All These Women* (1964), where the chief character is merely once visualized in the form of a hand, a device that Bergman may have borrowed from Cecil B. De Mille's *The King of Kings* (1927).[22]

In few Bergman films do gestures play such an important part as in *Winter Light*. When the film opens a few parishioners have gathered for Holy Communion in Mittsunda medieval church. The actual communicants are Jonas Persson and his wife Karin; Märta Lundberg, who has a relationship with the Rev. Tomas Eriksson, now officiating; and the sexton Algot Frövik. While they are all in their thirties, Magdalena Ledfors is in her sixties.

Jonas, we later learn, is greatly worried about a newspaper report that the Chinese can produce an atom bomb and are prepared to use it. To him, as to the characters in *The Seventh Seal*, Doomsday is close. This has made him doubt the existence of a benign god. During the Holy Communion his mood is that of Christ's: "My God, my God, why hast thou forsaken me?" (Matt. 27:46). Since suicide is on his mind, he may well be aware that this is his last Communion. To an extreme extent, he mirrors Tomas's despair. When Tomas reaches the end of the Lord's Prayer, we see him in profile with folded hands. When he says "The peace of God be with you," he is seen in long shot. There is a cut to Jonas and Karin. We see Jonas's folded hands and realize, in retrospect, how meaningful—or blasphemous—the minister's words must seem to him at this moment. Jonas is still in frame when the congregation sings: "O Lamb of God, that takest away the sins of the world." Bergman then cuts to Jonas's antithesis, church warden Aronsson who, indifferent to what is going on, coquettishly adjusts his tie and white handkerchief, elegantly stuck in his breast pocket.

The actual Communion is shown in two phases. When the wafers are delivered, the five communicants are treated as a homogeneous group, the minister's hand held blessingly over each of them. For the drinking of the wine—"Christ's blood shed for thee"—they are treated as five individuals. Algot Frövik receives the wine with clasped hands. Magdalena Ledfors places her hands over Tomas's hands that hold the chalice,[23] then clasps her hands. Both Algot and Magdalena are shown in profile. Jonas's face is shown in high angle. This links him with Tomas in the next low angle shot. Karin is seen in semi-profile in a medium shot, her hands clasped as she drinks. Märta, finally, is seen in profile in an extreme close-up, drinking from the chalice.

Not surprisingly, the camera gets closest to the fifth communicant, Märta, the most important of them. Significantly, we do not see her and Jonas's hands. The non-believers are unobtrusively separated from the believers, from those whose clasped hands indicate a sense of communion with God.

The altar piece behind Tomas is a richly decorated, symmetrically arranged, almost idyllic and very naïve piece of art, displaying the Holy Trinity. A fairly small Christ is hanging on a cross, consolingly held in the hands of his bearded Father and placed between His legs. On one of the arms of the cross the dove, symbol of the Holy Ghost, can be seen. When the congregation sings its praise of the Lord, this so-called *nådastol* (chair of grace) is seen in a medium shot.

After a shot of the bread and the wine follow two close-ups of the crucified Christ. In an extreme high angle shot—recalling the one of Jonas—we see the thorn-crowned head, then one of the nailed hands, missing three of its fingers. The contrast between the altar piece in the church and the crucifix in the sacristy—which Bergman found so important that he quite unrealistically inserted it in the Communion sequence—could be seen as that between an exoteric and an esoteric image of God. But more relevant in the context is the implied contrast between the feeling of confident communion with God and the feeling of desperate loneliness, of being forsaken by God.[24]

The thorn-crowned head and the nailed hand point also in the direction of Märta in her sheepskin coat. Sharing her age with Christ at the time of his crucifixion, she suffers from eczema on her forehead and hands, that is, at the places of stigmatization. The eczema "is the nail through the hands."[25]

The service ends with the singing of the final verse of hymn No. 400, the first lines of which read: "Last, my God, I pray Thee, / Take my hand in Thine."[26] When this is sung, Jonas and Karin are framed. *She*, the believer, is holding the hymnbook in one hand. *He* is supporting her hand. The man-God communion the hymn speaks of has a visual counterpart on the human level. We notice that one of Jonas's fingers is covered by a black bandage, linking it both with Christ's broken fingers and Märta's bandaged hands.

After the service, Karin and Jonas visit Tomas in the sacristy.[27] They have come to seek advice or at least consolation for Jonas's anguish. Tomas admits that Jonas's fear for the atom bomb is shared by everyone. He adds: "We must trust in God." When he says this Jonas, who has hitherto kept his face averted, looks Tomas straight in the face. During the long silence that follows, indicative of God's silence—which is made prominent by the ticking of the grandfather clock—Tomas faces the camera in close-up. Unable to meet Jonas's glance, he lowers his eyes. The camera tilts down to his right hand, hesitantly moving across the blotting pad on the desk. The lowered eyes, the silence, the emptiness of the blotting pad, the fumbling hand—everything contradicts Tomas's consoling words. Not least his gesture indicates that the clergyman has little faith both in God and in himself. We are very far from the Knight's confidence in his own hand.

Toward the end of the film, set in the church of Frostnäs, the non-believer Märta kneels and prays for Tomas and herself while the church bell is tolling. Her lowered face, in darkness, is silhouetted with light from the church windows. Her search for something to hold on to is visualized in her right hand grasping the back of the church bench in front of her. Her prayer ends in a groping for a faith: "If we could dare to show each other tenderness. If we could believe in a truth . . . " For the end of her prayer—"If we could believe . . . "—Bergman cuts to Tomas's head, brightly lit by a glaring lamp. Framed in the same position as Märta's, it shows another gesture: his clenched right hand touching his brow. While her prayer and gesture suggest her need to touch—to be in touch, to feel—his narcissistic gesture indicates rather that, like the Knight in *The Seventh Seal*, he is seeking a rational foundation for his faith. The hand of this doubting Tomas is very different from that of the believer Jacob, his colleague in *Private Confessions*, whose big hand is in fact compared to God's.

Prominent gestures can be found in all Bergman's films. But they become more frequent, more original, and more multilayered from the film trilogy in the early 1960s onwards.[28] The new approach, mirroring Bergman's orientation away from a belief in a benign "Pappa god"[29] towards a faith in the love solely between human beings, means "an even greater concentration on the human face."[30] It also means a greater focusing on the human hand[31] which, more than the face, is the tool of action. As Jacob in *Private Confessions* reminds us: "You do not need to say: 'I love you.' It is enough to do the deeds of love."

NOTES

[1] The dates refer to the Swedish premieres.

[2] Frank Gado, *The Passion of Ingmar Bergman* (Duke University Press, 1986), 322.

[3] Interview in *Film in Sweden* No. 2 (1971), 7. Quoted from Pais-

ley Livingston, *Ingmar Bergman and the Rituals of Art* (Cornell University Press, 1982), 243.

[4] Since gestures usually mean hand gestures, I shall in the following speak simply of 'gestures.'

[5] Erika Fischer-Lichte, *The Semiotics of Theater*, trans. Jeremy Gaines and Doris L. Jones (Indiana University Press, 1992), 43. Keir Elam calls the intention-fulfilling gestures "illocutionary markers." See *The Semiotics of Theatre and Drama* (London & New York, 1980), 75.

[6] Peter Cowie, *Max von Sydow: From "The Seventh Seal" to "Pelle the Conqueror,"* Chaplin Film Magazine Special, (Stockholm, 1989), 17.

[7] As Birgitta Steene has pointed out in her *Ingmar Bergman* (Boston, 1968), 112, the word is not invented by Bergman but is actually the Estonian word for 'hand.' When Bergman shot the film he was married to the Estonian pianist Käbi Laretei.

[8] The film was first entitled *God's Silence*.

[9] Bergman in Vilgot Sjöman, L136: *Dagbok med Ingmar Bergman* (Stockholm, 1963), 220. The mere fact that words in different languages—Swedish *hand* and Timokan/Estonian *kasi*, for instance—are different signifiers for the same signified proves that words create barriers, prevent communion.

[10] Thomas Elsaesser provides an illuminating reading of this sequence in "Ingmar Bergman—person and persona: The Mountain of Modern Cinema on the Road to Morocco," in Harry Perridon, ed., *Strindberg, Ibsen & Bergman: Essays on Scandinavian Film and Drama offered to Egil Törnqvist* (Maastricht, 1998), 42–44.

[11] Bergman never tells us whether he refers to Sophocles's or Euripides's *Electra*.

[12] Cf. Bergman's 1965 declaration that he considered art "as lacking in importance." See his "The Snakeskin," published in Ingmar Bergman, *Persona & Shame*, trans. Keith Bradfield (London, 1990), 12.

[13] In the script, Elisabet actually "begins to scream loudly and pierc-

ingly" as she watches the self-burning of the man, referred to as a "Buddhist monk." The implication here, disguised to the viewer of the film, is that the man can sacrifice himself for a cause because, unlike Elisabet, he has a faith.

[14] Marilyn Johns Blackwell, *Persona: The Transcending Image* (University of Illinois Press, 1986), 52.

[15] Bergman has staged each play three times.

[16] Marsha Kinder, "The Penetrating Dream Style of Ingmar Bergman," in Vlada Petric, ed., *Films and Dreams: An Approach to Ingmar Bergman* (South Salem, NY, 1981), 59.

[17] In an earlier discussion of this sequence, I have seen the boy's gesture as an ambivalent caressing and warding off. See Egil Törnqvist, *Between Stage and Screen: Ingmar Bergman Directs* (Amsterdam, 1995), 138-9. I now see no warding off in his gesture.

[18] The analogy relates to the comparison of Elisabet's viewing to Bergman's filmmaking in Birgitta Steene, "The Child as Ingmar Bergman's Persona," *Chaplin Special* (1989), 75.

[19] Cf. Bergman's remark that he was overcome with "despair" and "self-contempt" when he learned about the holocaust. See his *The Magic Lantern: An Autobiography*, trans. Joan Tate (Harmondsworth, 1989), 124.

[20] Cf. the first photo in a Sjöman book about *Nattvardsgästerna/ Winter Light* (1963), showing Bergman pressing his right hand against the window pane while discussing with Ingrid Thulin, who does the part of Märta Lundberg in the film.

[21] Emphasizing the meta-filmic aspects of Bergman's cinema, Maaret Koskinen sees the three boys' palm-against-the-window as Bergman-the-filmmaker's attempt to get hold of reality. It is every time, she finds, a gesture of conjuration. *Spel och speglingar: En studie i Ingmar Bergmans filmiska estetik* (Stockholm, 1993), 106, 123, 151.

[22] Hans Nystedt, *Ingmar Bergman och kristen tro* (Stockholm, 1989), 45.

[23] The information in the script that she is a widow gives an added, erotic significance to her gesture.

[24] Bergman suddenly realized that "the chief figure [Christ] should be seen during the hymn-singing," and he broke off one finger from the crucified hand. See Sjöman, 205. Why? Because three remaining fingers would erroneously have suggested trinity? Or because two fingers could represent the painful husband-wife relations (Tomas-Märta, Jonas-Karin) in the film?

[25] Bergman in Sjöman, 124, 169.

[26] This hymn is sung again in the fifth part of the TV series *Enskilda samtal* (1966), directed by Liv Ullmann. (The book has been published in English as *Private Confessions*, trans. Joan Tate [New York, 1997]). This occurs when Jacob (we never learn his surname) receives the Eucharist before dying. The wish to be "in God's hand" is a *leitmotif* in the series.

[27] This sequence is used as an example of Bergman's editing in Vilgot Sjöman's TV series *Ingmar Bergman gör en film/Ingmar Bergman Makes a Film* (1963), exclusively devoted to *Winter Light*.

[28] It is hardly a coincidence that Bergman takes a markedly increased interest not only in music but also in hands after his marriage to pianist Käbi Laretei in 1959. Bergman's growing concern with his own childhood in his later work may also play a part. Compare his remark about his mother in *Laterna magica/The Magic Lantern*, 287: "What I remember best, after all, is her hand with its deep life line, that dry soft hand, the network of veins. Flowers, children, animals. Responsibility, care, strength. Occasional tenderness. Forever duty."

[29] Sjöman, 28.

[30] Steene (1968), 113.

[31] Cf. Bergman's statement to Sjöman, in the TV series on *Winter Light*, that he wants "to learn to draw a human hand."

Professor Birgitta Steene
A Bibliography: 1959-2000

A. Gerald Anderson

1959

"Shakespearean Elements in the History Plays of Strindberg." *Comparative Literature,* 10:3 (Summer 1959): 209-220.

1960

"American Drama and the Swedish Stage, 1920-1958." Diss. U. of Washington, 1960. DAI 21 (1960): 268. [Entered under name: Kerstin Birgitta Steene] [Rev. typed. version also available in Uppsala U Library.]

"William Faulkner and the Myth of the American South." *Moderna språk* 14:3 (1960): 271-279.

1962

"The Critical Reception of American Drama in Sweden." *Modern Drama* 5:1 (1962): 71-82.

1964

"Arthur Miller's *After the Fall:* A Strindbergian Failure?" *Moderna språk* 58:4 (1964): [435]-438.

"*Macbeth* and *Rosmersholm*: A Comparison." *Proceedings of the 5th. International Study Conference on Scandinavian Literature.* London: University College, 1964. 198-216.

Rev. of *Seven Swedish Poets,* ed. and trans. by Frederic Fleisher. *Scandinavian Studies* 36:2 (1964): 163-165

1965

"Archetypal Patterns in Four Screenplays of Ingmar Bergman." *Scandinavian Studies* 37:1 (1965): 58-76.

"The Isolated Hero of Ingmar Bergman." [Revised version of above article] *Film Comment* 3:2 (Spring 1963): 68-76.

Rev. of *Sverige och svenskarna*, by Siv Higelin. *Scandinavian Studies* 37:2 (1965): 206-204.

Rev. of *Den sörjande turturduvan: Poesi och prosa, [av]* Hedvig Charlotta Nordenflycht; i urval samt med inledning och kommentarer av Torkel Stålmarck. *Scandinavian Studies* 37:1 (1965): 96-97.

"The Role of the Mima: A Note on Martinson's *Aniara*." *Scandinavian Studies: Essays Presented to Dr. Henry Goddard Leach on the Occasion of His Eighty-fifth Birthday.* Eds. Carl. F. Bayerschmidt and Erik J. Friis. Seattle: U. of Washington P., 1965. 311-319.

"Vision and Reality in the Poetry of Tomas Tranströmer." *Scandinavian Studies* 37:3 (1965): 236-244.

1966

"*Diktarens engagemang: Vietnampoesi eller Tranströmerska?*" Bohusläningen *28 Dec, 1966:* 4.

1968

Ingmar Bergman. *Twayne's World Authors. 32.* Boston: Twayne Publishers, 1968. Boston: St. Martin's P, 1972.

Rev. of *Rose of Jericho and Other Stories*, by Tage Aurell; trans. by Martin S. Allwood. *Scandinavian Studies* 40:4 (1968): 346-347.

1969
Rev. of *The Novels of August Strindberg: A Study in Theme and Stucture*, by Eric O. Johannesson. *Scandinavian Studies* 41:2 (1969): 203-206.

Rev. of *Den nya livkänslan: En studie i Erik Blombergs föfattarskap till och med 1924*, by Jan Stenkvist. *Scandinavian Studies* 41:2 (1969): 210-212.

1970
"Images and Words in Ingmar Bergman's Films." *Cinema Journal* 10:1 (1970): [23]-33.

1972
Bergman, Ingmar. "Words and Whisperings: An Interview with Ingmar Bergman." Interview by Birgitta Steene. *Focus on The Seventh Seal*. 42-44.

Focus on the Seventh Seal. Ed. Birgitta Steene. Englewood Cliffs, NJ, Prentice-Hall [1972]

"Introduction: *The Seventh Seal*: Film as Doomsday Metaphor." *Focus* 1-9.

"*The Seventh Seal*: An Existential Vision." *Focus* 92.

1973
Bergman, Ingmar. "Att filma är som at tala med en avlägsen släkting." Interview by Birgitta Steene. *Bohusläningen* 4 Jan. 1973: 4.

The Greatest Fire: A Study of August Strindberg. Crosscurrents/Modern Critiques. Carbondale: Southern Illinois UP, [1973]

Mailer, Norman. "Interview: Det är synd om kvinnorna." Interview by Birgitta Steene. *Chaplin* 14:8 (1973): 298-299.

"The Milk and Strawberry Sequence in *The Seventh Seal*." *Film Heritage* 8:4 (1973): 10-18.

1974
"About Bergman: Some Critical Responses to His Films." *Cinema Journal* 13:2 (1974): 1-10.

1975
"Bergman: A Retrospective." *The Thousand Eyes Magazine* 1 (1975): 7+.

"Bergman's Movement toward Nihilism: The Antiheroic Stance in *Secrets of Women, Brink of Life, The Seventh Seal*, and the *Chamber Film Trilogy*." *The Hero in Scandinavian Literature: from Peer Gynt to the Present.* Ed. John M. Weinstock and Robert T. Rovinsky. Austin: U of Texas P, 1975. 87-105.

"Erik Lindegren: An Assessment." *Books Abroad* 49:1 (1975): [29]-32.

"*Scenes from a Marriage:* Freedom and Entrapment." *Movietone News* 40-41 (1975): 16-19.

1976
"The Ambiguous Feminist." *Scandinavian Review* 64:3 (1976): 27-31.

1977
"Sju synpunkter på kulturutbytet." *Svenska Dagbladet* 5 Apr. 1977: 8

1978
"Ingmar Bergman: A Biographical Note." *Ingmar Bergman: Essays in Criticism.* Ed. M. Kaminsky, with Joseph Hill. New York: Oxford UP, 1978. 3-10.

Rev. of *Carl Jonas Love Almqvist* by Bertil Romberg. Twayne's Author Series. Boston: Twayne, 1978. *Scandinavica* 17:2 (1978): [165]-167.

"The Virgin Spring: Pro and Con." *Ingmar Bergman:*

Essays in Criticism. Ed. M. Kaminsky, with Joseph Hill. New York: Oxford UP, 1978. 215-222.

1979

"Bergman's Portrait of Women: Sexism or Subjective Metaphor." *Sexual Stratagems: The World of Women in Film.* Ed. Patricia Erens. New York: Horizon P, 1979. 91-107.

"Media Aspects in Modern Scandinavian Drama." *20th Century Drama in Scandinavia: Proceedings of the 12th Study Conference of the International Association for Scandinavian Studies, Helsinki, August 6-12, 1978.* Ed. Johan Wrede. Helsinki: U of Helsinki, Dept. of Swedish Literature, 1979. 329-335.

Rev. of *L136: Diary with Ingmar Bergman,* by Vilgot Sjöman; trans. by Alan Blair. *Scandinavian Review* 3 (1979): 88+.

1980

"Bergman, Ernst Ingmar." *Columbia Dictionary of Modern European Literature.* 2nd ed. Jean-Albert Bédé and William Edgerton, gen. eds. New York: Columbia UP, 1980. 78-79.

"Ingmar Bergman and the Theater." *Selecta: Journal of the Pacific Northwest Council on Foreign Languages (PNCFL).* 1 (1980): 91-94.

1981

"Alf Sjöberg's Film *Fröken Julie:* Too Much Cinema, Too Much Theater?" *Strindbergs Dramen im Lichte neuerer Methodendiskussionen: Beiträge zum IV. Internationalen Strindberg-Symposion in Zürich 1979.* Herausgegeben von Oskar Bandle, Walter Baumgartner und Jürg Glauser. *Beiträge zur nordischen Philologie* 11. Basel: Helbring & Lichtenhahn, 1981. 179-195.

"August Strindberg in America: A Bibliographical Assessment 1963-1980." *Structures of Influence: A Comparative Approach to August Strindberg: Festschrift in Honor of Walter Johnson.* Ed. Marilyn Johns Blackwell. University of North Carolina Studies in the Germanic Languages and Literatures. 98. Chapel Hill: U. of North Carolina P, 1981. 256-275.

"Film as Theater: Geissendorfer's *The Wild Duck.*" *Modern European Filmmakers and the Art of Adaptation.* Ed. Andrew Horton and Joan Magretta. Ungar Film Library. New York: Frederick Ungar, 1981. 295-312.

"Ingmar Bergman." *Contemporary Literary Criticism.* Ed. Sharon R. Gunton. Vol .16 Detroit, MI: Gale Research Company, 1981. 59-60.

1982

August Strindberg: An Introduction to His Major Works. 2nd. rev. ed. of *The Greatest Fire: A Study of August Strindberg.* Stockholm: Almqvist & Wiksell International; Atlantic Highlands, NJ: Humanities P, 1982

"Das Konzept der Fremdheit in der Litteraturgeschichte." *Die nordischen Literaturen als Gegenstand der Literaturgeschichte: Beiträge zur 13. Studienkonferenz der Internationalen Assoziation für Skandinavische Studien (IASS) 10.-16. August 1980 an der Ernst-Moritz-Arndt-Universität Greifswald.* Herausgegeben von Horst Bien, unter Mitarbeit von Gabriele Sokoll. Rostock: Hinsdorf Verlag, 1982. 190-199.

"Theatre in Scandinavia." *Seattle Intiman Scandinavia*

Today Program. Seattle: Intiman Theater, 1982 (October). 3-6

"Through a Glass Darkly: Two Books Explore Ingmar Bergman's Obsession with Artists, Magic, and Dreams." Rev. article of *Film & Dreams: An Approach to Bergman*, ed. by Vlada Petric and of *Ingmar Bergman and the Rituals of Art*, by Paisley Livingston. *American Film* 7:7 (May 1982): 62-64.

1983

"*Ett drömspel på Seattle-Intiman.*" *Meddelanden från Strindbergssällskapet* 67 (April 1983): 24-29.

"Ingmar Bergmans mottagande i USA." *Svenska Dagbladet* 3. juni 1983: 12-13.

"Konstsagan i *Bland Tomtar och Troll*: Ett försök till kategorisering." *Kortprosa i Norden: fra H.C. Andersens eventyr til den moderne novelle: Akter fra den XIV studiekonference for skandinavisk litteratur i Odense 1982.* Odense: Odense UP, 1983. 183-188.

Rev. of *Strindbergian Drama: Themes and Structure*, by Egil Törnqvist. *Scandinavian Studies* 55:2 (1983): 273-274.

"*Sjunde inseglet:* Film som ångestens metafor." *Svensk filmografi.* Ansvarig utgivare Jörn Donner. Bd. 5. Stockholm: Svensk filminstitut., 1983

1984

"Bergman, Ingmar." *McGraw-Hill Encyclopedia of World Drama: An International Reference Work in 5 Volumes.* Ed-in-chief Stanley Hochman. 2nd ed. New York: McGraw-Hill, c1984. Vol. 1: 328-329.

"Strindberg, August." *McGraw-Hill Encyclopedia of World Drama.* Vol. 4: 557-577.

"Strindbergs 'Kristina' i en fiskeby vid Stilla havkusten."

Meddelanden från Strindbergssällskapet. 68 (April 1984): 18-19.

"Swedish Drama: A Historical Survey." *McGraw-Hill Encyclopedia of World Drama.* Vol. 4: 585-596.

1986

"Strindberg in America: Glimpses from the 1980's." *Swedish Book Review: Supplement 2: August Strindberg (1986): 26-29.*

Rev. of *Frühe schwedische Arbeiterdichtung: Poetische Beitrage in sozialdemokratischen Zeitungen, 1882-1900,* by Birgitte Mral. *Scandinavian Studies* 58:2 (1986): 213-214.

"Royal Dramatic Theatre (Kungliga Dramatiska Teatern)." *Theatre Companies of the World.* Ed. Colby H. Kullman and William C. Young. New York: Greenwood P., 1986. 491-494.

Scandinavian Literature in a Transcultural Context: Papers from the XV IASS Conference. Eds. Sven H. Rossel and Birgitta Steene. [Seattle, WA] University of Washington, 1986.

1987

"Filmen som bokreklam." *Den svenska litteraturen.* Red. Lars Lönnroth, Sven Delblanc. [Stockholm]: Bonnier, c1987-1990. Bd. 4 [102]

"Hjalmar Bergman och filmen." *Den svenska litteraturen,* Bd. 4 [194-195]

Ingmar Bergman: A Guide to References and Resources. Reference Publication in Film. Boston: G.K. Hall, 1987.

1988

"Att röra sig mellan magi och havregrynsgröt." *Filmhäftet* 2 (1988): 51-55.

"Barnet som Bergmans *Persona*." *Chaplin* 215/216 (1988): 122-128.
"The Image of the Child in Swedish Cinema." Current Sweden 365. Stockholm: Swedish Institute, 1988.
"Ingmar Bergmans *Laterna magica*." *Finsk Tidskrift* 2-3 (1988): 78-90.
"Das Kind im schwedischen Film." *Ausblick: Zeitschrift für deutsch Skandinavische Beziehungen*. 38:3-4 (1988): 8-11.
Rev. of *August Strindberg: Selected Plays I and II*. Trans. by Evert Sprinchorn. Minneapolis: U of Minnesota P, 1986. *Scandinavian Studies* 60:3 (1988): 407-408.

1989

"Att skriva för filmen." *Den storsvenska generationen*. Stockholm: Bonnier, 1989. 260. Vol. 4 of *Den svenska litteraturen*. Red. Lars Lönnroth, Sven Delblanc. [Stockholm]: Bonnier, 1989. 7 vols. 1987-1990. Rpt. in : *Genombrottstiden*. Stockholm: Bonnier, 1999. 552. Vol. 2 of *Den svenska litteraturen* Eds. Lars Lönnroth, Sven Delblanc. [Ny rev. utg.] 3 vols. 1999.
Rev. of *Aspects of Modern Swedish Literature*. Ed. Irene Scobbie. Norwich: Norvik P, 1988. *Scandinavica* 28:2 (1989): 220-222.
Rev. of *Jorden är vår arvedel: Landsbygden i svensk spelfilm 1940-1959*. By Per Olov Qvist. *Scandinavian Studies* 61:1 (Winter 1989): 102-104.
"Selma Lagerlöf går på Svenska Bio." *Den svenska litteraturen*. Red. Lars Lönnroth, Sven Delblanc. [Stockholm] Bonnier, c1987-1990. Bd. 4. [104-105] Bd. 2. 393-394.
"Sommarlovets hägring är inte nödvändigtvis översättarens vision ...: Om Pelikanen, Kulturspråk och

Författarspråk." *Strindbergiana* 4 (1989): 56-66.

"Strindbergssymposium i Seattle." *Strindbergiana* 4 (1989): 67-72.

1990

"Bergman, Ingmar Ernst." *Dictionary of Scandinavian Literature.* Ed-in-chief Virpi Zuck. New York: Greenwood, 1990. 57-59.

"Bibliography of Selected Books and Articles on Swedish Children's Literature: Authors, Illustrators and Related Topics". With Laura Wideberg. *Swedish Book Review: Supplement. 1990: 89-91.*

"Breaking through Boundaries: Swedish Children's Literature since 1945". *Swedish Book Review.* Supplement: *Swedish Children's Literature*, 1990: 2-8.

"Film, erotik och pornografi." *Svenska Dagbladet* 5 Nov 1990.

"Den kvinnliga blicken." *Chaplin* 32:4 (1990): 193-196.

"Ingmar Bergman som dramatiker och teaterledare."
Medieålderens litteratur. Red. Sven Delblanc, Lars Lönnroth. Stockholm: Bonniers, 1990. [208-209] Vol 6 of *Den svenska litteraturen.* 7 vols. Rpt. in: *Från modernism till massmedial marknad: 1920-1995.* Red. Lars Lönnroth, Sven Delblanc, Sverker Göransson. Stockholm: Bonnier, 1999. 524. Vol. 3 of *Den svenska litteraturen..* Red. Lars Lönnroth, Sven Delblanc, Sverker Göransson. [Ny, rev. utg.] Stockholm: Bonniers,. 3 vols.

"Radio- och TV-teatern." *Medieålderens litteratur.* Ed. Sven Delblanc, Lars Lönnroth. Stockholm: Bonnier, 1990. [202-203] Vol. 6 of *Den svenska litteraturen.* 7 vols. Rpt. in: *Från modernism till massmedial marknad: 1920-1995.* 516. Vol. 3 of *Den svenska litteraturen.* Red. Lars Lönnroth, Sven Delblanc, Sverker Göransson. [Ny, rev. utg.]

Stockholm: Bonniers, 1999. 3 vols.
Rev. of *En hund begraven.* by Reidar Jönsson. *World Literature Today* 64:1 (Winter 1990): 136.
Strindberg and History. Ed. Birgitta Steene. Special issue of *Scandinavian Studies* 62:1 (1990).
"Strindberg and History: An Introduction." *Scandinavian Studies* 62:1 (1990): [1]-4.
Swedish Children's Literature. Guest ed. Birgitta Steene. *Swedish Book Review: Supplement, 1990.*
"Vita dukens magi: Ingmar Bergen och de nya medierna." *Modernister och arbetardiktare: 1920-199.* Stockholm: Bonnier, 1990. 260-270. Vol. 5 of *Den svenska litteraturen.* Red. Sven Delblanc, Lars Lönnroth. Stockholm: Bonnier, 1987-1990. 7 vols. Rpt. in: *Från modernism till massmedial marknad: 1920-1995.* Stockholm: Bonniers, 1999. 264-274. Vol 3 of *Den svenska litteraturen* Red.Lars Lönnroth, Sven Delblanc, Sverker Göransson. [Ny, rev. utg.] Stockholm: Bonnier, 1999. 3 vols.

1991

"Ingmar Bergmans *Bilder* och den självbiografiska genren." *Finsk Tidskrift* H.5 (1991): 274-86.

1992

"Barnvoksenfilmen: en ny genre?" *Z: [filmtidsskrift].* 4 (1992): 31-37.
"Bergman e il cinema svedese del dopoguerra." *Il Giovane Bergman.* Ed. Francesco Bono. Rome: Officina, 1992. 9-20.
Strindberg and History. Ed. Birgitta Steene. [Rev. and expanded ed.] Stockholm: Almqvist & Wiksell International, 1992.

1993

"The House as Setting and Metaphor in Strindberg's Chamber Plays." *Strindberg in Performance.* Combined spec. issue of *Theatre Research International* 18 (1993) and *Nordic Theatre Studies* 6:1-2 (1993): 37-41.

"Ett subversivt filmspråk: Ingmar Bergman i ett filmfeministisk perspektiv." *Nordisk forskning om kvinnor och medier.* Ed. Ulla Carlsson. Göteborg: NORDICOM, 1993. 141-158.

"Zwischen Hafenbrei und Zauberie." *Gaukler im Grenzland: Ingmar Bergman.* Herausgegeben von Lars Åhlander; [Übersetzungen aus dem Englischen von Christa Schuenke; Übersetzungen aus dem Schwedischen von Gisela Kosubek] Berlin: Henschel, 1933. 172-187.

1994

"Maria Gripe's *Agnes Cecilia* as an Adult Children's Book." *Scandinavian Newsletter* 8 (1994/95): 2-4.

1995

"Besatt viking eller uppskattad konstnär: Strindberg och Ingmar Bergman i USA." *August Strindberg och hans översättare: föredrag vid symposium i Vitterhetsakademiem 8 spetember 1994-.* Red. Meidal och Nils Åke Nilsson. Stockholm: Kungl, Vitterhets Historie och Antikvitets Akademien, 1995. *Konferenser* 33. 87-107.

"Manhattan Surrounded by Ingmar Bergman: The American Reception of a Swedish Filmmaker." *Ingmar Bergman: An Artist's Journey.* Ed. Roger W. Oliver. New York: Archade Publishing, 1995. 137-154.

"Strindbergs språk brände sig in i mitt kött." *Parnass*

(Stockholm) 1994:6/1995:1: 40-44.

1996

"En forskningsöversikt." *Ingmar Bergman: Film och teater i växelverkan.* Ed. Margareta Wirmark. Stockholm: Carlssons, 1996. 217-222.

"Gossen Ruda eller svensk ikon: Om Ingmar Bergmans mottagande i Sverige och utomlands." *Ingmar Bergman: Film och teater i växelverkan.* 187-216.

"Ingmar Bergman: En forskningsöversikt". *Ingmar Bergman: Film och teater i växelverkan.* 187-216.

"Kanske biet ser månen som en hexagon: Barndomsperspektivet i den kvinnliga och manliga självbiografin." *Litteratur og kjønn i Norden: foredrag på den XX. studiekonferanse i International Association for Scandinavian Studies (IASS), arrangert av Institutt for litteraturvitenskap, Islands universitet i Reykjavík 7.-12. august 1994.* Ed. Helga Kress. Reykjavik: Institute of Literary Research, 1996. 308-318.

"Liberalism, Realism, and the Modern Breakthrough: 1830-1890." *A History of Swedish Literature.* Ed. Lars G. Warme. Lincoln: U of Nebraska P, 1996. 204-272.

Måndagar med Bergman: En svensk publik möter Ingmar Bergmans filmer. Statistiskt samarbete, Eva Norin. Stockholm: Brutus Östlings bokförlag Symposion, 1996

1997

"Asta Nielsen och Strindberg: ett möte i stumfilmens tecken." *Strindbergiana* 12 (1997): 46-[61].

"Filmatiseringar och TV-produktioner av August Strindbergs verk." Med Elizabeth de Noma. *Strindbergiana* 12 (1997): 146-[175].

"Omvärdering av Bergmans kvinnosyn." *Svenska Dagbladet* 22 Jul 1997: 12-13.
Strindbergiana. Ed. Birgitta Steene. 12-14 (1997-1999).

1998

"Fire Rekindled: Strindberg and Ingmar Berman." *Strindberg, Ibsen & Bergman: Essays on Scandinavian Film and Drama Offered to Egil Törnqvist on the Occasion of His 65th Birthday*. Ed. Henry Perridon and Sven Hakon Rossel. Maastricht: Shaker, 1998. 189-204.

Ingmar Bergman's First Meeting with Thalia." *Nordic Theatre Studies* 11 (1998): 12-33.

"Med anledning av Ingmar Bergmans 80-årsdag: Bergmans första möte med Thalia." *Upsala Nya Tidning* 14 juli 1998: 11.

"Med Strindberg i Österrike." *Strindbergiana* 13 (1998): 21-36.

Rev. of *Strindberg, sagan och skriften*, by Boel Westin. *Samlaren* 119 (1998): 229-233.

"Strindberg, Ingmar Bergman and the Visual Symbol." *Strindberg: The Moscow Papers*. Ed. Michael Robinson. Stockholm: Strindbergssällskapet, 1998. 85-94.

"The Swedish Image of America." *Images of America in Scandinavia*. Ed. Poul Houe and Sven H. Rossel. Amsterdam; Atlanta, GA: Rodopi, 1998. 145-191.

"The Transpositions of a Filmmaker: Ingmar Bergman at Home and Abroad." *Tijdschrift voor Skandinavistiek* 19:1 (1998): 103-128.

1999

"Att filma Strindberg." *Parnass* 1999:1 12-17.

"August Strindberg, Modernism and the Swedish Cinema." *Expressionism and Modernism: New Approaches to*

August Strindberg. Eds. Michael Robinson and Sven Hakon Rossel. Wiener Studien zur Skandinavistik 1. Wien: Praesens, 1999. 185-195.

"Bergman's *Persona* through a Native Mindscreen." *Ingmar Bergman's* Persona. Ed. Lloyd Michaels. Cambridge: Cambridge UP, 1999. 24-43.

"Can this Bird Fly?: *The Wild Duck* on the Screen." *Edda.* 1 (1999): 31-39.

"Ingmar Bergman möter August Strindberg." *Strindbergiana* 14 (1999): 13-33.

Rev. of *Mitt personregister: Urval 98,* by Vilgot Sjöman. *Tijdschrift voor Skandinavistiek* 20:1 (1999): 85-102.

Rev. of *En afton på Röda Kvarn: Svensk stumfilm som musikdrama,* by Ann-Kristin Wallengren. *Scandinavian Studies* 71:1 (1999): 497-499.

"Sagotant eller litterär nydanare." *Den svenska litteraturen: Genombrottstiden; 1830-1920.* Eds. Lars Lönnroth & Sven Delblanc. Stockholm: Bonniers, 1999. 396-397.

"The Sjöberg-Bergman Connection: *Hets*: Collaboration and Reception." *Strindberg, Sjöberg and Bergman: The Artist and Cultural Identity.* Ed. Birgitta Steene and Egil Törnqvist. Spec. issue of *Tijdschrift voor Skandinavistiek* 20:1 (1999): 85-102.

Strindberg, Sjöberg and Bergman: The Artist and Cultural Identity. Eds. Birgitta Steene and Egil Törnqvist. Spec. issue of *Tijdschrift voor Skandinavistiek* 20:1 (1999).

Forthcoming Works

"Ingmar Bergman." *Twentieth Century Swedish Writers.* Ed. Ann-Charlotte Gavel Adams. Dictionary of Literary Biography. Detroit: Gale Group. 2001.

Ingmar Bergman: A Reference Guide. Amsterdam:

Amsterdam UP; Ann Arbor, MI: Michigan UP, 2000.
"Maria Gripe." *Twentieth Century Swedish Writers.* Ed. Ann-Charlotte Gavel Adams. Dictionary of Literary Biography. Detroit: Gale Group. 2001.

The above bibliography of Professor Birgitta Steene's scholarly writings contains the great majority of her works in the field of Scandinavian studies. It was not possible to retrieve each and every item from her formidable record of publication. Lacking from this list are various newspaper articles written and published in Swedish newspapers as well as published poetry and magazine features on the civil rights movement, the American South, and Native Americans.

The Contributors

A. Gerald (Jerry) Anderson, MA and MLS, completed his doctoral work in Scandinavian Studies, except the dissertation, at the University of California, Berkeley. He worked at the Library of Congress before assuming the position of Nordic Area Librarian at the University of Washington Libraries, Seattle. He is also an Affiliate Lecturer in the Department of Scandinavian Studies.

Marilyn Johns Blackwell is the Vorman-Anderson Professor of Scandinavian Languages and Literatures at The Ohio State University. She studied under Birgitta Steene in the early 1970's, learning from her how to "read" films, and has been working and publishing on Ingmar Bergman ever since. Her authored books include *C.J.L. Almqvist and Romantic Irony*, *Persona: The Transcendent Image*, and *Gender and Representation in the Films of Ingmar Bergman*. She has also edited *Structures of Influence: A Comparative Approach to August Strindberg*.

Harry G. Carlson, Professor of Theatre at Queens College and the Graduate Center of the City University of New York. He has published a number of translations and scholarly works on August Strindberg, both in the US and in Sweden. Carlson's books include *Strindberg: Five Plays*, *Strindberg and the Poetry of Myth*, and most recently *Out of Inferno: Strindberg's Reawakening as an Artist* (1996).

Inga-Stina Ewbank, Professor Emeritus of English Literature in the University of Leeds, was born and educated in Sweden. Apart from a book on the Brontës, her main research and publications have been on Shakespeare and the drama of his contemporaries, and on Ibsen, Strindberg and Scandinavian nineteenth-century theater.

Anne-Charlotte Hanes Harvey, Professor of Drama and Teaching Associate in Women Studies at San Diego State University. In addition to her scholarly work, she is active as a translator and dramaturg, with Strindberg and Ibsen, and the works of Unga Klara as special interests. She is the translator of the symphonic cycle *The Jewish Song*, the opera *Animalen*, and the play, based on Strindberg's poems, *Helluvaguy!!!*.

Maaret Koskinen, Associate Professor and (former) Head of the Department of Cinema Studies, University of Stockholm, film critic in the national daily *Dagens Nyheter*. Author of *Spel och speglingar. En studie i Ingmar Bergmans filmiska estetik* (1993), a study in the cinematic aesthetics of Ingmar Bergman, *Swedish Film Today* (ed., 1996) and (forthcoming) *Everything is, Nothing Represents*. Has also published numerous articles on film nationally and internationally, in journals and anthologies. Currently on the editorial staff of the scholarly film journal *Aura*.

Otto Reinert, Professor Emeritus of Comparative Literature and English at the University of Washington, was born and educated in Norway. He earned his Ph.D. at Yale University in 1952. His main research and publications have been on world drama. He has edited a number of drama anthologies and a collection of critical essays on August Strindberg in the series Twentieth Century Views.

Matthew Roy has studied drama under Birgitta Steene and is currently finishing his doctoral dissertation at the University of Washington entitled *August Strindberg's Perversions: On the science, sin, and scandal of homosexuality*. He has published articles on Scandinavian literature and Finnish folklore, including forthcoming entries on August Strindberg in Routledge's *Who's Who in Gay and Lesbian History* and on Jonas Gardell in the *Dictionary of Literary Biography's* volume called *20th Century Swedish Writers*.

Mark Sandberg is an Associate Professor of Scandinavian and Film Studies at the University of California, Berkeley. He has published articles on film, museology, and Norwegian literature, with a book forthcoming on museum spectatorship in turn-of-the-century Scandinavia.

Tytti Soila, Associate professor, Chair of Department of Cinema Studies at Stockholm University, Director of the Swedish Program at Stockholm University. Fulbright Scholar '92 at University of Michigan in Ann Arbor and '99 at Pembroke Center, Brown University, Providence, RI. A '98-99 Bunting Fellow at Radcliffe College, Harvard University. Co-author of Nordic National Cinemas (Routledge 1998). Publications in Swedish on feminist film theory.

Astrid Söderbergh Widding, Associate Professor in the Department of Cinema Studies at the University of Stockholm, and film critic in the Swedish daily press. Her research interests and publications include *Stumfilm i brytningstid: stil och berättande i Georg af Klerckers filmer* (1998), *Nordic National Cinemas* (Routledge 1998; co-author with Tytti Soila). She is the co-editor of *Cinema Studies into Visual Theory?* (1998) and *Moving Images: from Edison to the webcam* (1999).

Rochelle Wright, Professor of Scandinavian and Comparative Literature, Cinema Studies, and Women's Studies,

Affliated Faculty, Department of Theatre at the University of Illinois, teaches courses on Scandinavian drama, prose fiction, and film. Her research interests and publications include modern Swedish prose (articles on Ivar Lo-Johansson and Kerstin Ekman), Swedish film (*The Visible Wall: Jews and Other Ethnic Outsiders in Swedish Film*), literary history ("Swedish Literature After 1950," in *A History of Swedish Literature*), and literary translation (Lo-Johansson's *Breaking Free* and *Peddling My Wares* and Söderberg's *Doctor Glas*).

The Editors

Ann-Charlotte Gavel Adams, Associate Professor in the Department of Scandinavian Studies at the University of Washington, teaches courses on Scandinavian Drama, August Strindberg, Scandinavian Women Writers, and Modern Swedish Literature. She is the editor of the volumes *Inferno* (1994) and *Legender* (2000) in *Nationalutgåvan av August Strindbergs Samlade Verk*. She is presently at work on the volume *20th Century Swedish Writers* in the *Dictionary of Literary Biography* series. She has written several articles on Strindberg's works set in a French cultural context, most recently "Strindberg et l'occultisme en France" to be published by Cahiers L'Herne in Paris in 2000.

Terje I. Leiren has been a member of the faculty of the University of Washington since 1977 and Chair of the Department of Scandinavian Studies since 1995. An historian, he teaches courses in Scandinavian history and culture. He has written extensively on 19th century Norwegian and Scandinavian-American topics and is especially interested in questions of identity, national identity, and cultural development. He is the author of *Marcus Thrane: Norwegian Radical in America* and is currently completing a study of Thrane's immigrant plays and is at work on a biography of Sigurd Ibsen. He has authored over thirty scholarly articles in American and European journals and has appeared in several television documentary programs on Scandinavian history.